LONGMAN OI

Open L
for Adults

Edited by
Mary Thorpe and David Grugeon

Longman Group UK Limited
Longman House, Burnt Mill, Harlow, Essex, CM20 2JE

First published 1987

British Library Cataloguing in Publication Data

Open learning for adults.
1. Adult education—Great Britain—
Management 2. Distance education—Great
Britain—Management
I. Thorpe, Mary II. Grugeon, David
379.1′14 LC5256.G7

ISBN 0–582–90118–9

Printed and bound in Great Britain by
Biddles Ltd, Guildford and King's Lynn

Contents

Acknowledgements

We are particularly grateful to Diane Bailey, Judith Bell, Roger Lewis and Malcolm Tight for reading whole sections and providing comments while chapters were at draft stage. We also wish to thank Debbie Bailey and Janet Clarke for all their work in supporting the authors and editors from draft to handover stage.

The material on the WIT Project is drawn from a report submitted to the Manpower Services Commission *Women in Technology* on the retraining programme for qualified experienced women technologists. It is reproduced with the kind permission of Her Majesty's Stationery Office and is Crown copyright.

The model shown in figure 9.1 on page 84 is taken from *The Open Learning Toolkit* which is Crown copyright and reproduced with the kind permission of Her Majesty's Stationery Office.

The extract from *Servicing Video Recorders 2: Practical Book* on page 90 is reproduced with the kind permission of the publisher, Macmillan Intek.

Open Learning in industry (Johnstone et al, forthcoming) is Crown copyright and any material taken from it is reproduced with the kind permission of the Controller of Her Majesty's Stationery Office.

List of Contributors

Alan Woodley is a Research Fellow in the Open University's Institute of Educational Technology.

Alistair Wisker is Principal Lecturer and Co-ordinator of Adult and Continuing Education at Bedford College of Higher Education.

Roy Webberley is Director of the Open University's Centre for Youth and Adult Studies and is the University's liaison officer with the Manpower Services Commission.

Wendy Stainton Rogers lectures in Health and Social Welfare in the Centre for Continuing Education at the Open University.

Ailsa Swarbrick is a Senior Counsellor in the Open University's Yorkshire Region.

John Taylor is the Senior Liaison Officer of the Educational Counselling and Credit Transfer Service (ECCTIS), which is being developed by the Open University for the Department of Education and Science.

Mary Thorpe is a Lecturer in the Institute of Educational Technology at the Open University.

Andy Northedge is a Staff Tutor, Social Science in the Open University London Region.

Margaret Miers has researched into issues relating to primary health care and preventive medicine in the University of Wales, and lectured in Sociology at the Polytechnic of Wales. She has worked for the Open University as course tutor or tutor-counsellor since 1973, and is currently training as a nurse.

Steve Ryan is Senior Lecturer in Educational Development at the Centre for Educational Technology and Development, at Leicester Polytechnic.

Diana Laurillard is a Lecturer in the Institute of Educational Technology at the Open University.

Roger Lewis is Assistant Director of Student Services of the Open College.

Ian McNay is Deputy Director of the Yorkshire Region, the Open University.

Alistair Morgan is a Lecturer in Educational Technology at the Open University.

Tony Kaye is a Senior Lecturer in the Open University's Institute of Educational Technology.

Marion Jack is Deputy Scottish Director in the Open University in Scotland.

Patrick Kelly is Senior Counsellor in the North West Region of the Open University.

Janet Grant is a Senior Lecturer in the Institute of Educational Technology at the Open University.

Henry Goodman is Education Advisory Officer with the Business and Technician Education Council.

David Grugeon is Director of Student Services for the Open College, having most recently been Pro-Vice-Chancellor (Academic: Teaching and Students) at the Open University. He was the first editor of the journal *Open Learning*.

Ian Haffenden is a Staff Tutor in Adult Education at the University of Surrey's School for Educational Studies.

Angie Ballard is a Research Fellow in the Student Research Centre in the Institute of Educational Technology at the Open University.

Nicola Durbridge is a Research Fellow in the Institute of Educational Technology, at the Open University and a Tutor-Counsellor for its Arts Foundation Course.

Judith Fage has worked as a radio and television producer for the BBC, and is now a Senior Counsellor in the Open University London Region.

Diane Garrard is Assistant Chief Officer with the Business and Technician Education Council.

Jonathan Brown is a Senior Counsellor with the North Region of the Open University.

David Seward is presently the Director of Regional Academic Services and has responsibility for the Open University's student support services carried out through its thirteen regional centres.

Tony Bates is Professor of Media Research Methods at the Open University.

Joy Davis is Head of General Education at Rumney College, Cardiff and a Tutor in Mathematics at the Open University.

PART I ISSUES IN OPEN LEARNING

1 Moving into open learning

Mary Thorpe and David Grugeon

Introduction

'Open learning' is the recent buzz phrase to encompass the combination of old and new methods of learning (by print, written assignments, face-to-face, broadcasts, telephones and computers) to meet the growing needs of adults in the UK. Moving beyond the traditional classroom, we find substantial numbers of people studying in ways that have been adapted to suit their own life and work circumstances.

The UK provides some of the most advanced forms of open learning in the world. In particular, the Open University (OU), which started teaching students in 1971, was the first nationwide, integrated multi-media teaching and learning programme at degree level for adults; more recently it has developed its work in professional updating, personal and community education. We make no apology for drawing heavily on the experience of several authors who have worked, part-time or full-time, for the OU. Many of them are working or have worked in other areas of adult education and training; many of them have written in *Teaching at a Distance*, the OU's pedagogical journal, and its successor, *Open Learning*, jointly published by the OU and Longman.

Moving into open learning

It has not been our aim to provide the reader with a 'how do to it manual' for open learning. Others before us have already done so and we recommend consultation of the relevant publications from the Council for Educational Technology, the Further Education Unit and the Further Education Staff College. Our aim has been to contribute to the growing use and understanding of open learning, by a selective exploration of issues which seem to us generic and therefore relevant to a wide range of different systems.

Drawing heavily on the experience of OU staff and students, raises the question of whether distance learning is open learning, to which we would answer that distance learning is surely a sub-set of open learning – not synonymous with it, but a particular example of one type. 'Open learning' is an umbrella term which refers to a whole series of varied educational initiatives and provision. A general and sustained movement towards opening up education and training and providing more opportunities for all kinds of learning after basic education requires an appropriate slogan or umbrella term. It may not matter that, as Webberley and Haffenden state in chapter 4, 'There exists no universally agreed, adequate and comprehensive definition of open learning.'. This enables it to be given local interpretation and at least does not restrict that experimentation by individuals and small groups which is the preferred alternative of British educators and trainers, over centralised and monolithic provision. We do not see 'open learning' as an academic concept, something developed out of research and educational theory which we should expect to carry precise definition – at least not in this early stage of its development. Its current usage reflects developments in the last 20 years of educational practice, and more recently, the UK government's response to a perceived crisis in the relationship between education and training, and the needs of the economy as it has undergone the rapid changes of the last decade.

This is not to argue that we should not take open learning seriously, nor refrain from analysing its meaning and challenging some interpretations of it. However, this is not the context for an extended, definitional analysis, and it seems to us more productive to draw attention to thinking and practice which, broadly speaking, support moves towards 'open learning'.

Reaching a mass audience

There is, first, the incontrovertible evidence which the OU provided during the 1970s, that a multi-media approach could bring higher education to a mass audience. The application of modern technology in text, broadcasting and the administration of student support rapidly demonstrated that there were thousands (over 55 000 in 1985 and in 1986) of applicants annually for a place on the undergraduate programme, and growing numbers interested in taking one-off courses (over 10 000 in 1986 and in 1987). The OU, of course, was able to build on the methods and the educational commitment to students then established by the (non-profit making) National Extension College and to some extent, the correspondence colleges. But the innovations pioneered by the OU in the use of public network broadcasting, text design and local tuition and counselling led to the use of 'distance education' for a whole series of new institutions and programmes which were mounted worldwide during the 1970s and 1980s, drawing directly from the demonstrable success and experience of the OU of the UK.

Moving closer to the individual learner

A second strand within open learning is the shift in research and practitioner interest from teaching and instructional design towards learning and the particularity of individual student response. Such research and interest has, as often as not, taken place within the context of conventional full-time education, and some of the most influential (Dahlgen and Marton) with conventional university undergraduates. The re-thinking engendered by these studies, however, has been promoted by groups such as the Further Education Unit, the National Foundation of Educational Research, the Standing Conference on Educational Development Services, the National Institute for Adult Education, and many others, who would probably now see 'open learning' as incorporating a move towards student centred-ness.

A flexible response to changes in society

A third strand can be linked to the current historical context of the debate over purpose and values in education. The list of key topics is now a familiar one: the dissatisfaction of employers with the products of the school and university system; the mismatch between further educational provision, institutions for teacher training, and the declining numbers of school cohorts up to the end of the century; the escalating costs of education and training and the desirability of maximising use of existing provision and facilities; the priorities of political leadership, which have currently stressed a greater degree of private funding and a reorientation towards the vocational purposes of education. It is within this context that open learning has been promoted, by the Manpower Services Commission (through the Open Tech and now through the Open College), by the Confederation of British Industry, by the Institute of Training and Development and not least by the OU, as an approach to suit the times: a collection of techniques and approaches available to both education and industry with which to reach any conceivable sector of the population, to meet virtually any conceivable educational or training goal.

For our purposes here, of course, this is deliberate over-statement; it remains to be seen whether open learning can justifiably claim such universal coverage. And, having outlined some of the social and educational change out of which open learning derives, we can also summarise the common strands of thinking which have been associated with it.

Education responsive to the learner

The most productive route into this is probably through the idea of student-centred-learning, an approach which focusses less on what the institutions provide and more on what the learner wants to study, how the learner approaches study and the social and physical conditions which enable study to occur. Open learning, in fact, implies a critique of conventional provision, as being organised both socially and intellectually in ways which suit institutional providers primarily and only a small sub-set of the potential learner population, if at all. The Council for Education and Technology offered this neat definition in 1980: 'An open learning system is one which enables individuals to take part in programmes of study of their choice, no matter where they live or whatever their circumstances.' The implications of this approach for providers are summed up in the call for greater responsiveness and flexibility. In many ways, the admirably brief document produced by the FEU, *Flexible Learning Opportunities*,[1] provides the best definition of open learning because it recognises that open learning is a continuum rather than an either/or category, and that, rather than asking 'is this (example x) open learning' we should ask in what ways and to what extent an example displays openness. Roger Lewis provides a similar approach in his definition of open learning (Lewis, 1986).[2] One of the virtues of the currency of the phrase it seems to us, is that it has spawned a framework of analytical questions which can be applied to *any* form of education or training, as a means of determining the degree to which it responds effectively to learner requirements. Table 1.1 reproduces Lewis's 'open-closed learning continuum' as one example of this kind of interrogation.

Table 1.1 The open-closed learning continuum

Basic Question	Aspects Closed ←	→ Open
Who?	Scheme open to select groups only	Scheme open to all
	Set entry requirements, e.g. traditional exam success	Self-assessment and diagnostic facilities
	Scheme not marketed	Extensive publicity, regularly updated information
Why?	Choice made by others, e.g. tutor, employer	Learner choice
	No counselling or guidance	Pre-entry counselling
What?	Entire syllabus set out in advance, e.g. by validating body; no choice possible within it	Learner formulates own objectives and syllabus
	Limited to materials the tutor has produced	Uses wide range of materials drawn form many sources
	Whole course must be taken	Content tailored to need; individual learners can take different modules
	No guidance on selection of content	Guidance on selection of content
	Knowledge, facts, 'academic'	Experience, practice, feeling, attitude
	No recognition of past experience	Credit given for past experience
How?	Only one method/style provided for; little variation in learner activity	Choice of learning methods/styles; varied activities
	One route only through material	Choice of routes through material
	Package in one medium only	Package uses variety of media
Where?	One place only (e.g. at work)	Learner chooses place (e.g. home,work, while travelling)
	Regular fixed attendance required	Learner can attend, or not – as desired
	Practical work requires fixed attendance	Practical work offered through kits and/or drop-in access and/or place of work itself
When?	Fixed starting date(s)	Start any time
	Learner placed by a fixed timetable	Learner decides place of work
	Fixed ending	End at any time
How is the learner doing?	Externally mixed method of assessment e.g. formal exam	Variety of assessment methods; learner choice of assessment methods; learner constructs method of assessment
	Normative assessment	Criteria/competency based assessment
	No feedback on performance	Frequent, full, ongoing feedback on performance, available as desired
	Assessment dates fixed and non-negotiable	Learner decides when to be assessed
	Assessment available only for whole course	Assessment available for each module

Basic Question	Aspects Closed ⟵	⟶ Open
Who can help the learner?	No support outside course/package	Variety of possible kinds of support (e.g. advice, guidance, counselling)
	Only professional supporters (e.g. teachers) encouraged	Non-professional, as well as professional supporters; informal as well as formal support encouraged (e.g. mentor, family, friends)
	Support available only in one place, e.g. training centre	Support available in many places
	Support available in one mode only, e.g. face-to-face	Support, available in a variety of modes, e.g. letter, telephone, face-to-face
What does it lead to?	One destination	Various possible destinations

(This table first appeared in 'What is open learning?' and is reprinted with the permission of the Council for Educational Technology.)

Notes

1 It is possible to increase or to reduce the number of basic questions used to analyse a scheme.
2 It is also possible to increase or to reduce the number of aspects of each question. You can see, for example, that I have given two aspects for *why?* and six for *what?*
3 All schemes will, in practice, be open on some aspects and closed on others, either through choice or through lack of resources.
4 Some parts of a scheme, e.g. different modules or practical work, may be open to a different extent, or in different ways, from other parts of the same scheme.

(Lewis, 1986)[2]

This leads naturally onto the question, how 'open' does something have to be to qualify for 'open learning' status? Some have asked, for example, whether the OU, in providing a paced learning system with very conventional modes of assessment on the degree programme, should be excluded (despite its name) from the 'approved fold' of 'genuine open learning'. This seems to us the kind of purist approach which if implemented could lead only to a degree of logic chopping and divisive categorisation which would interest few, except professional educators. The development of complex typologies seems even less likely to benefit learners themselves.

Just to take the case in point, the fact that many adult learners want to define their own curricula and modes of assessment (if any), does not gainsay the equally undeniable fact that many adults want recognisable qualifications as well as other things (intellectual stimulation, pursuing an interest, boosting self-confidence and so on) and that structured learning and the 'external' pressure of having to complete assignments periodically, appear to contribute to the successful completion of course work, (see chapter 24 in this volume) – an end which the majority of OU undergraduate learners seem to desire every bit as much as its full-time staff and the Department of Education and Science.

Open to learners not otherwise reached

Equally divisive and self-defeating would be the (perhaps greater) danger of 'open learning' being used as a legitimating mechanism for provision which, on careful investigation, appears to have very little, if any, basis for claiming to be open. For, although we can speak of a continuum of openness along which any particular example may be located, there is surely a basic requirement that *institutional barriers to access* should be reduced enough to enable at least a proportion of learners to participate, *who would not otherwise have done so*. At present within further education the most common means by which such barriers are broken down is by the provision of materials which can be studied individually without tutorial support, and of a relaxation of the requirement (continuously or frequently) to attend the premises of a college for tuition, (which is offered, but at times and in ways which are accessible to students with other demands on their time during 9.00am to 5.00pm). In their study of Flexistudy at Abraham Moss Open College for example, Bagley and Challis[3] note that:

> . . . for the centre's Flexistudy students, the concept of the 'missed' population would appear to have held good: nurses, shift workers, postmen and others with variable working conditions were well represented. Other observations about the nature of the student population, derived from the internal evaluation, include:
> (a) females outnumbered by males by almost 2:1;
> (b) the vast majority (*c.* 85 per cent) fall within the age range 17–40;
> (c) the expressed reason for study divided fairly evenly between vocational aims and general interest or personal development;
> (d) over 80 per cent of the students lived within the normal catchment area of the centre.
>
> Only a small minority of the students had joined (Flexistudy) because they preferred it as a method of study; the vast majority found that it represented their only means of access to the centre's courses. A number joined (Flexistudy) only after they had attempted to enrol for traditional courses, found that the numbers were too small to allow the course to be conducted, and were then left with Flexistudy as their only alternative. (Bagley & Challis, 1985, pp 16–17)[3]

If we apply all the criteria for openness, there are few if any conceivable forms of (publicly funded) education and training which could be said to be completely open. And it is clear that very different forms of provision can be legitimately included under the 'open learning' umbrella – legitimately because there is at minimum a reduction of institutional barriers against access. Bagley and Challis, for example, refer to the three major subcategories suggested by the Council for Educational Technology in 1980:

> . . . college based systems, where all the teaching is done in the college but where students are able to study in the college at a time and pace to suit their own choice . . . local systems where most of the students live within travelling distance of the college but spend part of their study time at home . . . distant systems in which the students live at some distance from the college, and in effect pursue correspondence courses. (Open learning is often treated as synonymous with distance learning – a use of the term which can prove confusing and obstructive.) (Bagley and Challis, 1985 p 4)[3]

Common concerns of open learning

We intend not to fall into the misuse of the open learning term which Bagley and Challis were against. Distance learning is but one variant of open learning, and we do not seek to impose an OU model on open learning by masquerading distance learning in false dress, as it were. But, in the spirit of sharing what we feel is the extensive and interesting experience of adults pursuing ambitious learning goals by part-time study, we offer a number of *common (or generic) concerns* here which we feel arise as strong themes in a range of different kinds of open learning, including that provided by the OU.

Firstly there is the issue of adult learners, those who, whatever their age return to study after completing their initial education (in most but not all cases, terminated by schooling). The implications of studying while maintaining the adult roles of parent, worker, citizen, and so on appear in virtually every chapter of what follows, but a brief introduction to key issues is provided in chapter 8.

Secondly, there is the issue of learning to learn, especially where the familiar, often passive role of the traditional, classroom and teacher-based student must be replaced by a more independent, self-motivating approach. Early difficulties are exacerbated in systems, like the OU, which use technologies still unfamiliar to most adults as a means of learning (though incorporated increasingly into the school system). Again these issues are touched on in virtually every chapter, but readers might start with chapter 23 and then move into Section III; chapter 24 in the section on Student Assignments, gives more detailed consideration to a specific area.

Thirdly, there are all the implications of these changes in the process of learning, and of who is learning, for the role of the tutor/lecturer/trainer. Diane Bailey has referred to 'the melting of role boundaries brought about by open learning, with a consequent integration of teaching and guidance'. There is also a whole range of curricular decisions to be made in any new programme of open learning: how to advise and counsel learners before they start; whether learners need specially prepared materials for individual study; whether the use of several media would be effective; how much tuition and counselling to provide; what kind of group teaching/learning works best; how much intervention in the learning process is desirable; and so on. Then there is the experience of carrying out these decisions, which may require materials production more pre-planned and extensive than the familiar class 'hand out', an unfamiliar counselling role with learners, correspondence teaching, one to one and very small group teaching, and the development of a 'facilitator' role rather than 'communicator of subject expertise'. These issues are introduced in chapter 8 and the focus especially of chapters 23 and 26 to 30.

That there are generic issues across the field of open learning seems to us evident in the frequency with which similar concerns come up in accounts of learning situations which differ in their goals, methods and in the characteristics of learners. This is not to argue that all issues, always apply; even less that the forms these issues take, and the ways in which they can be effectively handled, are identical. For this reason the authors of each chapter have attempted to 'get below' the details of 'the OU system', to focus attention on underlying goals, processes and outcomes – unintended as well as intended – in order to make available experience which might be useful to practitioners working within systems, institutions and constraints very different from those of the OU.

We do not assume that the whole of this experience will be relevant to all readers. Nor that it can be directly applied to very different contexts. This *might* be possible, in the case for instance of a reader with a direct, practical interest in correspondence teaching, or the role of the tutor in group learning. Other times we anticipate the reader will need to reflect on the implications for their own situation of what has been communicated, and develop practical messages for themselves. A more accurate grasp of one's own problems and possibilities can sometimes come out of learning experience which is different from, or even opposed to, one's own, as well as out of experience which is the same.

This is not an exhaustive account of open learning: very large areas of the OU's work, not to mention that of other organisations, are not directly represented. We did not think it feasible, for example, to include analysis of materials' production and the work of the course teams – partly because so much of what would be communicated here revolves round those very particular and context-specific institutional factors which characterise an organisation and set it apart from others. And, while our intention is to write both for those who see themselves as trainers, as well as for those who are 'lecturers', 'tutors', or other education professionals, we are conscious of our lack of direct experience in industry and training. There *are* limits to the extent to which one can generalise out of very particular experience, and we anticipate that our readers are likely to be selective in their reading, and will be prepared to make that willing suspension of disbelief, at least initially, without which it would be difficult to learn from anyone's experience except our own.

And that is the spirit with which we have, collectively, pursued our writing. As we have said, not *all* our authors are OU staff; there are contributions from writers in the field of 'access' studies (chapter 10), Education Development Services in polytechnics (chapter 9) and accreditation of vocational education and training (chapter 3). A number of other chapters are based on collaborative work between the OU and other institutions – local government, professional bodies, the Open Tech and the Manpower Services Commission (see for example, chapters 2, 5, 11, 12, 13, 14).

Open and traditional learning

It is possible that the very scale of human and financial resources contributed to the OU annually has been an off-putting factor for many embarking on innovative programmes of flexible or open learning but on a much smaller and (less well resourced) scale. But, partly *because* of its nature as a public institution, we have taken the view that the experience gained since the OU was founded in 1969 ought to be made available in usable form to others, who may then have the option of acceptance or rejection as they see fit. The reader will judge the degree to which we have succeeded in that aim.

But perhaps the most important point to have communicated – one which was not in the forefront of our aims – is that a form of open learning has generated continuing commitment to student learning among a very large and disparate body of staff. Commitment, that is, to students primarily, and to 'open learning' only in so far as it is a means of reaching those students effectively. Consensus is hard to find in education but if there is one message the majority of these staff would concur with, it would be that commitment to the learner and the quality of their learning is as necessary for the success of 'open learning' as for conventional provision in education or training. Those 'old lags' who joined the OU in the 1970s (whether as part-time or full-time staff) might warn new recruits to the now fashionable movement of open learning, that it is more time-consuming and addictive than you think! To that extent we hope to encourage even more to 'jump onto the band-wagon'.

It may be that, as Lewis says:

> The phrase 'open learning' is regrettable in that it has an 'all or nothing' ring to it. In fact many traditional classes have some open characteristics . . . nor is it necessary to wait for new resources to open up learning. Teachers or tutors anywhere can open up one or more aspects of their work by an intelligent redirection of existing resources. (Lewis, 1986)[2]

We would agree that an over-rigid divide between conventional and open learning is undesirable, and though the latter has grown out of the experience of the former, we see it as equally desirable that experience with some of the 'new' forms of teaching should influence the conventional. Many of us, for example, would have liked our essays to have been 'marked' with the same care and creativity that a thoughtful correspondence teacher puts into 'marking' the scripts of a student learning at a distance. And many of the symptoms of low self-esteem, learning difficulties, anxiety over assessment and so on, can be found in students studying full-time in conventional programmes. They have more opportunity to resolve their difficulties, but might still value greater attention to 'counselling' needs and advisory support by their colleges, polytechnics, universities or training organisations. Indeed, one measure of the success of open learning might be the demise of the phrase itself, as having outlived its usefulness because, to a much greater extent, 'openness' pervades all education and training, to the benefit both of those who learn and those who teach and learn. We hope so.

References

L O Dahlgren and F Marton, 'Students Conceptions of Subject-Matter: an Aspect of Learning and Teaching in Higher Education' in *Studies in Higher Education*, Vol. 3, No. 1, 1978.

1 Further Education Unit, *Flexible Learning Opportunities* FEU, 1983.

2 R Lewis, 'What is Open Learning?' in *Open Learning* Vol 1, No 2, OU/Longman, 1986.

3 B Bagley and B Challis, *Inside Open Learning*, Further Education Staff College, Coombe Lodge, Blagdon, Bristol, 1985.

2 Organisation and staff development

Ian McNay

The manager of an open learning system can choose the sorts of hassle and heartache he (*sic*) will have but he cannot avoid them.
Tony Kirwan, Tutor Organiser
YMCA distance-learning scheme
(CET, 1985)[1]

Introduction

Those coming to open learning from now on may be like Amstrad, and other third generation PC manufacturers, and exploit the R & D work of the pioneers. There are other parallels – the market demand for open learning, and government pressure to develop it are now greater than in the sceptical early days. That still does not mean it is all now de-bugged and you can get on-stream quickly and easily. This chapter aims to disabuse any such notions while presenting questions and suggestions for three groups of people considering the possibilities of open learning to help them in planning and implementation in their institutions: senior managers, 'activity' managers and those responsible for staffing/personnel planning and development for both 'teaching' and 'support' staff.

Open learning, at the extreme, can turn an institution upside-down. For a start, it blurs the distinction between those two groups of staff – hence the quotation marks. It can invert the control mechanisms in teaching and learning, putting decisions more in the hands of the student than the teacher. It can shift the whole budget of an institution from a staff intensive service industry profile nearer to a production industry capital intensive model. It can abolish timetables, exams and all the other familiar maps and milestones of institutional topography. It changes roles; it demands new skills and attitudes; it threatens vested interests; it clashes with developed norms for measuring workload or allocating finance, and with established administrative practices. In two words, it can be disruptive and revolutionary.

You may think that this is worth risking, or even believe it's inevitable, because of a need to save money with current pressures for economy and efficiency. Forget it! It's true that the OU (Open University) is by far the most cost-effective degree awarding institution in the UK (McNay, 1986)[2] but it was *totally* designed *ab initio* for distance teaching, and it has a large market. Unit costs are low because of its size. Few, if any, other institutions can envisage enrolments of thousands each year on a foundation course and few could afford the substantial setting up costs and initial capital investment necessary. What this chapter assumes is the potential introduction of a significant initiative in open learning within an established institution. If that matches your need, carry on reading – unless you have been deterred by the previous paragraph in which case stop now and do something more useful like exploring early retirement provision!

Planning

This section deals with policy strategy and tactics – the why? what? and how? of planning. Your *why?* may have an overt agenda such as:

- making training and education more flexible;

or

- reaching clients and meeting their needs which traditional structures and processes cannot;

but may also have a hidden agenda including some of:

- increasing student numbers with limited accommodation by use outside a 9-5, five day structure, or by a shift to structured private study;
- providing an arena for innovation by young turks stuck low in established hierarchies – perhaps also challenging/threatening others to review and change;
- feeding back good material into traditional teaching sessions (as OU material has done through plagiarism by staff in other institutions);
- tapping the available funding to supplement decimated base budgets;
- getting on the current bandwagon as an 'image' management ploy.

The objectives you have set under *why?* will condition *what* you do but there will be other conditioners – what you *should* do and what you *can* do are often very different. What is possible is conditioned by the *context* – geographical, social, economic, political, by the *cash* available; by the *commitment* you can generate; and by the *controls* that operate – of exam boards or curriculum approval bodies. So, modular course structures are acceptable in Scottish 'O' grades, but less so within GCSE elsewhere in the UK. Money for outreach to urban immigrant communities may come from Urban Aid but for many scattered rural communities may come from the European Social Fund; and the first may need commitment to appoint extra staff with language skills working in community centres; the second commitment by a local radio station to cooperate, and special telephone conference networks. Very different skills are needed for these two examples. Staff attitudes are also crucial – for example, in an academic institution, outreach to the less able may be less welcome than introducing continuing education possibilities for traditional clients.

If these factors condition *what* you can do, they also set limits on *how much?* and *how quickly?* you can do anything. So, if you want to have an early manifestation of a new open learning ethos, the essence of which is client-centredness, this will also condition the *what?* Translation of a general leaflet into Bengali or Gujerati can be quickly done and funded under an existing budget head, though it may mean trimming on general publicity to get specific targetting, and you need to have capacity to match the demand you may generate. Negotiating a contract with the BBC, or designing and producing material to support radio programmes need longer planning lead times. But . . . whatever you plan, double the length of your original schedule before 'product launch', if you've never done something similar before. If you are, or are going to be, the activity manager make sure that you don't accept unreasonable deadlines – the case studies of open learning innovations are full of examples of staff frantically scrambling to keep ahead of students.

The *how?* will depend on staff attitudes, too, as well as their abilities. This was recognised by Chin and Benne (1973)[3] in defining their three approaches to planned change: power–coercive, empirical–rational and normative–re-educative. A useful FEU project report *Curriculum-led Institutional Development* relates these to beliefs about decision-making:

1 Things get done because powerful influences are able to impose decisions – for example, if you want a decision made in your favour, persuade the vice-principal.

2 Things get done because, when presented with clear objective information and argument, people will decide in a rational way – for example, if you undertake research, present findings and carefully construct conclusions, then everyone will agree to the presented solution.

3 Things get done through a process of reflection and review of existing practice, leading to mutually agreed changes in behaviour, attitudes and objectives – for example, if you give all the staff the opportunity to take part in discussing the need for change, then agreement will be reached.

(FEU, 1986)[4]

A mix of all three of these will probably be necessary. Which you give emphasis to will depend on where you are starting from: (1) is easy if you *are* the vice-principal with power; (2) will need open meetings to persuade; and (3) may need training courses to change perceptions.

If those are *process* approaches to the change to an open learning strategy there are *structural* issues too. Do you start with a small pilot and plan to expand incrementally or go for a 'big-bang' policy conversion following major debate? Is there to be a central team of missionaries/advisers, or an existing department which becomes a model centre of excellence, or designated individuals scattered among all departments? This last, by itself, is least effective because of the isolation such change agents suffer: they need support from like-minded colleagues at least. They will also doubtless have other duties which can crowd out their open learning tasks. A specific unit designation helps in providing a team base but must avoid being an 'innovation reservation' with a barrier round it – however invisible formally and whoever constructs it. Having a core unit also helps in cost identification and resource allocation which is the final task in the planning phase – any open learning project needs significant 'up-front' investment for materials preparation before students participate and pay fees, and it also needs criteria for efficiency evaluation which differ from the traditional lecturer contact load, class size, etc. Any new product launch also needs time to establish itself and a minimum life guarantee should be offered to any experiment.

Those putting forward plans for open learning therefore need to be clear:

why are the proposals being made?
who will programmes be aimed at?
what form will they take?
how will policy be developed and negotiated to approval?
how much will be done and ***when*** – over what time scale?
where will the institutional focus for such work be located?
how much will it cost?

Implementation and operation

There is a further question: who will prepare and present the new programmes once a policy has been approved in principle? It is with those chosen for these tasks that this section is concerned. The most likely approach is a team one but, although the team concept is now widespread in education, having arrived surprisingly late, it must be stressed that open learning demands a much more integrated team approach than many course teams currently adopt. I am assuming here that some of the characteristics of the programme involve private use of structured learning materials and lower student attendance at a college. Connections between elements cannot be made in response to student queries as they might in a face-to-face programme but need to be embedded in the design stage. There is, then, a dilemma at the stage of team formation:

– use a large team, where authors are writing on topics they know well, and you have problems of control and communication and have to put a lot of resources into the editing stage;
– use a small team, with competent generalists, and you have problems of overwork, possible reductions in the quality of the materials, and you have to put a lot of resources into the creation stage.

(Kirwan in CET 1985 pp 206–7)[1]

That raises two of the issues I wish to cover – *scheduling* and *standards*. The other two are *support* for the concept, for the team and for students: the balance between care and control; and *selling* – marketing would be a better, wider term but it's not alliterative!

Scheduling

Scheduling has several aspects. You may have some notion of how long it takes to prepare good writtern material, but if you haven't done it you will have underestimated, probably by a factor of 50 per cent. Do talk with those who have done work of this kind and adjust your critical path accordingly. Some OU units have been through seven drafts before final publication and if material is sequential and integrated the pace of the team is the pace of the slowest member. You may also depend on outsiders for illustrations, for typesetting and printing – be very clear about delivery dates and penalties in your contracts. Allow time for slippage even with in-house facilities – I recently suffered from two power cuts in the OU when up against a deadline which stopped all electric typewriters and reprographic machines.

Scheduling of study time is also important particularly if you are going to have a mixed ability group of students. The team needs to negotiate some norms but then be prepared to cope with different rates of progress by students in scheduling any supplementary input and in setting and receiving assignments. A modular structure will allow variable speed of progress from one module to the next, or of study load (the number studied simultaneously), but the issue of pacing *within* units of study still remains. And ... can they be structured in small sections which fit into otherwise 'wasted' time – e.g. bus journeys, waiting for the dentist?

Finally, there will be *some* contact time for students no matter how distant or independent the programme allows them to be. Is the contact schedule open – at their discretion? Or is it normal office hours? The OU has Saturday schools and I know one college running a Sunday programme (which was where much UK education had its beginnings) but this has implications for conditions of service and costs. OU tutors get phone calls at all hours unless they set limits, and even then there are emergency exceptions. Nor is it only academic staff who are affected – when can distant students get to a college library or computer terminal? These are issues for senior management but decisions on them set working limits for activity managers.

Standards

The *standards* topic concerns both form and content. I've already noted the problem of pacing and this relates crucially to content but, less obviously, to the way material is presented. Print in narrow columns with plenty of 'white space' is more quickly read than densely typed material. Illustrations break up the text and add variety. So do tables, but use of statistical data needs care if students are not used to it – there's no instant feedback from blank faces and silent students. An editor input to the course team is essential here, although resources will set limits to quality standards – OU texts have become more dense as funds have become constrained.

Support

The reference to the editorial role raises the third topic – *support*. Support staff play a prominent role in open learning – the librarians and computer-technician staff have featured already, and the role of secretarial staff in the preparation of written material is obvious. Again, there are issues here for senior management: negotiation on the shifts in the balance of the total staff cohort to provide such inputs. The role of the activity manager is to accord such staff the status they merit – a break with tradition – and to integrate them into the team. The support for open learning needs to spread beyond the team – the whole college needs to create an open climate and acknowledge the new clients. To use a support staff example again – it is no use designing a programme open to mature students on a second chance basis if an impatient or over-tired receptionist makes their first tentative approach to the college an experience they don't want to risk repeating.

Selling

Which leads to the fourth topic – *selling*. If you are opening your doors people will not come through unless they know, and are interested in what is on the other side. If you have answered some of the planning questions you will have some idea of which groups in the community you are aiming at and you need to go to them before they come to you. And 'after-sales' brings us back to support – such students will need a supportive formative approach and perhaps more substantial counselling than more established groups of students. There is a nice balance to establish between care and control. If much of the control in student centred learning passes to that student in terms of choice of study area and self-pacing how much progress chasing responsibility remains with staff? If there are course work assignments, these provide a check on student progress and can trigger supportive intervention which serves both care and control objectives . . . if properly approached.

The final aspect of marketing is client feedback to allow a better model to be produced next time. It is no use approaching groups only to 'sell' once – open learning equalises the teacher–learner relationship and, given the falling numbers in traditional market groups, education is a buyer's market so you need to *listen* to your clients, to evaluate in *their* terms, and negotiate provision to ensure its continuing relevance and accessibility.

Staff Development

The previous two sections have been a somewhat breathless coverage of some issues in product innovation – the planning, design, development and launch of an open learning programme. Some of the issues are developed later in this book. For college and activity managers there are useful checklists within *Inside Open Learning* (Bagley and Challis, 1985)[5] and the FEU/Open Tech Unit publication (1986) *Implementing Open Learning in Local Authority Institutions.*[6] The CET series treats management of different stages and facets in some depth with detailed guides. What I hope is now obvious is that open learning represents a substantial change from traditional practices and therefore requires training and development of staff of all categories if it is to be a successful, quality product. The final list in this chapter therefore identifies some of the topics for staff developers and also serves to recapitulate the issues I have covered:

- *an awareness raising programme* for all staff to establish tolerant attitudes if not enthusiastic acceptance of new client groups. 'Staff attitudes are crucial' is a message I constantly encounter in workshops. This is not only for the small group directly involved in an open learning programme: the open section cannot be shut off from the rest of the college and 'openness' cannot thrive if some sections of the college demonstrate hostility to new clients or refuse to accommodate to new attitudes to students and approaches to learning. So, even if only a small group is experimenting with openness, the whole environment needs to make *some* changes;
- *change management skills*, especially interpersonal skills, such as negotiation, political skills within key committees, paperwork skills for presenting proposals;
- *team management skills* to ensure integration of all members, including support staff, to establish consistent frameworks, to allocate responsibilities, to provide mutual support and to develop shared values in dealing with problems, crises, and common professionality in establishing standards and observing production schedules;
- *organisation skills* – devising appropriate structures for open learning with clear objectives and clear relationships with other organisation elements. This also allows development of clear job descriptions for staff which many throughout further education would welcome;
- novel *communication skills* related to written rather than oral presentation, to telephone contact rather than face to face in college;
- *counselling and support skill* – again, often at a distance – including judgements about timing of interventions;
- *skills in devising new learning materials* and assignments for assessment – again, there is an attitude shift here in accepting group discussion of assignments by students rather than the protected isolation usually imposed within 'examinations';
- *skills of partnership*, of acceptance of others' different views as legitimate, of working within teams with colleagues and clients in designing, developing and delivering learning and evaluating it in use, and of outreach to communities beyond a college's normal ambit.

Many of these reflect shifts which are already taking place in colleges but open learning concentrates them together and demands much more movement than has yet taken place generally.

References

1 CET, *Open Learning in Action*, Open Learning guides, Vol. 1, London, Council for Educational Technology, 1985.

2 I McNay, 'Open Market for the Open University' in *Open Learning* Vol. 1, No. 1, 1986.

3 R Chin and K D Benne, 'General Strategies for Effecting Changes in Human Systems' in W G Bennis, K D Benne and R Chin (eds), *The Planning of Change*, New York, Holt, Rhinehart & Winston, 1976.

4 FEU, *Developing the College*, draft of a project report submitted to FEU, March 1986, based on project RP116 *Curriculum-led Institutional Development*, in mimeo, to be published 1987.

5 B Bagley and B Challis, *Inside Open Learning*, Blagdon FE Staff College, 1985.

6 FEU/Open Tech Unit, *Implementing Open Learning in Local Authority Institutions*, London, FEU, 1986.

3 Accreditation of vocational open learning

Henry Goodman and Diane Garrard

Introduction

In further education there exist a number of major examining and validating bodies which together provide a comprehensive system of national accreditation for vocational education and training. There are also many professional associations which assume a more limited accreditation role in relation to their particular vocational area, linking association membership with the passing of their own examinations or with achievement of recognised qualifications.

The system has been criticised for being excessively complicated and the recently published DeVille Report[1] has led to the establishment of the new National Council for Vocational Qualifications (NCVQ). However, despite its complications, the system provides students with national recognition of their educational achievement and employers with some assurance that successful students have attained an appropriate level of relevant knowledge and skill.

The need for the existence of a national system of qualifications for young people preparing for a career is well accepted. However, the case for certification at adult levels and for open learning opportunities may seem less obvious. Adults arguably have clearer and more specific learning goals, are more likely to value the knowledge and skill gained for its own sake and be less impressed with paper qualifications. Also, open learning implies a friendly and informal pattern of learning, more concerned with meeting the real needs of the client than with fulfilling the requirements of an externally imposed syllabus. Is there therefore a need for accreditation within adult open learning?

Accreditation implies more than certification. It aims to establish standards and ensure quality as well as providing widely recognised qualifications. This can have benefits for those taking accredited courses and for others. In this chapter we shall consider the case for accreditation, and also dicuss some of the associated problems and issues, particularly in relation to adult open learning. First, however, it may be helpful to give a brief outline of the accreditation process.

The accreditation process

It is convenient to identify four aspects to the accreditation process:

- the establishment of appropriate qualifications and the determination of the criteria for awarding them (*accreditation of qualifications*);
- the devising and validation of particular courses leading to these qualifications (*accreditation of courses*);
- the approval of colleges and other study centres to operate these courses (*accreditation of course providers*);
- the verification of competence and the maintenance of standards (*accreditation of student achievement*).

These are dealt with in varying ways by the different validating bodies. For example, some rely more on centrally set examinations whilst others concentrate on verifying the expertise of the college or training centre before granting the college/centre itself responsibility for assessing students.

Establishing a qualification structure

The development of a national qualification structure can be a complex task, involving considerable consultation with employers, professional bodies and teachers. Adults have a wide variety of education and training needs which differ in both content and level. One person may need a short course to update himself or herself on new technology; another may require a more substantial management programme; yet another may be seeking to upgrade his or her level of membership of a professional body. Any system of qualifications for adults must take account of these differing needs. Also, although some needs may be met through courses designed principally for young people, ideally there should also exist a distinct provision specifically aimed at meeting the needs of adults.

The requirement for flexibility implies a modular system which can meet the needs of those who require short, specific updating as well as of those who want to build up a longer study programme. The existence of separate modules also facilitates the giving of credit and exemption for relevant study and experience. Ideally there should be compatability in structure between modules/units accredited by the various examining and validating bodies, and this will no doubt be a concern of the new NCVQ.

Defining and validating courses

Courses may be designed by a central examining or validating organisation to meet a nationally identified requirement. Or individual colleges, or other education/training centres, may design a course to satisfy a particular local (or wider) need.

In the former case a validating organisation may investigate the need and assemble a group of employers, educationists and others with expertise and experience in the subject area to advise it and to draft a course syllabus. Those designing the course need to ensure that the course is broadly equivalent to others at the same level. Centrally devised course syllabuses are normally reviewed periodically and revised when necessary to ensure that they are still relevant.

College-devised courses are usually designed within guidelines defined by the particular validating body. These parameters may include standard unit or module lengths and specific recommendations on, for example, assessment methods or proportions of practical or work-related activity to be included. The details of the course would then usually be submitted to the validating body for 'validation'.

Sometimes the distinction between these approaches is not clear-cut. For example, a validating organisation may provide an outline course syllabus but expect colleges/centres to modify it to suit local needs.

Approving centres

Some examining/validating bodies require education/training centres wishing to run their courses to seek approval before recruiting students. Such organisations normally need to be satisfied about the qualifications and experience of the teaching staff, the relevant facilities at the college/centre, and the teaching and assessment strategies to be employed. Students subsequently enrolled on the course are then registered with the validating organisation. In the case of college-devised courses, the processes of validation and approval may merge, college factors being considered alongside those relating to the course itself.

Maintaining standards

The maintenance of quality standards is a key aspect of the accreditation process. One way of attempting to achieve this is for the relevant validating organisation to devise, set and mark central examinations. It thus maintains central control of assessment and is in a position to compare results nationally. Often, such examining bodies do not require colleges/centres to obtain approval to run their courses, students registering in advance for the examination through any education/training centre, or sometimes applying direct to the examining body to sit their examination.

Other validating bodies avoid setting central examinations and place the responsibility for assessment with the colleges/training centres running their courses. Assessment may then take account of course-work including assignment and project work, as well as (or instead of) end-of-course examinations. The validating body ensures that standards are maintained by requiring part-time moderators or external examiners to visit colleges regularly, and/or by a system of major, periodic reviews.

The case for accreditation

The majority of adult vocational education and training does not involve any accreditation. This is particularly the case with short courses for updating and retraining purposes. Thousands of courses are run by training centres and further education colleges every year, designed to meet the needs of those working in business and industry; very few are validated or monitored by an external body or lead to a nationally recognised qualification. This applies to all study modes, including open learning.

How is the prospective adult learner, or their employer, to find their way through this profusion of education and training opportunity? There is a need for some touchstones, to provide a surer basis for choice and to give some assurance of quality. This may be considered even more important for open learning courses, where greater responsibility for learning rests with the individual.

Of course, accreditation is not necessarily appropriate in all cases. It involves a number of factors which make it valuable in some situations and less relevant or appropriate in others. The appropriateness of accreditation may be evaluated differently from the varying viewpoints of the community, the employer, the providing centre and the students/trainees themselves.

The provision of standard, accredited courses contributes to a degree of uniformity across the country. Although this may, in some ways be seen as a limiting influence, it does have the advantage of ensuring minimum standards, including making sure that certain key topics are adequately covered to a required level. For example, the need to remedy particular skill shortages cannot necessarily be left to local market forces, and central initiatives may be needed. An increasing number of professional bodies are recommending minimum standards of continuing education and professional development for their members. This training requires accreditation, either by the professional body itself or by a national validating body, to ensure that it meets the needs of the profession.

Accredited courses normally lead to the award of some kind of certificate or diploma. This may be restricted to those who have achieved a defined standard, or all students completing may receive a profile statement listing their achievements. Certificates may be awarded by the providing centre itself, but greater weight is usually given to externally validated awards which imply relatively common standards across providing centres and a wide recognition of what that standard entails. Whether or not a particular course awards a certificate may be of less importance to the student/trainee's present employer; however, accreditation does imply a standard of quality and can give the employer an assurance of the level and the effectiveness of the course.

In the course of the accrediting process, examining/validating bodies often make demands upon colleges and training centres. They may, for example, insist upon minimum standards of resources or upon appropriately experienced and qualified teaching staff. This may help centres to maintain their standards and may also have spin-off for other courses provided by the centre.

Employers familiar with the standard of a certificate, perhaps through having employed previous holders of the certificate, tend to assume a similar standard of competence from others. The qualification develops a reputation and possession of such a recognised certificate can often help the holder considerably in obtaining promotion or in finding a new job.

Also, accreditation usually implies assessment, and this may provide a valuable incentive. Learning can be hard work, and the knowledge that it is being monitored and appraised can be a stimulus to greater effort. Assessment can also influence the students' employers and course tutors: the students' success reflects partly on them, and so they also have a strong interest in encouraging and supporting them.

Accreditation can therefore bring significant benefits. What then are the problems, particularly as they affect open learning courses for adults?

Some problems and issues

Administrative problems

A potential drawback for course providers can be the time it can take from a decision to run a course to obtaining accreditation for it. Even when the college or other provider plans to offer a standard course, they may still need to obtain approval from the validating body to run it. Most accrediting bodies are very conscious of this problem and have streamlined their procedures for adult training courses. However, the anticipation of possible delays can still be a disincentive for many course providers.

Delays in validation or approval may arise when an organisation developing open learning materials leaves accreditation considerations until the course has been designed and the materials produced. If the course is not one of the examining/validating body's standard courses, it may still be necessary for its format and structure to conform to particular guidelines. In most cases these guidelines are unlikely to be overly restrictive if they are taken into account from the beginning, but trying to adapt the course later can sometimes be extremely difficult.

Even when materials are being developed for a standard course, it can be equally important to liaise with the examining/validating body from an early stage. Having spent time and effort in developing good quality open learning materials for a particular course, and to then find that the examining/validating body has just revised the syllabus, can be very frustrating indeed. Syllabuses have to be revised from time to time and usually there is reasonable notice of such changes. All accrediting organisations will happily provide information about their courses to materials publishers, provided they are asked.

The influence of assessment

Inevitably assessment has an effect on the learning process. The positive effects have been noted earlier, but if such assessment is insufficiently related to actual work competence, the need to pass irrelevant tests may dominate the course and distort what is learned. Unless opportunity is provided for local flexibility, the training may be seen as 'syllabus driven' rather than 'needs driven'.

It is necessary, therefore, to ensure that what is assessed reflects the needs of the students and that valid assessment methods are used. There should be no need for an examining or validating body to impose irrelevant or inappropriate assessment on a course provider. Normally, such bodies are just as keen as course providers to assess students' competence on the skills and knowledge they need, and to do it in appropriate and relevant ways.

Skills development

In most vocational education and training courses, skills need to be developed and assessed. This necessarily involves learner activity, often including 'hands-on' practice with materials and/or equipment, or interaction with other people. Examining and validating bodies have a responsibility to ensure that courses they accredit do fulfil this requirement. However, there is a tendency for much open learning material to be information-oriented and for many open learning courses to fail to adequately develop skills.

It is sometimes argued that it is unreasonable to expect open, and particularly distance, learning courses to develop skills. Such courses provide an important service for those unable to attend 'conventional' courses, and imposing demands of this nature on them reduces the openness of the course. A student based in the Outer Hebrides and without the possibility of access to any appropriate practical facility or even perhaps to many fellow human-beings, is sometimes cited in support of this attitude.

In practice, of course, the great majority of open and distance learning students are nowhere near so geographically isolated as this mythical Hebridean. The most common reason for choosing an open learning course rather than a class-based one is the inability to obtain day-time release from work coupled with a reluctance to commit oneself to regular evening classes. Overstating the problems associated with developing skills on an open learning course does not help the students, even those who are comparatively isolated, to meet their real training needs. Certainly there can be little defence for open learning materials which are just 'lectures in print'.

Many open learning courses tackle skills development and assessment imaginatively. Practical kits, work-based assignments, 'drop-in' or bookable practical facilities, simulations and case-studies are all used to encourage the development of relevant skills and to provide opportunities for their assessment.

Modularisation and work competence

A valued feature of much open learning is the division of the course content into study modules (often as short as six to eight hours). This enables the learner to take an incremental approach, progressively achieving a series of relatively limited objectives. A modular system also facilitates flexibility, enabling learners to take a 'pick and mix' approach and construct a personal learning programme to meet their needs.

Whilst making the course more flexible, manageable and motivating, this feature can have the drawback of concentrating attention on the development and assessment of easily achieved, knowledge objectives, rather than of work-related competence. In order to make effective use of learned knowledge and skill, the ability to apply them to relevant situations has to be learned as well. It is not sufficient to assume that learners will automatically integrate isolated chunks of knowledge and skill and apply them to their work. Opportunities for integration and application need to be built into the training programme. To overcome this problem, many open learning courses include work-based or work-related activities and projects. For the purposes of accreditation, unless such activities are undertaken and assessed, any certificate is unlikely to reflect work competence.

The role of the course tutor

Some enthusiastic designers of open learning material occasionally claim that 'good' material can be self-sufficient and provide all that a learner needs; the teacher/trainer is redundant. This partly stems from over-confidence in their product, but also from a genuine wish to place the control of learning with the learner. The movement towards open learning originates partly from learners' frustrations with class-based courses which seem to be designed for the convenience of the provider rather than for that of the consumer. The open learning ideal is to 'put the learner in the driving seat'.

All the evidence indicates that this rejection of the tutor is misguided. In most open learning courses tutors are essential, to encourage and support the learners and also to help with skills development. They certainly have a vital role in assessment which could not be dispensed with without resorting exclusively to formal tests and examinations, which are likely to have less validity. It is worth bearing in mind that it is not just tutors who can exercise control: badly structured materials, and in particular computer-assisted training which lacks user-friendliness, can often be as controlling and frustrating as any human-being.

Accreditation of study materials

If accreditation includes validation of courses, approval of centres, monitoring of assessment and certification of learners, why should it not include approval of open learning materials? Should validating bodies evaluate learning materials, particularly those designed specifically for their courses? Centres planning open learning courses often have difficulty in selecting published learning material and, given the option, would probably choose those bearing a validating body's seal of approval. This seal of approval would give some assurance of quality and perhaps imply a more effective course.

Validating organisations sometimes approve learning materials in the context of particular courses, and a few have themselves coordinated the development of open learning materials which may be published under their name. However, so far none has taken the step of giving any general seal of approval to learning material published by others. There are two main reasons for this. Firstly there is a reluctance to give an implied weighting to one aspect of the course implementation, and thus encourage the impression that just working through a set of learning materials could be sufficient in itself to achieve the desired competence; many other factors contribute to a course's effectiveness. Secondly it is recognised that assessing the quality of open learning materials poses considerable difficulty: although it is possible to identify certain desirable features of good open learning material, any evaluation could very easily over-weight superficial characteristics, such as presentation, and fail to adequately measure its effectiveness.

More realistic strategies might be based on agreeing some of the more critical features of good learning materials. A listing of materials might then indicate to what extent each of these features were present in particular material. It has also been suggested that just publicising these criteria could enable course providers, potential learners and employers to make more informed choices.

Future developments in accreditation

Most examining and validating bodies have policies relating to open learning and welcome open learning routes to their qualifications. However, further developments are possible and various ways of making the accreditation process more responsive to the needs of adult learners are under review.

For example, provided that a college or training centre has a successful record of running courses in a specific topic area, it should be possible to accredit the centre as a provider of courses in that area, without them needing to seek approval for each course separately. In this way course providers could be much more flexible in designing courses to meet particular needs, and would also be able to respond more quickly to requests from employers.

Also, many examining and validating bodies are already widening their policies in relation to giving credit for previous study. This must soon extend to giving credit for previous work and life experience. Such accreditation of experience is already common the USA and, although we may not adopt an identical system, a similar development is inevitable.

Rather than identifying open learning as a special provision, there is an increasing tendency to incorporate many of its features in adult education and training generally. These include flexibility in formal course entry requirements, a move towards resource-based learning and a relaxation in the degree of attendance felt to be necessary at a college or training centre. This gradual 'embedding' of open learning within the education and training system will provide a continuing challenge to accrediting organisations, to respond flexibly to the learning needs of adults whilst maintaining a necessary quality assurance role.

References

1 DES, *Review of Vocational Qualifications*, 1986. Business & Technician Education Council, Policies & Priorities into the 1990s, 1984.
Business & Technician Education Council General Guideline: Implementing Open Learning, 1987.
Council for National Academic Awards, *Handbook*, 1986.
City and Guilds of London Institute Handbook, 1986–87.

4 Limitations of the learning package

David Sewart

Introduction

This chapter highlights some issues which are perhaps brought into focus most sharply in the context of distance education, namely whether a package of materials, however sophisticated or well designed, can take the place of every essential facet of the teacher in the traditional teaching situation. Many open learning schemes involve individual study of specially produced materials i.e. learning at a distance from the teacher who was the originator of the materials. However, they also often include some traditional teaching support and, in the Open University (OU), a crucial aspect has been the student support provided through a system of tutors and tutor –counsellors. I shall be offering a rationale in this chapter for what may appear to be a very traditional element in a form of education based in most other ways on modern technologies.

Any system of teaching at a distance must concern itself with what and how it teaches and although there are now many different systems for teaching at a distance, most contain a package of attractively presented self-instructional materials. Printed material invariably forms the basis of this package but is often supplemented by audio-visual material, normally on cassettes, but sometimes offered through open circuit broadcasting. A great deal of thought is customarily put into the assembly of this package in large-scale distance education systems and it is made as attractive as possible for the student learning at a distance. The production of such packages is usually seen as the basis on which economic calculations are made and, since the production demands complex resources, both material and human, and requires longterm planning, it often dominates the system of teaching at a distance to the exclusion of all other activities.

Indeed there is a beguiling temptation to assume that the problems of teaching at a distance can all be solved by the production of an, as yet hypothetical, perfect package of material. This excessive concentration on the package is the institution-based approach to teaching at a distance and indeed it is characterised in the very use of the word 'teaching'. The student-based approach involves a more rigorous examination of *learning* at a distance. It is also inherently more difficult since, whereas the teaching approach can start from the known standard package of materials and tacitly assume the subordination of the needs of the individual to the package, the student-learning approach must involve an examination of an almost infinitely variable base which cannot be controlled or completely stabilised. Even where the teaching institution seeks to remove from its course materials the personality and idiosyncracies of the teacher, the fact remains that two students observing this package may well make different interpretations of it derived from their own assumptions and their own frame of reference.

In addition, the needs of the student at all education levels are not wholly related to the subject that is being studied, which is not to say that such needs are solely of a psychological nature, completely unconnected with the content of study. They may be of an educational, even an academic kind, but not strictly course related. The word 'teaching' is a simple definition of a complex interactive process and one might begin by dividing teaching – from the point of view of the institution – into 'subject matter' and 'advice/support'. The subject matter would embrace the strictly academic content of the course and advice/support would embrace general study problems arising from the individual circumstances of the student or the system of teaching peculiar to the institution. We might look at this in another way by saying that subject matter is information or knowledge and advice/support covers the way in which students as individuals fit new knowledge into their own pre-existing intellectual framework, even into their everyday attitudes and behaviour.

In a system of teaching at a distance what part does the teaching package play in the intermediary role? Does it or could it provide both subject matter and advice/support for individuals? While not wishing to exclude the theoretical possibility that the teaching package could perform all these functions, there are a number of reasons for suggesting that in practice it will always fall a good way short of this ideal, if only for reasons of complexity and cost.

While we might hope to define and delimit the subject matter through an institutionally centred analysis in a way which might receive general assent, advice/support, being student centred, is by comparison almost infinitely variable. Clearly course materials may cover some aspects of advice/support which are judged to be universal or at least common. But any package of materials which seeks to offer comprehensive advice/support for all its students must admit almost infinite variation and, moreover, entail unacceptably high costs.

I have suggested that institutions engaged in teaching at a distance have concentrated extensively on the production of the package of materials. For obvious academic reason these packages embrace the subject matter. For equally obvious economic and practical reasons, few of these packages embrace the function of advice/support. It does not seem unfair to suggest that there is an overwhelming tendency within the field of teaching at a distance to offer systems from the standpoint of the institution teaching at a distance rather than from the standpoint of the student learning at a distance. The response to the individual needs of the student learning alone and at a distance has often become lost in the overriding requirement to produce a grandiose package of materials.

I have argued that the standard teaching package cannot provide a wholly satisfactory individualised learning system for students and also that such a package suffers from a tendency towards tight curriculum control. It is only the introduction of the human element, capable of adapting to the great variety of student needs, which can counteract this sort of bias. Consequently, in the last two decades, the refinement of teaching by correspondence and of educational counselling has been added to the development of the carefully designed teaching package.

The technique and the approach of the correspondence tutor (discussed in much greater detail in chapters 23, 24, 26, 27 and 28) are not always immediately grasped by those who have been engaged in traditional forms of teaching. The correspondence tutor is not there to transmit information – all this is done in the package of materials. The role of the correspondence tutor is that of facilitator. This requires two things: the ability to convey through comments, advice for further study, and the ability to perceive the student's present state of knowledge and conceptual framework so that the advice may be as relevant as possible to the individual. Tutors must offer comments which are considered human, constructive and supportive. The formal nature of written comment, which is not susceptible to the inflection, tone and pause of speech, renders it liable to misinterpretation. Clarity is essential. While much is being done to refine the art of correspondence teaching, it is, as yet, in its infancy. It is clearly not the case that the skills of the traditional teacher are instantly transferable to correspondence teaching.

In the OU we have also seen the combination of the teaching package with an individual support system offered through correspondence tuition and general academic support provided by a tutor –counsellor who is responsible for the progress of individual students from entry in the University until graduation. This general service is supplemented by specialist tuition beyond foundation level.

The inter-relationship between the package of materials and the students has been achieved through the agency of tutor–counsellors and course tutors. Individual contact can be, and often is, by telephone and by post. But it is also very often achieved at foundation level through traditional face-to-face contact, usually at a study centre.

The study centre has been used for a number of functions in various distance teaching systems. In some it has been seen as a viewing centre where replay devices may be used. In others it has been seen as a library resource centre. In some it has been seen as a focus for student interaction and self-help groups, a substitute for the conventional campus. In yet others it has been offered as a site for practical experiments or the use of equipment, such as computing facilities, which are essential to study but which cannot be offered easily to the student at home. Finally, there are cases where study centres are valued as a tangible link between the otherwise impersonal distance teaching institution and the local community.

Can we then say that the study centre with its face-to-face contact is the dustbin of teaching at a distance? Is it the repository into which are emptied those functions or parts of functions which seem to be too difficult or too expensive to carry out by technological means? Is it there because we cannot feel completely confident as yet in our combination of teaching materials and correspondence tuition and because it is particularly useful in the provision of the advice/support function in which the necessity for individualisation is paramount? Is the presence of study centres a denial of the practical possibility, as yet of teaching at a distance? Might we so 'improve' teaching at a distance as to be able to dispense with study centres entirely?

Certainly cogent arguments against the use of study centres have been made. They are costly and, as far as can be ascertained in all systems of teaching at a distance, the use of and need for study centres on the part of the students, falls a long way short of their use and need as projected initially by the institution. It is clear that a large number of students either are not able or choose not to attend a study centre. Clearly many students choose to study by distance teaching methods because they prefer or require, for domestic or work purposes, to be free from the time and space constraints of traditional teaching methods.

However, I would suggest that the 'dustbin' view of study centres arises from a mistaken approach – one which sees them and what goes on in them, solely against the background of traditional education: namely as places in which conventional face-to-face contact between teachers and students takes place. In countering this view I would like to use the OU as an example. Within the OU the concept of a study centre is coloured by the objectives of study centres set out in the original report of the Planning Committee of the

Open University. The Planning Committee had initially seen two purposes for study centres: they were to be used as viewing centres and as places in which tutorials would take place. Such tutorials were envisaged as an essential element in this system of teaching at a distance. The reality, almost from the beginning, proved to be different. Over 260 study centres were created, but within the first three years it became apparent that they could not be used as originally intended. The open circuit broadcasting of radio and television did not always match the evening opening times of study centres. Furthermore, the store of audio and video tapes, particularly the latter, became too expensive to maintain and the replay facility provided by technicolour machines and audio-cassette devices lapsed. The increase in the number of courses after foundation level was not and could not be matched by increases in student numbers. The average course population rapidly fell below two students per study centre. The idea of local tutorials, other than for the high population foundation level courses, simply disappeared. Hence the concept of study centres as viewing centres and locations for essential tuition was not even the case, in practice, in the University's earliest years. It is even less the case today.

However, a significant element of the current role of study centres is implicit in the functions of the OU's tutor–counsellors (a case study of which is found in chapter 23). Tutor–counsellors are seen as the local and continuing support for students. The description of this support is given a physical presence in the study centre which is seen as the base for a tutor–counsellor's activity. A local study centre is a place in which the foundation level tutor–counsellors are able to offer face-to-face support both of a strictly academic and of an advisory/supportive nature to their first year students, all of whom live in the vicinity. The tutor–counsellor is seen as weaning students from the traditional method of face-to-face group teaching towards an approach to learning based on individual and independent study.

The study centre is, in reality, a transitional phase for the students in this process. For the student it has much of the appearance of the traditional classroom in that it is a physical location in which an authority figure, the tutor–counsellor, is present.

If this similarity between traditional and non-traditional methods holds good for the physical situation, it certainly does not hold good for the educational rationale. Tutor–counsellors do not lecture or profess a subject in the traditional way. Indeed they take the academic content more or less as given in the shape of the course units and broadcasts and set out instead to help students learn from this material, either by themselves or in groups. As such therefore, we might describe a study centre as an important element for most new students in the painful early steps of adapting to learning at a distance. It is a stepping stone from group learning of a traditional sort to individual and/or group learning of the non-traditional sort. While it is possible that some students do not need such a stepping stone, it seems clear from the attendance of students themselves that most students still require this element at some point. They may feel no need to attend a study centre tutorial for some time but later develop a need for contact and discussion with the tutor–counsellor and other attendants at the study centre.

It might be alleged that this argument does not hold equally true for more experienced students taking higher level courses and this is almost certainly the case. For post-foundation level students tuition is unlikely to be 'local' but face-to-face contact still exists, albeit less regularly, and provides for a large number of students a stimulus, both social and educational to the continuing process of study.

Study centres are places in which tutorials, day schools and self-help groups take place. Students do not use these facilities as often as the institution makes them available but they are nevertheless essential. We know that students do not read every word of the course units, let alone set books; some omit the radio and television broadcasts entirely; most are extremely selective. Some students do not complete all their home experiment kit activities and, indeed, a few do not even open the boxes in which they are contained. It would be clearly naive and simplistic to try to use student usage as the *sole* determinant of the value of an element in this system. It is the richness and variety, the multiplicity of provision which attracts and sustains students and what is offered in study centres is part of this richness of provision.

But are we to say that study centres are a contradiction of the feasibility of teaching at a distance? To say that they are is, I believe, to misinterpret the nature of teaching at a distance. If we consider the variety of teaching and learning processes, we might see at one extreme the continuous face-to-face dialogue between one teacher and one student, a totally supportive learning situation. Further along the spectrum we find a conventional primary school in which the authority figure of the teacher provides a continuous contact throughout the day with a group of pupils. Much further along the spectrum we find a traditional university teaching system in which the authority figure of the teacher appears less often and the students are more independent in their learning situation. At the far end of the spectrum we find the pure system of teaching at a distance in which the students are learning at a distance from those who have prepared the material; they learn at their own pace, whenever they wish to study and wherever they wish to study. Distance teaching institutions, like the conventional universities, may fall somewhere between the two ends of the spectrum although they are clearly further towards the end of pure distance teaching. Their position in the system is determined by a number of elements. These include the varying entry qualifications of their students, their domestic and work circumstances as adults learning part-time, their previous experience of learning and their perceptions of what they are capable of and the support they require. There is no contradiction between the notion of study centres with their face-to-face contact and teaching at a distance. For some students who do not take part in this particular activity, the institution might come close to pure (*sic*) teaching at a distance. For others it will come less close. More important, however, from the student's point of view, is that the institution offers a richness of variety in opportunities for learning such that its appeal is catholic. It is from this that its success will flow and, if the institution ever seeks to alter the balance of its provision or remove specific elements from the rich variety of this provision, it must do so only with extreme care and mindful of the fact that in so doing it will almost certainly be detracting somewhat from its universal appeal.

5 Adapting materials for alternative use

Wendy Stainton Rogers

Alternative use of learning materials

In this chapter I use the phrase 'alternative use of learning materials' for any situation where one person or a group of people make use of learning materials (text, videotape, audiotape, etc.) produced by other people, for a teaching purpose other than that for which they were originally designed. It includes materials designed for one set of learning objectives (undergraduate study, for example) being adapted for another (such as vocational training); use with a different kind of student (for instance, materials produced for study by nurses being used to train social workers); and adaptations to suit different timescales, different teaching settings and different levels of specialisation (such as materials produced for a general audience customised for the specific needs of management trainees).

The topic has been researched within the Health and Social Welfare Department of the Open University (OU), in an investigation of the educational and economic implications of the wide variety of alternative uses being made of materials produced by the department (Stainton Rogers, 1983).[1] The ideas and recommendations which follow arise out of that research.

There are good functional reasons for deciding to incorporate materials produced by somebody else into your own teaching. Very often such materials will have been produced by an organisation with access to skilled staff, and considerable resources in terms of facilities and equipment for the generation of high quality text, video– and audiotape, computer-aided learning software and so on. But even in terms of materials that have been produced by our own colleagues, it makes a lot of sense to extend their use beyond the specific purposes for which they were designed, since considerable time and effort has already been expended in their development.

However, it is important to recognise that alternative use, if it is to be functional, places strong responsibilities on both the original producers of materials, and the people who use them. Those who design and market materials must ensure that users are provided with proper support, information and advice to enable them to use them effectively. Those using materials need to inform themselves about the appropriate contexts in which they can be used, and ensure that they orient and guide the learner appropriately. Incorporating learning materials produced for other purposes into your teaching should never be seen as an 'easy option'. Rather, it shifts the relationship between the roles of teacher and materials in ways which can undoubtedly result in better learning, but certainly not less demanding teaching. To make clear why I say this, we need to explore in more detail the different roles of materials in different learning settings.

Differences between materials-based and teacher-based learning

In the majority of face-to-face teaching settings, the usual system of course design and dissemination is one in which learning is directed by the class teacher. Courses are organised by an individual or group of classroom teachers who specify the curriculum, plan and implement the teaching programme, set the work that students have to do, mark it, set the final examination and evaluate the students' performance at the end (albeit usually with some form of external monitoring). If materials are used, they are designed and/or selected by the teacher to augment their own role, not replace it, as shown in Figure 1.

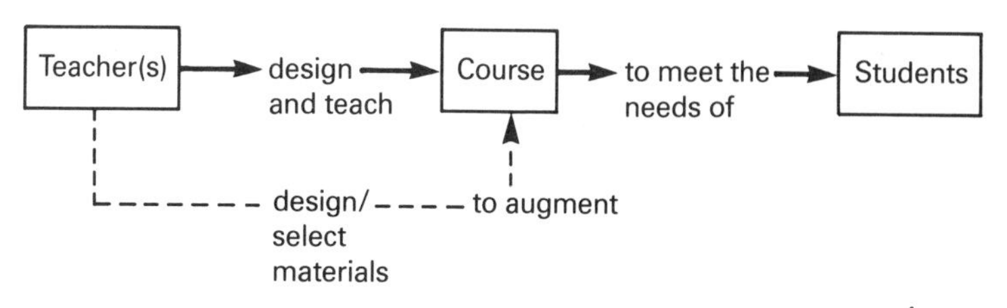

Figure 5.1

Where materials have, however, been designed as the major focus for a course, it is the materials which specify the curriculum and path to be taken by student through the course. Although there may be opportunities for face-to-face tuition built in, these are usually intended as augmentation, the mainstream implementation of the course being directed by the materials producers who specify the curriculum, design the materials to provide the teaching programme, set continuous assessment assignments and the examination, and evaluate students' performance at the end (monitored in the case of the OU by an external assessor and examiner). This system is shown in Figures 5.2.

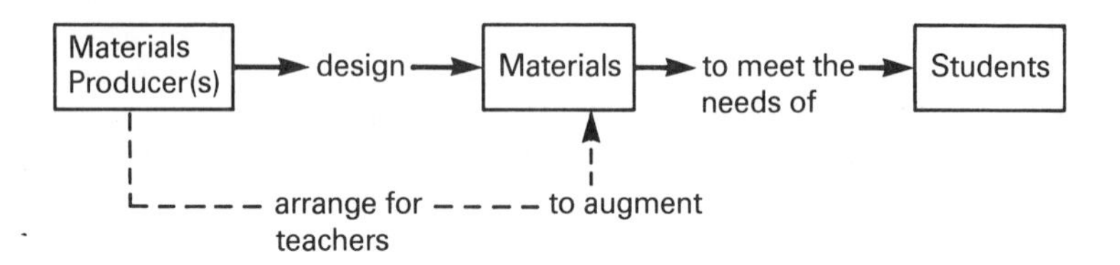

Figure 5.2

There is thus an important distinction concerning the use of materials in the two different situations. In a classroom course, it is the lecturer who assumes the teaching focus, with any externally produced materials acting as augmentation to their central role. In materials-based learning, it is the learning materials that assume the major teaching focus, tutorial input providing augmentation and support.

Where alternative use is made of materials that were originally designed for a materials-based course, the whole process of course design and dissemination becomes more complex. Materials that were designed originally to assume learning–directive functions now become used within a setting where the direction is undertaken by the class teacher. What the student experiences is an interplay between the teaching focus of the materials, and the teaching focus of the tutor, as shown in Figures 5.3.

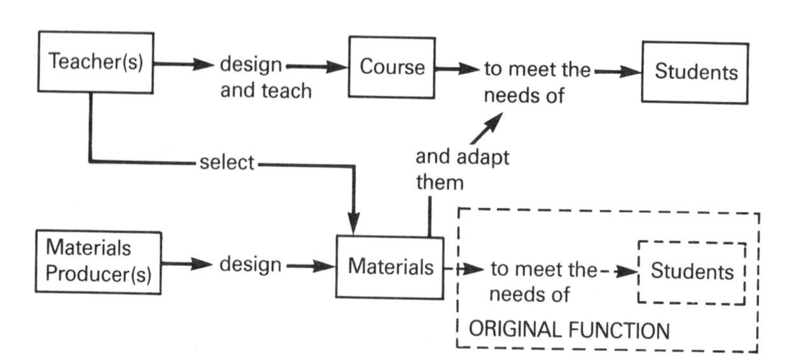

Figure 5.3

The implication is that when alternative use is made of materials in ways that ensure that these two sets of objectives are complementary, the learning experience of students is likely to be very productive, because they are exposed to consistent messages, and a series of learning experiences that progress systematically to a coherent outcome. However, where the objectives are in conflict, it is likely that learning will be confusing at best, and severely curtailed or even counter-productive at worst. What this demonstrates is the crucial importance in the alternative use materials of ensuring an effective mapping of objectives between the producers and users of materials, both those of students, and of teachers.

What are the advantages for the student?

Transferring a portion of the curriculum content to learning materials does two things. Firstly, it offers students a range of learning experiences far broader than any individual tutor could provide. The student can see videotapes, listen to audiocassettes and read case studies of a quality the individual teacher is unlikely to be able to equal. They can gain access to first-hand accounts, which can be far more compelling than a tutor's second-hand account. For example, one of the most effective teaching items I have observed in use is a tape-recording [1] of one woman's problems – and her emotional reactions – arising from caring for her elderly mother suffering from senile dementia. No class teacher's description could have the impact of this harrowing story as told by the person who experienced it.

Secondly, when major parts of the curriculum are covered by distance study prior to classwork, a diverse group of students – from very different backgrounds, with varying experience and prior education – can meet together with a common store of experience and knowledge. Thus group sessions can focus on activities like discussion and group exercises. The tutor, released from an information-transmission role, can give more attention to the role of stimulating and managing learning.

Take, for example, the teaching of interpersonal skills, crucial, to many forms of learning from counselling to personnel management. To acquire competence at such skills, students need to be able to gain three forms of competence; knowledge competence (gaining a knowledge-base sufficient to make decisions about what to do); performance competence (acquiring and being able to perform the appropriate skills effectively) and outcome competence (being able to monitor and fine-tune performance to achieve a desired outcome). Clearly some aspects of this require the intervention of a teacher to provide immediate feedback, but much of it can be done very effectively by way of materials such as text (for communicating information for the knowledge-base) and videotape (providing role models of performance, or as the basis for critical analysis). By shifting a large proportion of students' learning experience onto materials, the teacher is able to devote proportionately more time and effort to those learning management aspects which can only be done within a face-to-face context.

Another example would be in the teaching of subjects which require computer programming literacy. Self-study materials (usually in the form of a combination of teaching text and user-friendly computer software) enable students to acquire the basic programming skills prior to face-to-face teaching, thus allowing the teacher to concentrate on developing more advanced skills, and directing students' powers of critical analysis.

However, learning materials themselves offer particular learning opportunities beyond the effective transmission of curriculum content. Media such as audiotapes have intrinsic properties that make them very effective for other aspects of learning such as attitude change (Stainton Rogers, 1986).[2] The tape of the daughter with a mother suffering from senile dementia is a good example. It was not only that it was a first-hand account, but the spoken word had the ability to communicate feelings and emotions, and gain empathy and a sense of what the world looked like through one woman's eyes.

One student who listened to this tape was a highly experienced head of an old people's home. Her response to the account was to change her whole conception of the relatives of the older people in her care. Previously she had seen them as cold and unfeeling, simply 'dumping' their relatives when they were fed up with them. 'So we kept them at Sunday afternoon's visiting distance. Why should we concern ourselves with people who could be so callous to their Mums and Dads?' The account on tape made her realise that what she had seen as coldness was in truth the result of overload, where entry into a home became the only option in a crisis. So her policy in the home changed: she began involving relatives much more into the care of the residents, and the result was a far happier atmosphere for her staff, the residents themselves, and their relatives. The student made the point:

> To make the change, I had to know how it felt to be a daughter, I had to see the behaviour in terms of what it felt like to be her. It was hearing a real person, all the emotion in her voice, hearing her crying and describing breaking point. It was that which convinced me.

Clearly, then, learning materials have an important educational role to play in a variety of settings, including face-to-face teaching; they are not in competition with conventional methods, but offer useful opportunities to augment and facilitate them, so long as they are carefully chosen and properly used in ways that complement their learning objectives. What does this indicate about alternative use?

Ensuring that alternative use is effective

Whether materials are alternatively used for other distance learning functions (for example, where a change in student population leads to a course designed for social workers being used by student nurses) or alternatively used by being incorporated into classroom-based teaching programmes, it is evident that there are requirements both on the user and the producer to make sure they are effective.

One critical aspect of alternative use is the extent to which existing materials can and should be modified. Usually it is assumed that such modification is for student-related reasons. Centrally produced materials which, for economic reasons, must be marketable, are inevitably generic in their applicability. When used by an individual tutor for a specific student group, they need to be tailored to specific needs – this course, our time-constraints, these students, our local conditions. However, there are a number of other motivations for change which need to be taken into account.

Many people find that they only really understand and 'feel on top of' materials they have produced themselves. Studies of expository writing (Wason, 1980)[3] for example suggest that only by writing about a particular topic or issue can you really begin to understand what you think and understand. The act of writing is an act of comprehension. So sometimes, tutors re-write materials, not for the students' needs, but for their own need to understand.

Other people may change materials because they fail to familiarise themselves with the pack or course as a whole. They read a bit, listen to just some of the audio tapes, or watch only some of the videotape, and feel they need to introduce material which they assume is missing. This comment, which was made during an interview with a Health Visitor Tutor about her use of a teaching pack about Child Abuse, illustrates such a case:

> I wasted a lot of time extending the case study because I felt it only concentrated on physical needs and I felt emotional needs were important. It wasn't until I read a later part of the course, maybe a year after, that I realised it was in the course, but taken up in a later section.

Some people change materials to demonstrate their competence – using somebody else's materials is somehow 'cheating'; others to demonstrate their autonomy: 'Nobody is going to dictate to me how I am going to teach my course'. Yet others feel a need to customise, to put a personal stamp on anything that isn't theirs. All of these responses, of course, can be functional, though I would suggest (as an inveterate changer of materials myself!) that it is sensible to think carefully first before being beguiled into changing materials. Often a teacher's time is better spent on using the opportunities that materials provide, and the time saved, than in change for change's sake.

Being an effective alternative user

Having said that, the whole point of alternative use is that as it is, by definition, a process of adapting materials produced for one purpose to suit another, some degree of modification will always be necessary to meet genuine student-related needs. I have identified four main kinds of modification that need to be considered:

1 *Transformation*, which consists of re-working and re-formulation such as rewriting text, using a different medium, changing the form (e.g. putting a diagram onto an OHP transparency). Changes may include level of difficulty, degree of specificity, or the context used.

2 *Selection*, where some parts of the material are chosen as appropriate, and others discarded, to ensure that students only tackle that which is appropriate.

3 *Augmentation* by introducing additional material or input, to make the materials more up-to-date, topical, locally relevant, or to increase conceptual depth or specificity.

4 *Integration* whereby materials are linked to other teaching inputs so that students experience coherent learning rather than a series of isolated and even conflicting elements.

Being an effective alternative user requires all four kinds of modification. Transformation and selection must be carried out with care to make sure that crucial aspects of context are not lost in the process, but both are very likely to be necessary. Augmentation and integration are, however, essential if materials are to be adapted properly to serve different objectives.

Being an effective producer

When people design learning materials for their own use alone, it is tempting to be single minded: to set a specific task, and concentrate on designing materials suited to particular objectives. Certainly this approach is easier. However, in education generally and in our area of Health and Social Welfare in particular, there are enormous and growing educational demands, and very limited resources. Increasingly it makes more sense to design materials which are flexible and therefore appropriate for a variety of different forms of alternative use.

I suggest that those involved in materials production need to see themselves far more as the providers of resources than of strictly confined, unifunctionally structured courses. I believe this has two main implications for the producers of open learning materials. Firstly, we must design materials with potential for flexible use, for example, by modularisation, with sections that can be self-standing or combined in different ways for different functions. Secondly, alongside production of the materials themselves, we need to make their purpose much more explicit, and to provide information that will enable them to be customised for different settings. We need not only to provide learning resources, but also teaching resources; not just learning materials, but advice, information and skills so that alternative use can occur readily and lead to effective learning.

Hints for the successful alternative use of materials

I will end, therefore, with a brief checklist intended to help potential alternative users make best use of any materials they decide to incorporate into their teaching:

1 Check carefully not just the content of the materials you intend to use, but their learning strategy and design. Where these are consistent with your own, you will not need to make changes – but where there is a potential conflict, make sure you amend them. Ensure that students will experience a systematic and coherent study path.

2 Check that the materials are appropriate in form as well as content, and be willing to change them to suit your students' needs.

3 Select materials carefully, and make sure that they are given sufficient context to make them effective.

4 Decide what kinds of augmentation need to be provided. This may well be little more than a brief introduction and explanation before use, but such additions are essential for materials to be used effectively.

5 Look at your teaching overall, and see that materials are properly integrated with the other elements in the programme.

6 Avoid change for change's sake – ensure that your transformation, selection, augmentation and integration suit the needs of students.

7 Having decided to make use of materials to serve particular teaching functions, have the confidence to allow them to do so, and make use of the time, resources and opportunities to direct your efforts into those aspects of teaching for which your role is crucial.

Notes

[1] This tape recording is itself a good example of the Open University engaged in alternative use. It was modified for our 'Caring for Older People' course from a tape called 'Where's the Key?', originally produced for Age Concern.

References

1 W Stainton Rogers, 'Alternative uses of materials', in *Teaching at a Distance*, Vol 24, pp 49–54, 1983.
2 W Stainton Rogers, 'Changing attitudes through distance learning' *Open Learning*, Vol 1, No 3, pp 12–17, 1986.
3 P C Wason, 'Dynamics of Writing' in *Visible Language*, No 14, p 423, 1980.

6 Introducing Computer-Based Learning

Diana Laurillard

Introduction

Computer-Based Learning refers to any way of using computers in education or training. Computers are frequently used, reasonably enough, to train users of computer systems, or students of computer science, but they can also be used in areas quite unconnected with computers. They can act as simulators, to allow learners to practise using complex equipment; they can act as infinitely patient tutors, allowing learners as much time and practice as they need to master a procedure; they can test levels of competence on certain kinds of skill and knowledge. These unique features of CBL features, together with all the other advantages of open learning methods, such as savings on residential courses, better timing of training, etc., can make it a very competitive method. When we consider the task of training and retraining a workforce of 20 million to an adequate standard in a rapidly changing world, it becomes clear that new technology must play a part in modernising the training industry, as it does for every other industry.

CBL has been available for more than twenty years now, and widely available, with the advent of cheaper microcomputers, for more than five years. There is a widespread conviction that computers have a valuable contribution to make as a teaching medium, a conviction backed up by the allocation of government funds for computers in schools and even to some extent in industrial training. Yet Computer-Based Learning has not yet fulfilled its potential. It is still a very low-profile activity.

The role that has been promised for computers in education and training is the radical one of taking over a substantial part of the learning process from the inefficient, inflexible classroom. This has not yet begun to happen. The computer is still relegated to the minority specialist areas, and to the committed bands of enthusiasts. This article outlines the conditions under which CBL might be more likely to flourish.

Investigations into Computer-Based Training

In 1985 the Open University (OU) was asked by the Manpower Services Commission to investigate the state of the art in Computer-Based Training (CBT) in the UK, and to produce a multi-media pack entitled *Introduction to Computer-Based Training.*[1] The aim of the nationwide survey of industrial trainers and training managers was to assess the degree of interest in CBT.

The introductory pack is intended to help trainers decide whether they need to use CBT for their particular training applications. The material for the pack was based in part on visits to 12 UK companies, experienced in the introduction of computers for training, and on a literature search of more than 200 papers and reports on CBT.

For the survey, a questionnaire was sent to training personnel in all areas of industry. A relatively low response rate of 14 per cent gave 371 replies, on which the survey results are based.

Replies showed that 26 per cent of companies who responded are currently using CBT, of whom most (64 per cent) were members of companies of 1000 employees. CBT is far less economical for smaller companies at present, because there is no existing bank of training courseware for them to make use of, and because they have too few employees over whom to spread the cost of developing CBT or any other form of self study. Smaller companies cannot be expected to use CBT until it becomes sufficiently well used in larger companies for a bank of usable courseware to be established.

Among companies who responded and who are not currently using CBT, approximately half planned to do so in the near future. Comparing UK with USA figures over the last ten years the UK is consistently about five years behind the USA in adopting CBT. Current USA survey figures are running at over 40 per cent usage of CBT among respondents. If the trend continues, only half of the UK companies who plan to introduce CBT will actually do so in the next five years.

Although these figures suggest a reasonable degree of penetration into the industrial training world, much of this usage will refer to applications such as word-processing, or data processing, where it would be hard not to use a computer in training. These are perfectly legitimate uses of CBT, but they cover only a narrow range of its potential applications. We cannot assume, on the basis of these figures, that CBT holds the place it should in the trainer's repertoire of methods. It is most likely, for example, that in companies that say they use CBT, the great majority of their training is done in the classroom, or perhaps with text-based materials.

The other main finding of the survey was that respondents showed a wide range of familiarity with CBT, from those who wanted more information about the concept itself, to those who knew about it already and wanted technical help with the implementation of CBT. Even those companies which have already adopted CBT feel the need for support and further information on how to use it. Of the respondents to the survey, more than 70 per cent felt they needed to know more about:

- the case for and against expenditure on CBT;
- the identification of likely sources of CBT courseware;
- the assessment of different types of computer for CBT;
- implications for staff development once CBT is introduced.

In fact the replies showed a need for more information in areas other than those concerned with new technology. For example, 39 per cent indicated that they needed to know more about how to identify training needs. For one of the traditional areas of expertise among training managers, this is a surprisingly high score.

The low response rate, together with the lack of confidence in using new technology for training displayed by the respondents to the questionnaire, suggests that there is a considerable awareness-raising job to be done among professional trainers, if CBT is to be used more widely.

Three principal determinants

For the case studies, the course team visited 12 UK companies that have recently introduced CBT, and talked to the managers, trainers and trainees involved, to determine the components of a successful implementation. From these case studies, coupled with the literature search, it was possible to isolate three principal determinants of a well-established CBT programme: institutional integration, pedagogical fit and staff awareness.

Institutional integration

There are basically two ways of introducing CBT. Either a company launches a full costed and staffed programme for a limited period at the end of which a decision is taken about its feasibility on a full scale within the company; or the initial phase is the small-scale pilot program, written by an enthusiast who has acquired a work-station within his departmental budget, where the aim is to produce something that will convince others that CBT is useful. The first is much more likely to work than the second. The use of computers in teaching or training requires a minimum critical mass of activity before its benefits become visible. There are very few situations where it is particularly useful on a small scale. The development of courseware is a major creative project that almost certainly cannot be done by one person, and certainly not in his or her spare time. It is most likely to require a team effort, involving trainers, managers, programmers and trainees. Companies that assign a budget, staff and a limited time-scale with defined objectives are much more successful at making CBT work. It becomes an integrated part of the organisation's activity, accountable to a senior manager, instead of being an optional extra. It is sensible to start with a pilot study, but it must be planned, as must any other innovative project.

Pedagogical fit

Sometimes CBT is introduced for the wrong reasons; the bandwagon effect is very common in projects connected with new technology. While this may be a perfectly valid reason for taking an interest, it is important that CBT be pedagogically appropriate for its intended use. There are many examples of existing CBT where the question 'Couldn't you do the same thing more efficiently with a text (video/workbook, etc.)?' would be an embarrassing one. Even if the full institutional integration has been achieved, if the programs themselves are pointless, boring, or time-wasting, they will not be used.

Staff awareness

Once the two conditions above are met, the next most important component is the involvement of the individuals whose work will be affected by the innovation. There are many legitimate reasons for staff to resist the introduction of CBT, according to their particular role in the institution. Senior managers will be concerned about initial investment; line managers will want assurance that their staff can be trained to the same level in the same time, or better; trainers will see CBT as a threat to their jobs; trainees will be wary of the data-gathering capabilities of computers. Involvement of all participants in advance of the introduction enables an institution to accommodate the concerns, and meet them where necessary. A complex innovation of this sort is inevitably vulnerable to opposition from any one of many staff groups or individuals.

If these three components are taken into account, then the introduction of computers into training is much more likely to succeed. And although the survey and case-study information was based on industrial training, much the same considerations apply to computers in education.[2]

With this basic information gleaned from the survey, the literature search, and the case studies above, we can now consider the conditions under which CBT could be expected to flourish as a widely used and efficient training and learning method.

Conditions for the success of Computer-Based Learning

Computer-Based Learning itself can be seen as a kind of manufacturing industry. It produces a marketable product, namely the computer-based teaching programs; it has a measurable objective, namely the increased efficiency of learning or training; and it requires a 'business plan' to be able to function properly. At the national level an innovation of this type, if it is to have a major impact on our education and training, needs a supporting infrastructure. This will involve collaboration between computer manufacturers (to orient their marketing towards this new audience), industrial training and teacher-training organisations (to undertake the professionalism of trainers and teachers with respect to the use of new technology), further and higher education (to provide courses on developing CBL), and government agencies, such as the MSC and the DES in the UK (to allocate resources for and promote the use of new technology). Only the latter two have begun to happen so far.

Existing course provision on how to develop and implement CBL is very low. There are short courses and seminars at an introductory level, run by educational institutions and private companies. There are a few introductory books. But this is scarcely sufficient to support an adequate educational programme, given that widespread use of CBL presupposes a large number of highly trained CBL designers. The absence of CBL courses occurs because there is no established base of expertise in the subject. Very few people have much experience in CBL. The skill base is only likely to be established as a consequence of government funding – no other organisation will take the responsibility for it. This has been minimal, however. Over the last ten years, the DES in the UK has awarded only £11m for the whole of CBL education, for industrial training funding only began three years ago. With only a handful of individuals able to provide training in CBL it is not surprising that the process of building up the skill base is still slow.

Considering where CBL should be, the infrastructure it needs, and where it is now, what is needed to bridge that gap? The collaboration of the groups I mentioned above will help to quicken the development of the skill base. Educational institutions, such as the OU, can begin to play their role as course providers, but this will not be effective unless the other key organisations also collaborate in the programme of promotion, awareness-raising and resourcing.

The OU has begun to play its role by developing an introductory pack *Introduction to Computer-Based Training*, funded by the Manpower Services Commission.[1] The pack addresses the fact that for whatever reason an institution is interested in CBT, they need some basic information to help them decide whether it is appropriate for their conditions. The decisions taken in designing the pack took account of the following points, based on the investigations described above. Although the examples and the information base are taken from industrial training, the theoretical points are equally applicable to education:

- the use of CBT is often confined to small-scale, under-financed projects. Therefore, there is a need to foster the implementation of CBT as a properly resourced and accountable project;
- CBT is often introduced for the wrong reasons. Therefore, it is important to ensure that the right reasons, such as pedagogical appropriateness, are considered;
- as all participants in CBT must be aware of its value and limitations, a multi-media design will help to provide easy access to the description of CBT for various staff groups;
- the introduction of CBT requires a complex decision-making process. Therefore the pack should assist managers to do this by providing an Action Plan for them to complete as they work through the information, applying it to their own situation as they go;
- CBT is often introduced by people who are relatively inexperienced in buying and using computer hardware and software. Therefore, the pack content must cover all the basic information relevant to the introduction of a new computing system, including the types of hardware and software available, how to critically evaluate them, how to cost them, and how to plan the logistics of using them;
- because many people using the pack will be going beyond its scope (i.e. the decision whether to use CBT or not) and will have begun implementation, it must also provide follow-up help in the form of information about providers of CBT support.

If the pack succeeds in its aims, it will create a large number of trainers and managers capable of making realistic and efficient plans for the introduction of CBT.[1] It is not a how-to-do-it pack, however, and if the use of CBT is to become widespread and successful in the UK, one of the critical problems to be solved will be the provision of sufficient numbers of trained, professional CBT designers. A 'how-to-do-it' pack is therefore essential.

Concluding points

CBL in both education and training must still be regarded as being in the early stages of development. We have to recognise that although provision appears to be changing rapidly, usually because of the acquisition of more work-stations, this is only a superficial change, an artefact of the sudden reduction in the cost of hardware. The real changes will come when the infrastructure of the development of course material changes. But it takes a long time for infrastructures to change. Converting from an on-line process (classroom teaching) to a batch process (individualised learning) requires a major upheaval in the way we train and use teachers, which cannot be expected to happen overnight. And the work being done now should be carried out with this in mind. Within this longterm framework, decisions taken about the planning and resourcing of CBL will be quite different from those taken with the short-term perspective of 'having something working next week'. Longer term planning will lay more solid foundations, and will enable the use of CBL to take its place as a major teaching and training method, alongside the other open learning methods.

References

1 For more information on the pack, please contact the Learning Materials Service Office, Centre for Continuing Education, The Open University, PO Box 188, Milton Keynes, MK7 6DH. Telephone (0908) 74066.

2 D M Laurillard (1981), The promotion of learning using CAL, in D Wildenbury (ed), *Computer Simulation in University Teaching*, North Holland.

Further reading

P Barker and H Yeates, *Introducing Computer-Assisted Learning*, Prentice-Hall, Hemel Hempstead, 1985 – useful for its descriptions of integrating computers with other media, including video.

C Dean and Q Whitlock, *A Handbook of Computer-Based Training*, Kogan Page, London, 1984 – some detail on course design, evaluation and authoring.

G Kearsley, *Computer-Based Training – A Guide to Selection and Implementation*, Addison-Wesley, Reading, MA, USA, 1983 – more mainframe oriented than micro-based, and with an American emphasis.

7 Understanding adult student drop-out

Alan Woodley

Introduction

A popular story in educational circles was that, just as Colmans made their fortune from the mustard left on the side of people's plates, private correspondence colleges only remained solvent because of high student drop-out. If all the students who paid their registration fee sent in their assignments for marking, the profit margin would disappear. Which, if any, colleges actually displayed such a callous indifference to the fortunes of their students is open to question, but what is apparent is that today's 'open' and 'distance learning' schemes are obliged to take the matter of student progress very seriously. Employers who run their own schemes want to ensure that it is a sound investment, and where the programme relies upon subsidies from public funds there is also a need to justify continued funding. Also, on strictly humanitarian grounds, any programme which is based on the philosophy of 'open-ness' should be concerned about its drop-out rate.

In our experience concern with drop-out is sporadic rather than continuous. Panics occur when a particular course is seen to have a high drop-out rate or when drop-out rates in general are greater than last year. During these panics it is common for the wrong questions to be asked and for simplistic solutions to be put forward. Drop-out is actually a very complex phenomenon and can be looked at in a number of ways. In this chapter we attempt to illuminate the problem by isolating what appear to be the key questions and by suggesting certain explanatory frameworks. To do this we draw heavily on our OU (Open University) experience and in particular on our investigations of increasing drop-out rates on third-level courses (Woodley and Parlett, 1983).[1]

Defining drop-out

'Drop-out' is a term frequently used in a variety of educational contexts and, by and large, people share a general conception of what it means. Roughly speaking it concerns students who start a course but do not complete it. However, there is wide variation in how the term is applied in practice and especially in the area of open and distance learning. Which students are considered to have started the course? Those who accept the offer of a place? Those who make the first fee payment? Those who turn up to the first class? Those who send in the first assignment? Withdrawal during the first stages of a distance course can be quite high and choice of a baseline will crucially affect drop-out rate calculations.

Again non-completion of a course can take many forms. As well as students who formally withdraw there are those who effectively 'choose' to withdraw by not attending classes, not submitting assignments, not attending exams, not paying fees, etc. Withdrawal can also be made compulsory by the institution if the student breaches certain regulations or fails to make the required academic progress.

How you choose to define 'drop-out' will depend upon the nature of the course and the definitions used by courses elsewhere with which you wish to make comparisons. It is then up to you to state the definition, to explain its underlying rationale and to apply it consistently. For illustration we reproduce below an attempt to do this in the context of the OU undergraduate programme:

> Here we are concerned with performance in a given year rather than with graduation rates of continuation from one academic year to the next. Even within a given year there are various ways of defining and measuring student performance. In considering the global question of student drop-out we have chosen to use the following four measures of performance which seem most suited to the OU context:
>
> i) ***Non-completion of final registration***
> This only concerns new undergraduates. The number not completing final registration is expressed as a percentage of those who were provisionally registered on January 1st.
>
> ii) ***Withdrawal rate***
> Students are considered to have withdrawn if they finally registered but did not sit the end-of-year exam.
>
> iii) ***Failure rate***
> Students are considered to have failed if they sat the end-of-year exam but did not gain a course credit.
>
> iv) ***Overall wastage rate***
> This is the percentage of students who finally registered but who did not gain a course credit. In other words it includes both 'withdrawal' and 'failure'.

A further complication is that each of these four rates can be 'student-based' or 'course-based'. In the former case students are generally considered to be unsuccessful if they do not gain any course credit in a given year. Therefore a student who has withdrawn from three courses but has passed one is still classified as 'successful'. In the tables that follow we have specified whether they are course or student-based but it should be pointed out that the two types of analysis actually produce very similar results. The great majority of OU students only finally register for one course (78 per cent of students in 1980) and those who register for more tend to either pass them all or pass none of them. In 1980 only 5 per cent of all finally registered students could be classified as 'drop-downs' – i.e. those who succeeded in some but not all of their OU courses.

(Woodley and Parlett, 1983)[1]

This statement was then followed by a table (Table 7.1) which summarised the position in 1982:

Table 7.1

OU undergraduate performance in 1982 (student-based)

		Total	New students	Continuing students
i)	Non-completion of final registration (Base = all provisionally registered)	NA	28%	NA
ii)	Withdrawal rate (Base = all finally registered)	24%	17%	27%
iii)	Failure rate (Base = all who sat exam)	6%	6%	7%
iv)	Overall wastage rate (Base = all finally registered)	29%	22%	32%

Source: Woodley and Parlett, 1983[1]

On the face of it the table presented reasonable and objective measures of student performance. However, even these need interpretation and critical assessment. Firstly, the distinction between 'failure' and 'withdrawal' is not a clear-cut one. Are those students who do not sit the exam because they think they will fail very different from those who actually fail? Secondly, the decision to allow new students a trial period of provisional registration, while justifiable on education and moral grounds has profound effects on the statistics. If the percentages in Table 7.1 were based on all new provisionally registered students then the overall wastage rate for this group would be 45 per cent rather than 22 per cent. Finally, these are performance rates as measured for administrative purposes and do not necessarily reflect the subjective perceptions of the students themselves. For example those who were not studying with the intention of gaining a course credit or who left to transfer to another course would probably not consider themselves to be 'drop-outs'.

'Drop-out' can be taken to include all unsuccessful students but is more commonly used to describe those who decide not to complete a course. Therefore, for the remainder of this chapter we will equate 'drop-out' with withdrawal from a course and 'wastage' will include both drop-out and failure. However, some imprecision inevitably remains as a result of inconsistent definitions in the research literature and variations in regulations between courses and institutions.

Is drop-out a problem?

If you are running a short open learning course for six employees, say, it's possible that everybody will successfully complete it. However, given life's vagaries and the problems of part-time study, it is likely that your course will have at least a few drop-outs. Then you must ask yourself 'Is this drop-out rate acceptable?'. A drop-out rate of 50 per cent may seem very high but is it about what you would expect given the nature of the course and the characteristics of your students? It is natural to look for comparative figures in other institutions and we present below some of the data currently available on adult students.

Distance study

Glatter and Wedell concluded from their review of research around the world that drop-out on correspondence courses is much higher than would be expected in full-time courses and that it is particularly heavy in the early stages of a course (Glatter and Wedell, 1971).[2] Drop-out rates varied with the length and type of course involved but sometimes ran as high as 70 per cent.

Glatter and Wedell only recorded two British studies. The first concerned a 12-assignment introductory economics course provided by the University of Nottingham, Department of Adult Education, in conjunction with a television series where it was found that 17 per cent of the students who enrolled on an individual basis, sent in no assignments and 56 per cent completed ten or more assignments (Wiltshire and Bayliss, 1965).[3] In the second 21 per cent of students who had enrolled for a GCE 'O' level Physics correspondence course provided by the National Extension College, and who replied to a post-course questionnaire, said that they had not used the course at all, even though they had each paid £12.50 each for it (Wedell and Perraton, 1968).[4].

Harris (1972)[5] attempted to follow up the students surveyed by Glatter and Wedell as part of the 1967 'Enrolment Survey' (Glatter and Wedell, 1971).[2] These students had embarked on a correspondence course leading to one of three commercial qualifications equivalent to degree level, or to a London external degree, the BSc (Econ), or to GCE 'A' levels in any of a variety of subjects. On the basis of the follow-up questionnaire, Harris concluded that 33.5 per cent of the students had dropped out from these courses between 1967 and 1970. However, this is likely to be an underestimate of wastage for two reasons.

Firstly, it is based on questionnaire returns and the response rate was only 51 per cent. It seems highly likely that those students who had dropped out would be less inclined to return the questionnaire. Secondly, many of the respondents were still continuing with their courses. Harris himself speculated that the final wastage rates for the five courses might range from 48 per cent to 57 per cent.

Student performance for OU undergraduates in a given year has been shown in Table 7.1 Wastage rates in terms of failure to graduate can never be calculated exactly because students are allowed to accumulate credits at their own pace. However, it can be said that 57 per cent of those who finally registered as new students in 1971 have been awarded an Ordinary degree, and that the final figure is unlikely to be much higher. It seems that figures for subsequent intakes will be somewhat lower but will still exceed 50 per cent (McIntosh, Woodley and Morrison, 1980).[6]

The University's associate student programme is designed primarily for adults who have had practical experience in a given field and wish to develop or broaden their skills and understanding to a higher level. Some of the courses have been specially prepared to cover identifiable professional areas whereas others were originally introduced as part of the undergraduate programme. Students may work towards a Course Certificate obtained by passing the continuous assessment and the examination, or a Letter of Course Completion, obtained by passing the continuous assessment. In 1981 there were 7478 associate course registrations. Forty-nine percent resulted in the award of a Course Certificate and 13 per cent in a Letter of Course Completion. This gives a wastage rate of 38 per cent, but it must be remembered that many of the students will have enrolled on these courses with no intention of completing the assessment component.

Part-time study

Part-time degree study is relatively rare in British universities. Birkbeck College is the notable exception and there is some evidence on performance, albeit somewhat dated (Academic Advisory Committee on Birkbeck College, 1966).[7] It was found that one in four of the students entering in 1957, 1958 and 1959 did not return for the second year, but of those who did, some two out of three subsequently graduated. This gives an overall wastage rate of approximately 50 per cent. A more recent study of adults taking a part-time degree in psychology at Goldsmiths College revealed a drop-out rate of 65 per cent (Vinegrad, 1980).[8]

Part-time advanced study is more common in the public sector but data on drop-out is just as hard to come by. A recent report by Her Majesty's Inspectorate revealed high wastage rates on part-time engineering courses at the South Bank Polytechnic with only half of the students passing (Santinelli, 1986).[9] In another polytechnic, it was shown that on a Diploma in Management Studies course, which could be taken one year full-time or three years part-time, the wastage rates were 36 per cent and 54 per cent respectively (Woodley *et al.*, forthcoming).[10]

Shaw (1972)[11] carried out a study of wastage in part-time adult GCE classes in colleges of further education and technical colleges. The sample consisted of over 2000 students enrolled for day and evening work in five large colleges in a major conurbation in northern England. Drop-out was measured between enrolment at the beginning of the sessional year and sitting the examination nine or ten months later. A drop-out rate of just under 70 per cent was found and this figure would be larger if it were to include in it students dropping out after failure at the examinations.

There have been a number of studies concerning drop-out on Local Authority adult education classes and, although there are variations in definition and the range of courses surveyed, the results are reasonably consistent. A study of evening class students in the Huddersfield area, where drop-out was defined as 'a student who leaves a course three weeks or more before the end of the period paid for' showed a drop-out rate during one term of 16 per cent (Roberts and Webb, 1980).[12] In another study at the City Literary Institute the overall drop-out rate was estimated to be 26 per cent (Glynn and Jones, 1967).[13] A third study considered the progress made by some 3000 students on over 150 courses at four different centres (Woodley *et al.*, forthcoming).[10] It was found that 21 per cent dropped out during the Autumn term (i.e. did not attend any of the last four sessions) and that 58 per cent of those who had initially enrolled in the Autumn term did not re-enroll for the second term.

Full-time study

A study of mature student performance in British universities showed that 17 per cent did not gain a degree compared with a figure of 13 per cent for those aged under 21 (Woodley, 1984).[14] In terms of degree performance, there was virtually no difference between the two age groups with approximately one in three gaining a First or Upper Second. Wastage rates are not available for polytechnics but the evidence on degree performance parallels that for universities (Bourner and Hamed, 1986).[15]

There appear to be few published statistics concerning performances at longterm residential colleges. One estimate for the women students of Hillcroft College put the wastage rate at between 16 and 24 per cent (Woodley *et al.*, forthcoming).[10]

It must be admitted that these findings, while of some interest, are of little practical use. Unless you can match your own course in terms of course length, level and subject, admission criteria, student characteristics, etc. (and of course by definition of drop-out), then there will always be legitimate grounds for rejecting precise comparisons with other courses. The findings merely provide a general context in which to place the figure for your own course.

In the absence of directly comparable courses elsewhere, much can be learned by looking at patterns and variations in performance on courses within your own institution. For example, Table 7.2 shows that in 1981 the wastage rates for OU Maths and Technology courses were above average at each of the three course levels, whereas for Arts and Social Science courses they were consistently below average. (Wastage rates also appear to increase with course level, but it must be remembered that the Foundation rates are artificially low due to the Provisional Registration procedure for new students that was mentioned earlier.) One response to these figures would be to concentrate on improving higher level courses, especially in Maths, Science and Technology. However, there is actually greater scope for reducing the volume of student wastage on Foundation and second level courses because that is what the great majority of students are taking.

Table 7.2

OU overall wastage rates in 1981, analysed by faculty and course level (course-based)

	Foundation	Second level	Third and fourth level
Arts	22%	30%	32%
Social Science	22%	33%	34%
Education	NA	31%	38%
Maths	26%	39%	45%
Science	23%	32%	40%
Technology	28%	41%	41%
Total	24%	34%	37%

Source: Woodley and Parlett, 1983[1]

Changes over time are also of interest. Figure 7.1 shows that there have been important trends within the OU undergraduate programme. On third and fourth level courses, for example, wastage rates increased consistently for seven years, and then fell in each of the next four years. If drop-out on your own course is increasing each year, it is clearly important to know whether this is a departure from or part of the prevailing trend within your institution. It is also vital, of course, that the institution should attempt to understand the causes of such trends and we shall return to this question later.

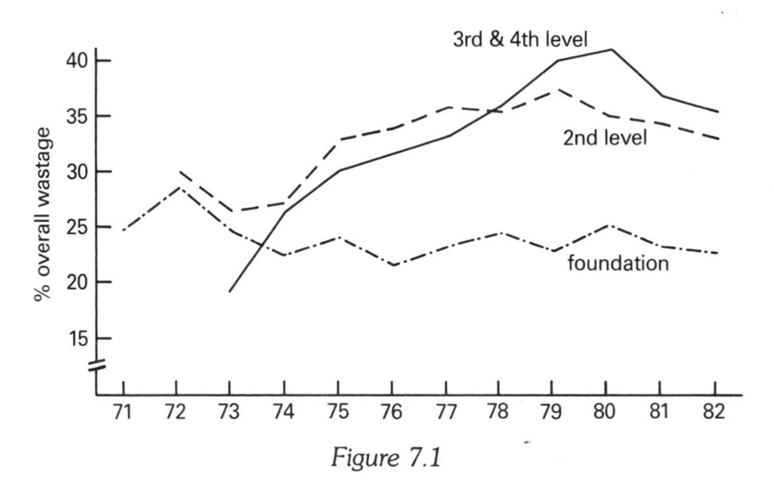

Figure 7.1

Explaining drop-out

It has long been acknowledged that lack of ability is not the sole cause of student drop-out. On the one hand there are other influential student factors such as motivation, personality and background and on the other there are institutional factors concerning how students are selected, taught and treated. Drop-out rates result from the interaction of these student and institutional factors. Furthermore, these factors are certainly different and probably more numerous and complex when considering adults in open learning situations. As an introduction, we list below some of the factors which can underlie drop-out from the students' perspective.

1 Course factors

- Course found to be too difficult or not sufficiently advanced.
- Course required too many hours study each week, i.e. 'overloaded'.
- Course badly designed and/or taught.
- Content found uninteresting.
- Content not as expected from the course description.

2 *Institutional factors*

- Inadequate classrooms, equipment, parking, accommodation, etc.
- Administrative errors, e.g. not sent the teaching material.
- Required to leave by the institution.

3 *Study environment factors*

(a) ***Unforeseen/unplanned changes***

- Personal/domestic changes such as illness of student or relative, change in marital status, having a baby, having to care for ageing relatives, moving house.
- Work changes such as increase in working hours or responsibilities, more travel, e.g. sent abroad, became unemployed, changed job, started work.
- Other changes such as withdrawal of financial support, loss of a quiet place to study, clash with other leisure activity.

(b) ***Chronic factors***

- Little time or energy given to other domestic, work and leisure commitments.
- Lack of money.
- Lack of encouragement by spouse or employer.
- Transport problems.

4 *Personal blame*

- I was too disorganised.
- I was not clever enough.
- I lacked the necessary study skills/background knowledge.
- I was too lazy.
- I lacked self-confidence.
- I had unreal expectations of the course.
- I couldn't face the assessment/exam.
- I took on too much along with my other commitments.

5 *Motivational factors*

- Student no longer needs to complete the course as original goal has been achieved, e.g. gained promotion, learned something about painting.
- Original goal has changed, e.g. enrolled on course in order to become a teacher but now has decided to remain in present job.
- Goal met better elsewhere, e.g. student transfers to a course elsewhere which better meets his-her needs and circumstances.
- Realised goal would not be achieved, e.g. enrolled on class in order to meet people but did not get on with other students.
- Other goal has taken priority, e.g. student decides to spend more time on another hobby, trade union activities, voluntary work, etc.

'Explaining' drop-out can take a number of forms. One approach is to attempt to identify which types of student are more likely to drop-out. In Table 7.3, for example, we analyse the performance of OU undergraduates by their previous educational qualifications. Generally speaking, the lower these qualifications were, the less likely the students were to gain a course credit. This held true for new and continuing students but the difference in wastage rates were more marked among new students.

Table 7.3

OU overall wastage rates in 1981, analysed by previous educational qualifications (student-based)

	All students	New	Continuing
No formal qualifications	47%	48%	46%
CSE/RSA	44%	42%	45%
'O' levels	35%	29%	37%
ONC/OND	32%	27%	35%
'A' levels	29%	22%	31%
HNC/HND	27%	16%	30%
Teacher's Certificates	25%	11%	29%
University Diploma	27%	17%	30%
University Degree or equivalent	27%	13%	32%

Source: Woodley and Parlett, 1983[1]

Student drop-out within the OU has also been shown to be related to age, occupation, sex, region, credits held, length of study and workload (Woodley and Parlett, 1983).[1]

Another approach to explaining drop-out is to look at the courses themselves and to look for those features which are associated with high or low wastage rates. In the case of the OU we have already looked at variations by course level and by faculty, but it has also been shown that courses tend to have high wastage rates if they have no summer school, are half credits, have been presented for several years, have few TV and radio programmes, have few students, or have few set textbooks (Woodley and Parlett, 1983).[1]

These approaches are likely to shed some light on the drop-out phenomenon but they will not be conclusive. It is most unlikely that you will ever be in a position to say that all students displaying characteristic 'x' will complete the course and all those not displaying it will drop out. Furthermore, even when a variable is strongly related to student progress, there are often difficulties in interpretation. For example, the relationship between previous qualifications and OU performance suggests that academic ability or at least educational experience is a determining factor, but there are other possibilities. Those with low qualifications tend to be in jobs where they are less likely to receive encouragement and financial support from their employer. As they receive no credit exemptions they will also face many more years of study before gaining a degree, so there may be motivational factors involved.

Some problems can be overcome by adopting multi-variate statistical models, but, while this has led to the identification of some 'high risk' student groups, their overall explanatory power has been limited (Woodley and Morrison, 1976).[16] In part this may have been because important independent variables were missing such as motivation and strength of commitment, but some causal factors such as illness, changing jobs and transferring to a better course are essentially unpredictable. An attempt to explain the variability in course wastage rates using the characteristics of the course itself and of the students taking it was more successful (Woodley and Parlett, 1983).[1] The resulting model was used subsequently to show that most of the increase in wastage rates on OU higher level courses could be explained by a combination of changes in the type of course on offer and in the student population. However, even this model failed to predict the sudden down-turn in rates on higher level courses which occurred in 1981 and which was almost certainly a consequence of the large increase in student fees (see Figure 7.1).

Another approach to the explanation of drop-out is to ask the students themselves for the reasons behind their decision. We summarise briefly below the results from a number of such surveys.

The Open University

A sample of new students were asked in an open-ended fashion to give their main reasons for not completing final registration (Woodley and McIntosh, 1980).[17] Of all the reasons given, 77 per cent were related to domestic and work circumstances, 21 per cent referred to study problems caused by the form and content of the courses and 2 per cent were administrative problems.

In a survey of students who had dropped-out from third level Maths courses, the questionnaire gave a list of 12 possible reasons for drop-out (Phythian and Clements, 1982).[18] Students were asked to give a main reason and also a second and third reason, if there were any. Domestic and job factors were given by 61 per cent of respondents as their main reasons, 27 per cent mentioned problems with the courses themselves and 12 per cent gave motivational factors. When 'second reasons' were added in, the figures for the three categories were 53 per cent, 36 per cent and 11 per cent respectively.

Correspondence courses

Glatter and Wedell (1971)[2] reviewed five studies of drop-out from correspondence courses in the USA and Australia and striking similarities were found between them. In each study, lack of time due to work and other commitments was by far the most frequently cited reason for dropping out. Other common reasons were illness, changed intentions and interests, and transfer of place of work. Course factors were mentioned by less than one in five of any group.

Adult education classes

Glynn and Jones (1967)[13] carried out a survey of students who had dropped out from courses at the City Literary Institute 'to try to identify the extent to which dissatisfaction with the class was a decisive factor and to define the nature of the dissatisfaction'. Seventy-three percent of the respondents said that they left their class for reasons unconnected with the course or the Institute. When criticisms of the course were made, they generally related to the subject being presented in an uninteresting manner or turning out to be less to their taste than they had expected.

The majority of surveys indicate then, that mature students tend to withdraw for reasons unconnected with the course itself or the institution. However, it seems to us that there are a number of reasons why such findings should be treated with a great deal of caution.

1 The response rates for drop-out questionnaires are generally low. This leaves great scope for response bias, particularly if those students who are experiencing academic difficulties are less willing to give their reasons for withdrawal.

2 Many researchers feel that the reasons given by respondents tend to be rationalisations. It seems likely that students who find the courses too difficult or who fail to put much effort into them will seek to protect their self-esteem by attributing their withdrawal to external pressures such as lack of time.

3 Even a 'genuine' response of lack of time conceals as much as it reveals. In the sense that it means that students prefer to spend their time on other activities, it is clearly related to the perceived value and interest of the course itself.

4 When main reasons are 'unpacked', features of the courses themselves are often revealed as contributory factors. For instance, 'increased work pressures' might be expanded as follows:

'Work pressures meant that I had less time for study – but I guess that I would still have stuck with the course if I had found it more interesting.'

Changes in goals or intentions may also arise from the course itself: 'I decided not to become an accountant because I realised from the course that I couldn't cope with the maths.'

5 Certain factors can be attributed to the institution or to the students themselves. For instance, if students cannot cope with the

level of the course, they may blame either themselves or their teachers. It seems likely that mature students returning to education with some trepidation would adopt the former position.

If we are to arrive at a more complete understanding of why an individual drops out, it seems that we must move beyond the usual 'check list' approach. We must take into account what participation means to an individual and the total context in which he or she is studying. We must treat dropping out as a complex process in that it generally involves numerous inter-connected causal factors and often builds up over time. Finally, we must have a greater awareness of how people explain their behaviour, both to themselves and to other people. We outline below a model which begins to deal with some of these complexities.

To the extent that they have consciously thought through their decision to enrol, mature students have said to themselves:

- This course appears to offer me what I want, or at least it is the best one available for my purpose.
- I can cope with the level of the course.
- I can afford the cost of the course.
- The course fits in with my personal/social/domestic/work commitments.
- I am prepared to put in the time and effort required by the course.

Essentially they have performed an individual cost-benefit analysis and decided that it is worth their while to enrol. However, this is a continuing analysis and, as the course begins, they learn more about what the course actually offers and what the real 'costs' of attending are in terms of money, time, domestic rearrangements, curtailment of other activities, etc. Also new factors may enter into the analysis such as changes in their personal or work situations.

Although we are not suggesting that students are constantly engaged in a rational, mechanistic weighing-up of the costs and benefits involved in continuing with a course, it is certainly the case that all students are subject to a complex interplay of positive factors which encourage them to continue and negative factors which push them towards withdrawal. What the relevant factors are will depend upon the individuals concerned and the courses that they are taking, but by way of example we present below the 'positive' and 'negative' factors acting on an imaginary individual studying with the OU.

Open University student

Negative factors
- Wants to spend more time with family.
- Course is very difficult.
- Fees are high.
- Doesn't like course tutor.
- A part-time degree is available in a nearby town.

Positive factors
- Wants degree to get promotion.
- Likes to finish something once started.
- Very interested in the subject matter.
- Spouse is very encouraging.
- Employer allows time off for studying and summer school.

Each student will have a different array of factors which is relevant to his or her situation, and each factor will be weighted in importance by the individual. Drop-out will occur when, in some sense, the sum of the negative factors outweighs the sum of the positive ones. Some students will begin their course with the positive factors barely outweighing the negative, and these 'marginal' students will be particularly vulnerable. Any small new negative factor such as a cold classroom or missing one class may tip the balance. In other cases, the positive factors greatly exceed the negative ones and it will take a dramatic new negative factor, such as a death in the family or being sent abroad to work, to cause withdrawal.

When students are asked why they dropped out, they frequently give the most important or most recent negative factor as the reason. In many cases this is a valid and sufficient response. For instance, if a person says that he has moved to a town 100 miles away, he is unlikely to return each week to attend his evening class. However, many of the reasons, while valid in themselves, do not provide a complete explanation. For example, while moving house, changing jobs, pregnancy, etc. may be given as reasons for dropping out, there will also be students who underwent similar experiences but still persisted with their course. To understand these different outcomes, one needs a deeper awareness of the various positive and negative forces operating within a given individual, and the weight which that individual assigns to them.

Conclusion

We began the chapter by saying that drop-out has to be taken seriously. However, in reality it is possible to live with all but the most catastrophic performance figures by using a variety of arguments:

- 'A high drop-out rate demonstrates the academic rigour of the course.'
- 'A certain level of drop-out is inevitable due to events such as death, illness, marriage, etc.'
- 'Our drop-out rate may look bad but it is even worse on course x.'
- 'Many students transfer to other courses or just stop when they have learned enough.'
- 'We did a survey of drop-outs and the reasons they gave were mainly things we couldn't influence.'

We consider it unwise to use such arguments to conclude that drop-out is not a problem. Drop-out generally involves loss to the individual. At a minimum this may only involve loss of time, but it can also involve a financial loss to people who can't afford it. At the worst, it can involve a loss in self-esteem and a final rejection of the educational system. When places are restricted it also means that access has to be denied to another student who could perhaps have benefitted more from the course. Drop-out also involves loss to the institution in terms of wasted resources.

It is possible that a high drop-out rate may be caused by a single, identifiable factor such as a poor teacher. However, experience at the OU suggests that it is more usually a multi-causal problem and therefore one that requires multiple partial solutions. These solutions will vary from institution to institution but should all be aimed at improving the ratio of 'positive' to 'negative' factors for its students. Greater efforts can be made to enrol the 'right' students by improving selection procedures, admissions counselling, course descriptions, etc. Increased support can be given during the course in the form of extra tuition, counselling or financial assistance. Higher quality courses can be designed which engage the students' interest to a greater extent. All of these initiatives will increase the student's attachment to a course and counteract negative factors that the institution cannot influence.

The novelist Robertson Davies noted several disadvantages in getting a degree extra-murally (Davies, 1986).[19] The first was that 'the student has no-one to make him work, and no companionship to lighten his work'; the second that 'he must take in a great deal of information in circumstances which are, as a general thing, uncongenial to such an exercise'. Finally, he notes the feeling of relative deprivation experienced by the student in relation to a full-time student: 'his position is comparable to a man who is in a house where a wedding feast is going on, but who is forced to remain in the cellars and suck his portion of the cheer through a long tube'. These are fundamental problems confronting all designers of open and distance learning courses and any steps to reduce them will almost certainly reduce student drop-out.

References

1. A Woodley and M Parlett, 'Student Drop-out' in *Teaching at a Distance*, No 24, pp 2–23, Autumn 1983.
2. R Glatter and E G Wedell, *Study by Correspondence*, London, Longman, 1971.
3. H Wiltshire and R Bayliss, *Teaching through Television*, London, National Institute of Adult Education, 1965.
4. E G Wedell and H D Perraton, *Teaching at a Distance*, London, National Institute of Adult Education, 1968.
5. W J A Harris, *Home Study Students*, Manchester Monographs 1, Department of Adult Education, University of Manchester, 1972.
6. N E McIntosh, A Woodley and V Morrison, 'Student Demand and Progress at the Open University – the First Eight Years' in *Distance Education*, Vol. 1 No 1, pp 37–60, 1980.
7. Academic Advisory Committee on Birkbeck College, *Report*, University of London, 1966.
8. M D Vinegrad, 'A Profile of Part-time Adult Degree Students' in *Studies in Adult Education*, Vol 12 No 2, 1980.
9. P Santinelli, 'Poly Drop-out Rate Unacceptable' in *Times Higher Education Supplement*, 26.9.1986.
10. A Woodley, O Fulton, L Wagner, M Slowey and M Hamilton, 'Coming Back for More – a National Survey of Mature Students', SRHE/Open University Press, forthcoming.
11. A Shaw, 'Part-time GCE Students in Colleges of Further Education', Unpublished thesis, 1972.
12. G L Roberts and W Webb, 'Factors Affecting Drop-out', in *Adult Education*, Vol 53, No 2, 1980.
13. D R Glynn and H A Jones, 'Student Wastage' in *Adult Education*, Vol 40, No 3, pp 139–149, 1967.
14. A Woodley, 'The Older the Better? A Study of Mature Student Performance in British Universities' in *Research in Education*, No 32, pp 35–50, November 1984.
15. T Bourner and M Hamed, 'Entry qualifications and degree performance', a project for CNAA Development Services, Brighton Polytechnic, (mimeo), 1986.
16. A Woodley and V Morrison, 'The Explanation of Student Performance – a Multi-variate Approach', IET, The Open University (mimeo), 1976.
17. A Woodley and N E McIntosh, *The Door Stood Open – an Evaluation of the Open University Younger Students Pilot Scheme*, The Falmer Press, 1980.
18. T Phythian and M Clements, 'Drop-out from Third Level Maths Courses' in *Teaching at a Distance*, No 21, pp 35–44, 1982.
19. R Davies, *The Salterton Trilogy*, King Penguin, 1986.

PART II EDUCATION AND TRAINING FOR ADULTS

8 Adult learners in open learning

Mary Thorpe

Introduction

Open learning, as with other forms of learning, expresses the values and the views of learning of those who control it. Its flexibility, its utility in meeting quickly and efficiently specific (possibly very short-term) needs for education and training, is surely one of its strengths – something potentially as much to the advantage of the individual consumer as to the institutional paymaster of education and training. The potential of open learning, however, is much wider than this. It is used for programmes with an instrumental function certainly, in much current provision, including that of the Open University (OU); but it can also be instrumental in achieving personal and social roles (parent, school governor, voluntary worker, etc.) as well as work roles. In addition it may be used for programmes with primarily intrinsic cognitive or expressive functions, as in the case of a degree programme, non-degree packs on art appreciation, East Anglian Studies and so on.

In short, looking at open learning is not an excuse to side-step values and purpose for the more detailed concerns of techniques and media. None of the contributors to this section, for example, sees it as a mere offshoot of mainstream education, but as an approach which, rather like the Trojan Horse, has brought back more urgently into the strongholds of institutions of education and training, a set of issues about whom we should be providing for, to what purpose and by what means.

For while 'open learning' may be seen as merely a convenient bag of tricks with which to target education and training more accurately and economically on particular sectors of the workforce or potential workforce, these same techniques also bring counteracting pressures. Because open learning is so demonstrably powerful in the range of subjects it can cover and the sectors of population that can be reached, it has brought pressure to bear on government more effectively than ever before, to meet a wider range of needs than job training (largely for those in employment) alone.

By opening up access to education and training, open learning opens up demand for education and training. Groups previously excluded from study after 16 because of its inaccessibility, now know that they can study and can demonstrate that they want to study. For institutions of education within the community, it means that the traditional exclusion of all except a very limited category of entrants cannot any longer be justifiable. Chapter 10 in this section discusses the issue of 'access' in greater depth, and looks at the growing provision of opportunities which enable entrants lacking conventional qualifications to gain access to higher education. 'Access' courses remove some of the barriers against entry and therefore provide one of the forms open learning may take in further and higher education. To take another example, at a time when a dominant political ideology within the UK has recalled the serviceability of Victorian values – including 'a woman's place is in the home' – there has been growing pressure from women for educational and job opportunities. Some of this pressure is fuelled by the economic effects of male unemployment, pushing many women into the labour market to supplement an inadequate family income. However, chapters 10, 12 and 13 in this section suggest that education for many women also has an intrinsic value, associated with a commonly expressed need to prove self-worth and intellectual ability.

Those of us engaged in encouraging open learning need to maintain a critical self-awareness – about our own goals as well as those of our institution more generally. Is the role of open learning to be defined solely in relation to the needs of employers, responding appropriately as these wax in one area and wane in another? In whose interests would it be, were it to be so defined? In the long term such a restricted view of education and training could not serve the interest of employers, let alone students or trainees.

Fortunately, we are able to present evidence in the chapters in this section of the very varied uses to which open learning has already been put and which have broadened the scope of education and training rather than narrowed it down. They also demonstrate the very wide range in circumstances, interests and motivations of those who become 'open learners' of one kind or another. The purpose of this chapter, however, is to consider a number of issues which appear to cross-cut such differences and which are associated in one way or another with learners who take up study during adulthood.

It would be impossible, in a single, brief chapter, to introduce the field of adult learning* as a whole, or to provide a comprehensive picture of adult learners. Those whose interests go beyond this chapter might at least start with the report of the national survey of mature students, sponsored by the DES, which provides a breakdown of demographic, motivational and other characteristics of students (21 or over on entry) attending fee paying courses in 1980/81 at a variety of institutions – colleges of further and higher education, polytechnics, universities (including the OU) and university extra-mural departments, correspondence colleges, residential colleges, adult education centres and the Workers' Education Association (Woodley *et al.*, 1987).[1]

The aim of this chapter is a more limited one, and it is to highlight a number of points about adult learners which have emerged in the reports of various kinds of open learning, and which appear to have important implications for teachers and providers. At this very general level of concern, distinctions between education and training are often not useful, and points made here are intended to be relevant to readers whose context is that of education, training or a mixture of both. I shall look first at motivation, approaches to learning and the student's context, and in the process refer the reader to other chapters in the book which develop much more fully the agenda of selected concerns listed here.

Motivation for learning

Successful study is often related to the strength of motivation of individual students, and where study is voluntary, as is usually the case for adults, motivation is of even greater significance. It is not just the strength of motivation, but its quality which matters. A student who is desperately anxious to succeed can be extremely deflated by early study problems or poor performance, and can drop out as a result. Others may drop out because their motivation is not sufficiently clearly defined, or is less strongly felt than the motivation to respond to other demands which compete for their attention at the same time. Chapter 23 provides useful case studies here, including the example of a student whose career involvement 'prevents' him from completing the assessment requirements for an OU foundation course. He is officially a 'drop-out', although he still feels positive toward returning to study when he has made a more realistic assessment of the 'space' available in his life to do so.

The examples in chapter 23 are also a reminder that the initial, starting motivation needs at least to be confirmed by the early experience of study, if the learner is to make an effective commitment to learning. The 'induction period' will throw up different problems in different systems of learning; the important point is that it exists, that starting to study is not accomplished by the simple act of enrolling on a course. There is a period when the learner consciously reassesses whether study, and this course in particular, was an appropriate choice for them. The design of materials, and the approach of teaching and support staff need to reflect an active awareness that students will be reflecting on their decision to enrol, possibly with considerable anxiety, during the earliest stage of course work.

One perspective on the induction period (and on motivation more generally) is to attempt not only to support, but to develop student motivation. It is possible, for example, for students to discover new reasons for study – reasons which may become more important even than those they started with. For example, in learning where vocational motivation is likely to remain a major factor, it is nevertheless possible to enrich and broaden this by emphasising the intrinsic value of skill or knowledge improvement rather than mere certification. In a study of 16 Open Tech students, Strang identified, as one would expect, that the most important reasons for study were vocational, but that those who wanted to learn to improve job performance in some way, got higher grades on the whole than those studying for reasons extrinsic to course content, such as 'they said it would look good on my records ... enrolling on this course' (Strang, 1986).[2] Strang recommends that trainees should be encouraged to recognise or to develop intrinsic reasons for studying. She notes that:

> many students simply had not thought through their reasons, but only had a few vague ideas. As some of our examples show, the more specific the reasons, the clearer their influence on concerns in studying. We found a slight tendency for students with a greater variety of reasons for study, to perform better on course assessment than those with only 1 or 2 reasons. (Strang, 1986)[2]

Certainly in the OU context students usually have a mixture of reasons behind their initial decision to register, and a (relatively intensive) admissions and initial counselling service has been established partly in order to help students clarify their ideas and to make sure that they realise the nature of their decision. (Chapter 21 gives a fuller account of this process.)

Where successful, the OU student often experiences a growing commitment to learning during the first few years, and this has been linked with the sense of participating in a significant enterprise, of involvement in a national institution and sharing with other students similar aspirations towards study and personal achievement (Goodyear, 1976).[3] In a recent study of the possible effects of cuts in services to OU students, there was also a common theme in student interviews that direct contact with tutors and other students was vital, and not an optional extra. To a lesser extent, the provision of several media for learning was also linked to the need for an enjoyable and rewarding experience of study, as well as for effective learning. The need for a variety of stimuli, and some person-to-person contact during study is felt by most students and not just a minority of 'gregarious learners'. (Those who want to study absolutely alone, with no direct contact with another by preference, are a very small minority, in the OU system at least.)

Providers of open learning might consider the importance (reflected in sustained student motivation and completion rates) of providing (as far as possible) an interesting and enjoyable as well as a useful and effective experience of study. Firstly, many of its courses are, and will continue to be, vocationally oriented and therefore possibly at risk of a narrowly utilitarian approach. Secondly, although particular courses may be designed to last only a few weeks, the promotion of the open learning idea is based on the assumption that the need for further education and training will recur. It would be unfortunate, therefore, if a bad experience with one open learning course put off those learners from further study via open learning methods.

Approaches to learning

Motivation is not, of course, the sole determinant of effective learning; most importantly learners themselves have different views of the meaning of learning and go about the process of study in very different ways. (Some illuminating insights into the experience of starting to study again are offered in chapter 15.) This is not simply associated with poor educational attainment hitherto. The majority of adult learners who choose to return to study which is assessed in some way, do so not because they lack any qualifications at all, though they may want to better them. Only a minority (18 per cent of the OU's students and 31 per cent of the mature student survey referred to earlier) have no formal qualifications at all. Nonetheless, most of those studying by correspondence and distance education have attained either no qualifications or qualifications up to 'O' level only, at school (Table 8.1).

Table 8.1: School-leaving qualifications of distance students

	OU-UG	OU-ASSOC	NEC	NALGO	Private
	%	%	%	%	%
None	18	16	35	8	22
'O' level or less	45	33	41	34	48
'A' level	36	48	22	58	27
Other	1	4	2	1	3

(Woodley, 1986)[4]

Whether or not they have taken other qualifications since, negative school experiences can intrude unhelpfully into the learning process for many students. Dislike of the experience of schooling may indeed effectively prevent many from ever studying again, and chapter 13 in this section describes the experience of participants in the Strathclyde Open Learning Experiment who perhaps surprised themselves by enjoying working through OU materials, proving (in the words of one) that 'we're not as stupid as they made out we were at school'. However, through its associate programme, the OU now also has experience of adults who already have a degree and return to study. Such students *also* find that the process of study is itself something they must come to terms with.

For these, as for other students, there is first the problem of finding time to study and balancing study demands against family and work commitments. In the Mature Students Survey (Woodley *et al.*, 1986)[1] the most important problem experienced by most students studying qualifying courses was 'Organising my time in a disciplined way' and to a lesser extent 'Family demands restricting my study time'. Such problems are predictable, and chapter 21 suggests how they can be taken up through counselling, especially helpful at the pre-study stage.

Less easily identified, and more difficult to handle are problems learners experience in studying itself, whether difficulties of 'concentration', 'remembering', 'making sense of it all', or whatever. Similar problems are doubtless experienced by young learners as well as adults, but there is likely to be a greater self-consciousness among adult learners, which brings such attitudes into the foreground. Also, where adults study mainly alone, they may continue for a long time with unhelpful approaches which frustrate their own progress. Research analysis relevant here has concentrated most often on the 'deep learning' versus 'surface learning' approaches identified initially among conventional university students studying full-time.

Within this paradigm, rote learning and memorising are associated with the less effective approaches of surface learning. Strang, for example, reports the case of a very well motivated learner whose poor progress she links to his view of learning as merely reading and *remembering* the content of his course. In their study of the progress of 29 students over four years (1980–83) Taylor and Morgan[5] also report remembering facts and ideas as one of the ways in which many new students conceived what learning was about at the beginning. The mismatch between student expectations and those of the course forces those students who do not drop out as a direct result of these early difficulties, to revise their expectations and develop new ways of studying. Some of the early confusion and pressure to adapt is evident in this student's comment on learning in the first year of OU study:

> I just think that I harp back to school days too much and I am surprised there aren't the facts there presented for me and – I don't know – I do find some of the course text – I read it through and I think, 'oh, I don't know what on earth I have read there'. I read it through page after page.
>
> (extract from Taylor and Morgan, 1984, p 29)[5]

Learners *do* develop more complex or sophisticated views of learning with practice, however, and course work can encourage this. Some of the more successful experience of recent OU foundation courses has in fact capitalised on the self-consciousness of adult learners, requiring students to reflect on how well they are learning, and on skills associated with learning, as part of their study of the course. (Chapter 15 looks at these issues in more detail.)

One feature of this development which may also cause dissonance in students' early experience of a course is that they bring expectations of what a course is like from their pasts. Some OU students, for example, stick fast to their hard won experience of 'how to study an OU course' based on foundation course work, when the approach of higher level courses is quite different. Presumably adults in open learning may enrol on a variety of courses from different institutions and need to be alerted to the distinctive character of each course they come to. Having once mastered an unfamiliar mode of learning, they may be unprepared for the need regularly to adapt to the many different forms open learning can take. Again, OU experience provides a useful warning, when Taylor and Morgan wrote:

> After the first year, however, most of the things students did when studying were quite firmly fixed ... students seemed remarkably inflexible in their approach to different courses .... Some students failed to respond to the different structure of the course, where they were expected to choose their own route through the material and to concentrate on some parts rather than cover everything in equal depth ... These robust ideas that students develop (in their first year) about 'how to study with the OU' could be a major problem in producing courses with rather different demands but which are packaged in a very similar way.
>
> (Taylor and Morgan, 1984, p 27)

The student's context

I have already commented on aspects of students' existing experience in discussing their motivation for study and orientation to learning. However, two further points deserve inclusion here.

The first is the dynamic impact on a student's studies of circumstances at home or work. Even within the duration of courses lasting only a few months the effects of events like unexpected job loss or promotion, bereavement, ill health or some other change in family circumstances are likely to affect several members of the group. An insight into individual cases is offered in chapter 23 – a case-study of the tutor and counsellor role for new learners – which also illuminates the inner changes learning can bring about in adults. Many of those who return to study, even if they do have qualifications, are chronically underconfident and perceive themselves as largely failures in terms of school education. Therefore, to study successfully as an adult is a vindication of their wish not to accept a low opinion of their own abilities. Many OU students, for example, perceive the OU not as a second chance, but as their only chance, to prove to themselves and to others that they have ability.

A proportion of adult learners is also likely to find the cost of studying a problem, and others will be effectively prevented from starting. In an ACACE survey[6] of the 2500 adults, it was reported that cost was the single most important reason among respondents who had not been able to study a course they wanted. And Lowen's study of mature students on second chance courses in the Central and West London Open College network,[7] found that around half the students in the sample found difficulty in paying fares, childcare expenses and buying books and other materials needed for study. In her report on the financial barriers to access, Ames notes that, in learning which does not follow traditional learning routes after school, 'neither the learners nor the providers seem able to rely on standard sources of support' (Ames, 1986).[8] She documents the various ways in which the provision of the DHSS, LEAs, colleges, MSC and others can lead to confusing and uncertain funding circumstances, and on occasion, inequities and hardship. Those particularly at risk, as one would expect, are the unemployed, young people up to 25, women with no independent income source and the elderly. However, adults generally (and especially those in their thirties and older) have existing financial responsibilities which mean that the costs of studying have implications for their immediate family as well as for themselves. It may not always be possible for providers to do much to change the funding provisions locally, if there are problems, but it is clearly vital to be alert to the possibility of financial difficulty among students or trainees. Early advice and counselling is at least better than none until it is too late.

The second major point here is that students can only make meaning out of what they are studying by bringing to bear their own relevant experience. Learners need help and encouragement to do so, however, and this may be particularly difficult where 'academic study' is at issue. Chapter 15 uses the contrast for most people between reading a novel and trying to read on OU text, or some other study material very fruitfully. One brings to a novel a very well practised ability to read it, whereas

> ... with educational texts, instead of images of people and events, one is working with more abstract internalisations, such as conceptions of the economy, or the role of the health visitor ... unless one has the beginnings of the relevant train of thought already available at the forefront of one's attention there is little the words on the page can trigger off. This is the problem for beginning students. Until they become launched into the system of discourse within a given field of study, sequences of words may mean very little.

This may pose the difficulty at its most extreme, but it is not limited to the academic context. Chapter 14 in this section outlines the particular difficulties for a project aimed at Supervisors on the Youth Training Scheme. They were not likely to be strongly motivated to learn, indeed were very likely to reject an obvious attempt to 'teach', or to impose unrecognisable versions of the reality of their work position and their experience of having to relate both to shop floor trainees and to management. The approach that worked was to develop course materials out of the language and anecdotes used by supervisors themselves, who were prepared to use the materials developed in part because they were credible and used language they recognised; in the words of a participant – 'It isn't stuffed shirt or jargonese, it's plain and deals with real issues'.

It has become a truism to say that those working with adults need to take into account the fact that their learners are experienced, perhaps more widely than themselves. There are no neat formulae, however, for 'how to take experience into account'. Chapters 11, 13 and 14 in this section offer approaches appropriate in very different contexts, and an indication therefore of the range of ways in which open learners can use their own experience in learning which does not assume that it will be irrelevant.

The implications for open learning providers and teachers

The variety of work coming under the heading of open learning makes it difficult to generalise about the impact of open learning on lecturers, trainers and teachers who have previously used face-to-face methods primarily. For some it will mean the new discipline of materials production. Perhaps even more will be affected by the less obvious but nonetheless real changes in their tutoring role, brought about by adult learners, and the increase in demands which could include a counselling role. In a (1982) study of three open learning schemes in further education colleges (Bagley and Challis, 1985),[9] the authors note:

> It has always been difficult to define the role of teacher in further education, but what is apparent is that open learning schemes make the task of definition more complex and hazardous. A teacher in one of the open learning schemes studied in the project compared the role with that of the traditional classroom teacher: 'And of course, your role changes. As a teacher in a classroom – you know, you perform, you're up there performing. But in this scheme, you're all sorts of things – tutor, helper, counsellor. It's a different thing altogether – your role changes.'
>
> (Bagley and Challis, 1985, p 63)[9]

In the OU context, tuition and counselling is carried out largely by a core of (around 5000) part-time staff, most of whom are employed in other forms of education as well. A study of how lecturers in colleges, polytechnics and universities developed the necessary skills for OU tuition and counselling concluded (in agreement with Bagley and Challis) that a more diverse range of skills and human abilities was required for satisfactory performance of the role, than in many cases was necessary in conventional teaching.

> They are required to develop new forms of teaching, to develop an ever widening repertoire of appropriate responses to the particularity of each student's contribution, in writing or face to face, as well as to the substantial minority of students who fail to make a contribution appropriate to the requirements of their course. They are required to balance a number of seemingly contradictory stances; between on one hand, putting themselves in the position of the student and resolving difficulties, whilst on the other recognising that students need to be independent if they are to succeed in the long term; between providing teaching and support to help individuals succeed and representing more impersonal standards of academic achievement against which students are measured. And while their role overall may be different in degree rather than in kind, some of the activities it requires are quite new for most people, notably teaching by correspondence, frequent contact (for tuition and counselling) by telephone, and, when it occurs, the attempt to facilitate learning rather than to lecture.
>
> (Thorpe, 1986)[10]

In 1987, the OU will be spending £244 300 on staff development for its part-time staff, in recognition of the continuing need to train and support those with key roles in making open learning and part-time study successful for the adults who undertake it. Although OU part-time staff do not themselves produce course material (unless as consultants to course teams) their role is nonetheless demanding and surprisingly diverse. The tutor–counsellor especially needs to be a manager of information about students and systems, able to intervene where necessary in offering help and counselling. Both tutor and tutor–counsellor need to be able to expound and explain, but also to elicit responses from students and to exercise intuition in working out the sources of confusion or inadequacy in students' developing frameworks of learning. They need to be adept in setting up effective group learning as well as sensitive about their own interactions with individuals and with groups. And they need to be able to carry out all these things in writing and through telephone conversations, as well as face to face. (Chapter 23 offers an extended account of the tutor–counsellor role.)

The breadth of the tutor or tutor–counsellor role in open learning, and the range of skills required is also evident in very different contexts than the OU, as the work of the Industrial Training Research Unit demonstrates, in a survey of five open learning projects: Shoe and Allied Trades Research Association, Site Management Open Tech, Kingston Open Learning Action Project, the Electricity Council's Power Systems Protection, and the Open University (Clarke *et al.*, 1985).[11] Forty-eight tutors completed questionnaires, covering 27 courses, 15 leading to a national qualification (BTEC, ONC, etc). On average tutors had been involved in open learning for 5 years, about two-thirds were lecturers and only 14 said they had received any training. The report notes the considerable variation in the role of the tutor across the different schemes, including (in the case of the Kingston Open Learning Project) even marketing the course and in-company negotiations. There is a mine of useful material here on the tasks of the tutor, including a composite list of 15 major task areas, each of which has a list (often lengthy) of component sub-tasks and skills.

In brief, the change in the form and content of the teacher (lecturer or tutor) role which is generated by open learning programmes for adults is significant, requiring major rather than minor adaptations for staff experienced in conventional teaching hitherto. This needs to be recognised in setting up open learning programmes, and in providing support and development opportunities for staff on a continuing basis.

References

1 A Woodley, O Fulton, L Wagner, M Slowey and M Hamilton, *Choosing to Learn: Adults in Education*, SRHE/OU Press, 1987.

2 A Strang, 'Open Learning: Identifying the Hidden Barriers', in *Open and Distance Learning in Management Education and Development: Issues in Theory and Practice*, Centre for the Study of Management Learning, Lancaster University, 1986.

3 M Goodyear, *Open University Student Motivation*, IET, Open University, Milton Keynes, (mimeo), 1986.

4 A Woodley, 'Distance Students in the United Kingdom', in *Open Learning* Vol 1, No 2, Longman and The Open University, 1986.

5 E Taylor and A Morgan, *Students' Open University Careers*, Study Methods Group Report No 14, IET, Open University, Milton Keynes, (mimeo), 1984.

6 ACACE, *Adults, their Educational Experiences and Needs: the Report of a National Survey*, 1982.

7 D Lowen, *Barriers to Access*, Central and West London Open College; ALBSU (1985) Special Developments Project, Report No 4, November, 1986.

8 J C Ames, *Financial Barriers to Access*, UDACE, 196 de Montfort St, Leicester, LE1 7GE, 1986.

9 B Bagley and C Challis, *Inside Open Learning*, The Further Education Staff College, Bristol, 1985.

10 M Thorpe, for IET Student Research Centre, 'The Human Dimension in Open University Study', in *Open Learning*, Vol 1, No 2, Longman and The Open University, 1986a.
M Thorpe, *Moving into Open Learning*, IET, The Open University, Milton Keynes, (mimeo), 1986b.

11 A Clarke, M Costello and T Wright, *The Role and Tasks of Tutors in Open Learning Systems*, Industrial Training Research Unit, Cambridge, 1985.

* Much of the experience drawn on here and in the rest of the book is of adults 21 and over. Clearly there is a 'grey area' between 16–21 where youth and adulthood overlap, and some parts of what I have to say may not be relevant. Perhaps the most applicable definition is that of learners in *post-compulsory* education, most of whom did not continue in full-time study immediately following schooling.

9 Open learning in industry

Roger Lewis

Introduction

The mid 1980s have seen a growing trend in industry towards open learning as a means of delivering training. There are many reasons for this: firstly, the greater cost effectiveness that can be demonstrated over more conventional forms of training; secondly, the flexibility offered by open learning: training requirements can be met immediately, as they arise, and for any number of employees; and thirdly, training can be better-targetted: the modular approach of open learning enables a company or learner to pick just the skills required without having to work through a whole course. Open learning is seen, in addition, as strengthening the involvement of line managers in training. Furthermore, the philosophy behind open learning – the development of individual independence in learning – is in keeping with the spirit of the times: adaptability and autonomy are seen as key skills needed for industrial regeneration.

This paper identifies some key developments in the application of open learning to adult training. It is important to stress that we are talking about open learning and not distance education. *The Open Learning Toolkit* (Lewis *et al.*, 1985)[1] defines open learning as 'a term used to describe education and training schemes which are designed to meet the varied requirements of individuals – for example as to what, where, when and how they learn'. The *Toolkit* goes on to outline some of the forms of open learning that may be developed:

> Learners may, for example, attend a centre that is open flexible hours and contains a variety of learning materials. Or they may study mainly at home with only occasional attendances at a local centre. Or the learning may be carried out entirely at a distance from the providing centre. This last variety, 'distance learning', is

best known – but newer schemes, for example those funded by the Open Tech Unit of the MSC, rarely use pure 'distance learning'.[1]

In industry open learning may be provided by well-established management or further education colleges, diversifying from more conventional means of training; by the LEA 'delivery projects' set up by the Open Tech to market and support open learning packages; or by the company itself. As I shall show later, this last route is becoming increasingly important.

The *Toolkit* uses the model in Figure 9.1 to show the main elements of an open learning scheme.

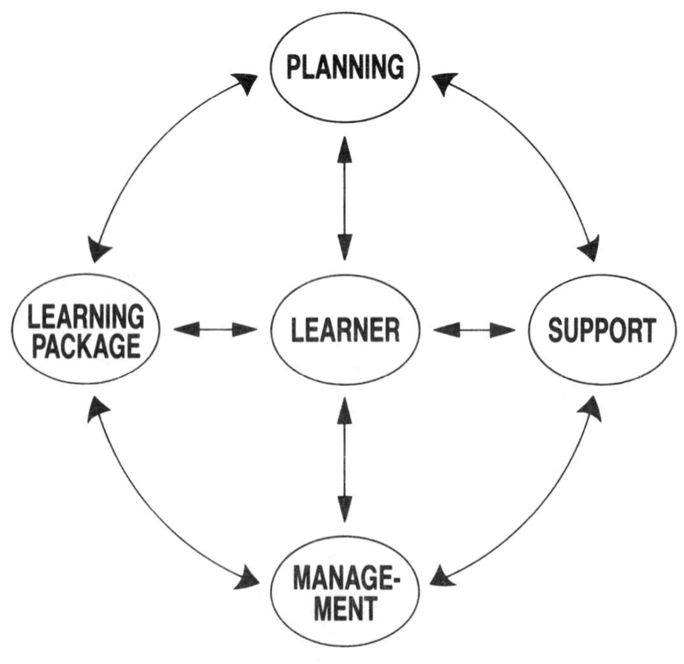

Figure 9.1

The learner is at the centre of the provision, but in industrial training the company context is particularly important and pressing. The learner will often be sponsored by their company and the learning may well take place on company premises and in the company's time.

At the *planning* stage decisions are made about the nature of the learning package, the support systems and the management framework necessary to run the scheme. Once the scheme is in operation the three major components – *package*, *support* and *management* – are in constant interaction. The whole system exists to respond to and meet the needs of the target learners. Since this model has been influential in training I shall use it as a structure for this paper. But first, what models of open learning were available to trainers before the MSC's Open Tech Programme was created during the mid 1980s?

Open learning models pre Open Tech

Four main models of open learning existed before Open Tech: correspondence courses, the Open University (OU), FlexiStudy and Learning by Appointment Centres. None of these had much appeal, or relevance, to industrial and commercial training – partly because of the subject areas (mainly liberal education) and partly because of inappropriate delivery arrangements. Some of the characteristics of these models are set out in Table 9.1

Table 9.1

Model	Package	Support	Management
Correspondence only	Typewritten, photocopied material; in the past, often not illustrated	Correspondence tutor; student contact largely through submission of assignments	Central record keeping by correspondence college
Open University	Well-produced packages, using wide range of media including radio and television	Regional tutor; correspondence tuition; some face-to-face tutorial time; self-help learning groups encouraged	Central, computerised systems; regional network to implement central procedures
FlexiStudy	Centrally-produced (mainly by National Extension College); attractive, printed	Local support by variety of means – post, telephone, face to face	Decentralised; all management activities (e.g. fee collection, storage of materials) carried out by local centre
Learning by Appointment Centre	Programmed learning packages; short home-produced, often print	None or very basic (e.g. receptionist)	Simple booking and materials maintenance systems

Correspondence courses had been used for many years by individuals seeking advancement in professions such as banking and accountancy. But the early reputation of many courses was low and continued even after improvements to the quality of materials, and to support for students, had been made.

Learning by Appointment Centres used material developed from a Skinnerian behaviouristic philosophy. By and large they provided little in the way of learner support and they suffered from the general disfavour into which programmed learning fell in the mid 1970s.

The Open University (OU) made correspondence education respectable by providing an effective opportunity for thousands of part-time adult students to study for a degree which has been recognised by other British universities. The OU produces high quality learning packages and a complementary personal support system for learners. But, until the Business School was started in the 1980s, the OU responded solely to individual needs rather than to corporate training requirements.

FlexiStudy showed an alternative and more collaborative way of delivering education and training. In FlexiStudy packages of material were produced centrally by the National Extension College and bought in by local colleges, mainly colleges of further education. The centre and the local provider each worked from a position of strength. The local college – not the central producer of the packages – 'owned' the student and thus had freedom to offer whatever support fitted the needs of its particular clients.

Unfortunately the FlexiStudy model was never fully developed to meet company needs. FlexiStudy was confined to general studies departments and GCEs; suitable packages for industry did not exist.

The Open Tech and PICKUP

When the MSC was deciding how best to foster open learning as a means of delivering training it could easily have turned to a centralised model such as that offered by the Open University. However, the Open Tech Task Group Report (1982)[2] decided against the centralised model and opted instead for collaborative arrangements. Funding was dispersed to projects of widely different kinds based in institutions of many different types and meeting very specific industrial needs. Some types of project funded by the Open Tech are summarised in Table 9.2.

Table 9.2

Type of project	Purpose	Current example
Materials production	To produce open learning materials (and, in some cases, also to deliver them)	Hotel and Catering Industrial Training Board
Delivery	To market existing open learning packages and to offer tailored support (e.g. tutorials, consultancy)	Staffordshire Open Learning delivery project
Practical training facility	To provide access to up-to-date hardware on a flexible basis	Dudley Open Access Centre
Support	To back-up all the above (e.g. by maintaining a central record of open learning packages, by research into aspects of open learning, by consultancy)	Materials & Resources Information Service (MARIS)

For the first time in open learning, government funding – via the MSC – encouraged industry to look at its own needs and to meet these either itself or through collaborative open learning arrangements with education providers. Open Tech thus adjusted the focus of open learning to include not only individual development but also the developmental needs of organisations. Packages were produced in a wide variety of media, and support and management systems showed a similar diversity. Similar developments resulted from PICKUP (Professional and Industrial Updating), the parallel DES initiative.

By 1986 open learning had established a firm hold in training. The extent of this was apparent at the April 1986 SPRING OPEN exhibition and conferences – the first of its kind in Britain and attended by over 3500 trainers and managers in two days.

Growth has been helped by shrewd allocation of MSC funding. The 'Big Companies' project, for example, dispersed small sums of 'seedcorn' money to 18 major companies such as Boots, British Rail and British Caledonian. The companies used the money to buy in and pilot open learning packages. At the conclusion of the project all but two of the companies had plans to use open learning as an integral part of their training arrangements.

The MSC has also contributed to the growth of open learning by a carefully managed public relations campaign. Three promotional videos, together with printed case studies and glossy brochures aimed at senior managers, have given open learning an image it would not have been able to establish as quickly by any other means.

The following case studies were developed during preparation of Open Learning in Industry (Johnstone et al, 1987) and we are grateful to the writers for their agreement to allow access to this material.

Case studies

Manufacturing company A large manufacturing company in Britain decided to invest heavily in open learning centres at its manufacturing plants. Employees could learn new skills which were directly relevant to the company, for example, moving from conventional draughting practices to CAD/CAM, and managers could be taught interpersonal skills, such as negotiation and delegation.

While this compulsory in-work element of the open learning system was the primary purpose, any members of the company could also come to the centre for self-development in their own time.

All the centres used Computer-Based Training (CBT) as their main medium of instruction. Fairly basic support was available on demand; more specialist support was available by phone. The company was so impressed by the success of these centres that they contracted to develop a total of eight centres instead of the five originally planned. The centres are open nearly all day and night.

Oil industry A large oil company wanted to make more resources available to managers wishing to engage in self-development, especially after appraisal interviews. The company bought a large, wide-ranging library of open learning materials in a variety of media. These could be borrowed by management staff who would look at the index of materials available and select an appropriate package (say on time management). This would be delivered to them, together with any necessary hardware. Users would then report back on the effectiveness of the package, and on what new skills had been learned.

Service industry A company in the service industry was about to be affected by new legislation and government directives on profit centres. Whereas all financial matters had previously been handled centrally, now the managers of the various departments would have to take on budget control and loss monitoring.

The senior managers needed fast skill-development in financial management. The company decided to enrol them on an Open University Business School course and to supplement the OU tutoring by contributions from senior staff within the Finance Section.

Retail industry A retail company was attempting to alter the management style of staff within one particular operation division. New working practices had broken down the traditional strong hierarchy and managers had to be trained to cope with this.

For speed and efficiency major elements of the retraining course could be handled by open learning. The interpersonal skill development sections required face-to-face interaction, and this would be provided at short, highly intensive residential sessions.

Heavy industry A major British heavy industry needed to train its process workers in the applications of fast-developing technology. The workers were used to VDUs and keyboards and disliked reading, so CBT and interactive video were chosen. Packages in metallurgy and electrical engineering subjects were written and employees used these in areas adjacent to their workplace.

Their managers were enthusiastic and on hand to help with any problems in understanding the package or applying it to work conditions. Some managers also ran regular, informal discussion groups to consolidate individual learning.

The learning package

Open Tech has led to changes in the types of *package* produced for use in open learning.

Previously, packages were overwhelmingly print-based. However, the Open Tech Unit has allocated funding to developments in new media such as CBT and interactive video.

Secondly, open learning has broken down curricula into chunks smaller than before, allowing the learner to study something meaningful in a short space of time, such as half an hour for example.

Thirdly, there has been a move to making courses more modular. This enables students to study just the material they need, rather than having to take a total package, and learners can often combine modules over a period of time to acquire a qualification.

These developments are illustrated in Figure 9.2a.

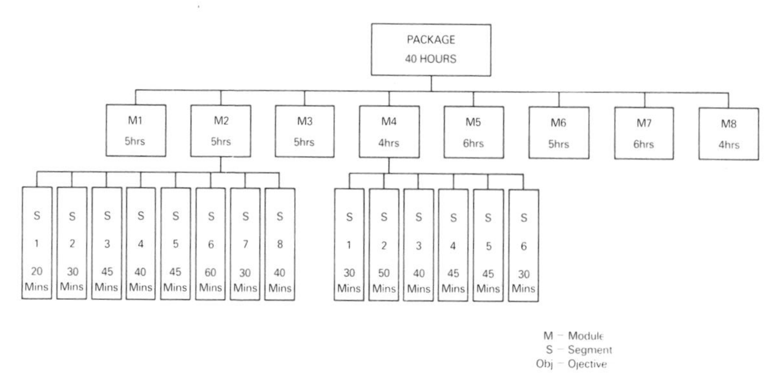

Figure 9.2a

A fourth new feature is the content of the training packages and the outcomes to which they lead. There is increased emphasis on material that will affect learners' practice, produce changed behaviour and show immediate results. Instead of 'objectives' we see 'business payoffs'.

The early Open Tech packages concentrated on cognitive skills; now increasingly, practical skills are covered. This has been an area of the curriculum previously considered (by some) not amenable to open learning. However, there are now successful examples of materials teaching practical skills. The Skillcentre Training Agency packs on bricklaying, complete with model bricks, are just one example. Such packages feature 'activities' rather than 'self assessment questions', case studies rather than theoretical analysis. They are also much less didactic than previous models (see Figure 9.2b).

Practical 2

Aim

At the end of this Practical you should be able to:

- Follow the luminance signal path up to the FM modulator.
- Recognize typical waveforms in this part of the circuit.

It will take approximately 30 minutes with the recorder stripped down to the luminance panel.

You need

Video recorder – service manual – television receiver for monitoring – double beam oscilloscope – colour bar generator.

What to do

1 With the recorder in the stop mode, connect the colour bar generator to the aerial input socket. Check that you get a colour bar display on the television receiver.

2 Sketch the waveform at the input to the luminance panel from the tuner/IF panel.

3 Is it possible on your machine to display the signal immediately after the keyed AGC circuit? If so, are there any differences?

....

....

4 Try varying the input signal from the colour bar generator. Note the amount of variation in the waveform amplitude.

....

5 Sketch the waveform at the output of the low pass filter circuit. (In case you can't find this easily, note that it will be similar to the input to the clamp circuit.)

What has happened to the signal?

....

....

continued over . . .

Figure 9.2b

Where are these materials coming from? In the early days of Open Tech much money went into funding the production of materials from scratch. Increasingly the problems of this became apparent to all: few organisations had experience in package production; it took much longer to produce packages than the newcomers expected; money and time were wasted; organisations tried to undertake activities for which they were ill-prepared; not enough packages were produced to give sufficient density for a scheme to take off; packages produced in newer media prompted a host of technical development problems.

The MSC had identified from the start the need to encourage organisations to buy 'off the shelf'. MARIS – the Materials and Resources Information Service – was one of the earliest projects to be commissioned. Run, since 1982, by the National Extension College in England and Wales and the Scottish Council for Educational Technology in Scotland, MARIS-NET provides instant access to information on over 8000 packages suitable for use in open learning.

Organisations now see the logic of checking carefully to see whether existing materials can be bought in. There is a greater interest also in adapting other peoples' materials so that they fit a particular company's image. Adaptation can be major or minor and can include:

- using an existing package with updating/errata;
- reprinting an existing package with the company logo;
- adding 'bolt-on' elements such as a practical activities booklet, a supporter's handbook, computer-marked tests, a glossary of terms;
- adding a study guide which directs learners to key parts of the package or to different parts of several different packages, which themselves remain unaltered.

Some materials producers – such as the National Extension College and Henley Distance Learning Ltd – offer adaptation and customisation of their packages at all these levels.

The development of new materials also continues to take place. Larger organisations, such as the Civil Service, British Gas and British Telecom, have always produced their own packages and are allocating considerable resources to open learning, particularly to the use of newer media such as computers and interactive video.

Support

In the *Toolkit* model *support* is defined as 'the arrangements made by an open learning scheme to provide help to the learners additional to that already contained in the learning package'.[1] In the early 1980s the main means of providing support to learners in existing open learning schemes was the tutor – either provided centrally as in the OU, or by the local college as in FlexiStudy. This was inappropriate to industry which usually needed support available in company, with knowledge of company procedures and from a practical rather than an academic base.

The inappropriateness of existing support models unfortunately drove new training schemes away from the whole idea of support as such. A touching but misplaced faith was put on the package itself: 'Our packages are so good that support is not needed'; 'We use the powerful new media of information technology'; 'If our packages cannot stand alone they are not doing their job'. These statements are not heard so often now. Industrial schemes have found that additional support to the package *is* necessary but that this has to be provided within the company rather than bought in from outside (for example, from a college).

Schemes running for some time now assert that support is needed throughout all levels of an organisation, the nature of the support differing with the level. Senior managers, functional specialists, trainers, line managers and the learners themselves all need to be involved. The work of Diane Bailey shows the great variety of support – in type, in source and in means of delivery – that now exists. Not all of it is 'people support'; new technology has, for example, been used for careers counselling and for feedback on learning.

Much support is provided directly by the organization itself. But some interesting collaborative schemes with educational providers can be found. Support in the Kingston Open Learning Project, for example, is a partnership between the learner, his or her supervisor and the training department.

The learner's immediate boss – the 'first-in-line manager' – has a vital role to play both in legitimising the open learning process and in offering practical help to the employee wishing to apply their learning. The importance of this 'coaching' role is described in *Open Learning: the ICI Experience* (ICI, 1986).[5]

Another developing role is that of mentor – a para-professional source of help often chosen by learners themselves. Schemes in pub management and the dairy trade provide materials for learners and mentors to help both to make maximum use of this form of support.

Many industries are setting up open learning centres. Learners come to the centre to access packages. In these schemes the learning centre administrator, or receptionist, plays a key support role.

The role of the self-help group or their industrial equivalents – for example, action learning groups, management development groups, quality circles – is also important.

A number of challenges remain in the support area. First, can lecturers in colleges and polytechnics adapt quickly enough to play a key role in supporting learners in industrial schemes, particularly when they have not themselves produced the learning package in use? Second, how can organisations activate the necessary support at *every* level in the organisation? This is where planning an open learning scheme must be seen more generally as part of organisational development. This point leads us to consider the final two circles in the *Toolkit* model.

Planning and Management

Planning and management are related. Planning a scheme can be seen as the first step to managing it. Planning issues include the identification of training needs that can be met by open learning; decisions about which aspects of the learning process are to be opened and how far; the strategic plan to be used for introducing and embedding open learning; and links with other company training and organisational development. The MSC has recognised these as important issues and is producing a guide to trainers, *Open Learning in Industry*, to help organisations facing these challenges (Johnstone *et al.*, 1987).[3]

The introduction of open learning is often taken as an opportunity to upgrade the professional skills of a training department. Trainers need new skills to play the enhanced role that the previous paragraph outlines. They have to ensure that specific company objectives are met and that training is cost effective, meeting both company and individual needs. The Open Tech has itself supported trainers by funding projects on such skills as the diagnosis of training needs, promotion and marketing, and financial and business planning.

Once a scheme is in operation the key management activities can be summarised thus:

- manage resources;
- choose and train staff;
- market;
- choose suitable delivery systems;
- maintain records;
- monitor the scheme;
- review the scheme.

One open learning model proving popular in training is the resource centre. This can be developed as a central collection from which resources are loaned out, or as a room immediately available in a works, for example, adjacent to the shop floor. The management demands of this model include:

- selecting and displaying resources;
- furnishing and equipping the centre;
- ensuring access;
- monitoring learner progress;
- evaluating packages.

Conclusion

Developments are currently rapid. Organisations wishing to introduce open learning are moving with increasing speed and confidence. Current training needs require the flexibility of open learning and this form of training is seen no longer as a poor cousin but as a key to solving problems otherwise inaccessible to change. Companies show a welcome preparedness to consult with each other and devise schemes which fit their own cultures and circumstances.

There are tensions at the heart of these developments. First, how is the traditional focus on the learner to be reconciled with the organisation's development priorities? The interests of the individual may not always be consistent with those of the company. Second, how longterm a view of investment in individuals should the company take? Short-term investment to develop key skills currently in demand? Or a longer-term investment in individuals to produce a more flexible and committed workforce.

In the best schemes there is a commitment to the learning process as a powerful means of development both for the learner and the company; when the individual is learning that in itself releases power and resource within the organisation.

References

1 R Lewis *et al.*, *The Open Learning Toolkit*, National Extension College (MSC Trainer of the 1990s), 1985.
2 Open Tech Task Group, *The Open Tech Task Group Report*, Manpower Services Commission, 1982.
3 M Johnstone, R Lewis, J Meed and N Paine, *Open Learning in Industry: a Guide for Practitioners*, Manpower Services Commission, 1987 (forthcoming).

* As, for example, in materials on how to meet the needs of your market, for learners working in the catering industry.

10 Developing access to higher education

Alistair Wisker

A number of major educational agencies have in recent years issued statements about access through further to higher education. In a number of cases this has been more than just a statement: it has been guidelines or surveys and in some instances it has been funding support for research initiatives. The educational agencies busy in this area include the Further Education Unit, the then National Advisory Body, the Department of Education and Science, the Council for National Academic Awards, the Inner London Education Authority, the Commission for Racial Equality, the National Association of Teachers in Further and Higher Education and others. A number of federations and consortia of polytechnics and colleges have arisen and are presently being developed. These include the Open College of South London, the Open College of the North West, the Manchester Access Unit, the Essex Access Consortium, and schemes based on Middlesex Polytechnic and North London Polytechnic. There are many other colleges and polytechnics currently running or planning a programme of access studies. I myself am working to develop a package of access studies at Bedford College of Higher Education. All of these schemes have been devised to meet identified educational needs and often to provide alternative routes into higher education for non-traditional mature entrants, particularly those from minority ethnic groups. Many such schemes involve negotiation between institutions of further and higher education, and often lead to negotiated and individualised learning programmes for the students.

The power to rise has often seemed to be given or taken away by education – by its accessibility. This has been one of the central social, political, racial and gender issues of our modern world. One hundred years ago, the novelist Thomas Hardy was absorbed by the possibilities and attendant difficulties of rising in the world, of moving between the old world and the new. In his novel *Jude The Obscure* the great university city is seen to be miles from Jude's experience, under a halo, a dream, a heavenly Jerusalem, a city of light, a seat of 'l'arning'. As he regards this paradise of the learned, Jude believes that 'all that silence and absence of goings-on is the stillness of infinite motion' – and he may well have been right! Jude soon abandons hope of gaining access to this learned Jerusalem and the whole of his scheme bursts 'like an irridescent soap-bubble under the touch of reasoned enquiry'. Our hero reflects:

> it would have been better never to have embarked on the scheme at all than to do it without seeing clearly where I am going, or what I am aiming at ... I must get special information.[1]

If only Jude could have benefited from active educational guidance! He would have been reassured that it wasn't his problem alone, applauded for his accurate and succinct summary of the situation and provided with at least enough special information. But we must not be complacent. There have been many improvements in educational opportunity during the intervening years but as we approach the next century we need to see that opportunity is maintained and developed. Access needs to be available for those who merit it for reasons and by methods which make social sense. It must be access to a valuable and valued higher education. Progression rather than perplexity, progression not prerogative, might well be the guiding principle and objective for access through the education system and into higher education.

In the last 10 to 15 years there has been an outburst of innovative schemes, collaborations and publications aimed at fostering opportunities for access. Individuals (and here I think particularly of the work of Ken Millins, the Director of the Department of Education and Science Evaluation Project *Access Studies to Higher Education*[2] which reported in January 1984) and institutions (particularly of course the new universities, the polytechnics, and the OU) have considered new forms of access to higher education. In 1975, for example, the OU guaranteed admission to a number of students who had been studying at the Rowlinson Adult Education Centre in Sheffield. These students remained together as a group studying the Social Sciences Foundation Course. Since then the OU has granted group admission on a number of occasions, for students attending, for example, 'New Opportunities for Women' and 'Fresh Start' courses. Such students – unlike Hardy's Jude Fawley – *have* got special information. As a result of new institutional arrangements they have gained access to higher education and achieved some success.[3]

These new institutional arrangements have developed thinking about entrance requirements, patterns of attendance and modes of study. Whilst broadening and easing access, there always remains the central concern of maintaining standards. Beyond that there are questions about who gains access to higher education, how they gain it, and what it is they have got into. Late in the 1970s the scene was certainly set for real innovation to focus on developments of opportunity for access to higher education.

Early in August 1978 the Department of Education and Science accepted this challenge and gave some focus and impetus to a rethinking of access to higher education. After consultation with various bodies, including the Advisory Committee on the Supply and Education of Teachers and representatives of a number of ethnic minority groups, a number of local education authorities were invited to initiate developments in the area of special access courses. The authorities were Avon, Bedfordshire, Birmingham, Haringey, Inner London, Leicestershire and Manchester. The invitation was to create what were called 'special pilot courses for entry to higher education' for people who have special needs which were not being met by existing educational arrangements and who possess valuable experience but lack traditional qualifications. Such courses were to serve a number of objectives within the concept of educational disadvantage. For example, for some they might provide an opportunity to enter higher education for its own sake, while for others they would provide an opportunity to enter teaching, nursing, youth and community leadership or other social work areas, a major factor in this commitment being that such students would eventually undertake responsible careers which would bring them into contact with the community. It was made clear that in this way the representation of ethnic minorities in a number of professions might be increased. There were thus to be new opportunities for non-standard entrants to higher education. Implied in this new initiative was the forging of new links between institutions of further and higher education. The majority of the invited authorities mobilised resources to effect the establishment and delivery of such courses.

The Department of Education and Science initiative in 1978 meant that an educational strategy preceded and informed educational opportunity and planning. This, it seems to me, tended to generate and ensure a high degree of interest and debate and offers a lesson to policy-makers at all levels in education. This is not to say that definition has become any easier in this area, indeed it is hazardous and sometimes all too *ad hoc*. The notion of access currently means different things in different areas and in different institutions. Many people now use 'access' as a way of describing different stages in a progression through the education system.[4] This seems to me to be encouraging rather than the reverse in that it provokes a timely rethinking of all aspects of entry to further and higher education.

It is, of course, most important that this rethinking is underpinned by research. Although there are a number of research projects being conducted already in different places, and particularly a number funded with the support of the Council for National Academic Awards, there is a selection of topics which need new or further exploration:

- ways in which special access initiatives or provision mesh with adult education more generally;
- the resourcing of access courses and especially grant aid for students;
- recruitment strategies with particular reference to ethnic grouping and to gender;
- the experience and attainment of students from access courses as compared with that of more traditional entrants;
- the curriculum response in institutions of higher education to the contribution made by non-traditional entrants from access courses;
- the importance of institutional collaborations, particularly between institutions of adult, further and higher education;
- specifically rural problems as distinct from the urban developments in access studies;
- the relationships between local needs and regional or national policies on access with particular reference to the accreditation of access courses.

I could continue the list and I know that the hobby-horses of a number of people are not included. But I hope that I have made my point. Rethink access and you rethink process and outcome.

Of course, the question of standards is uppermost in the thinking of many people. The National Advisory Body publication *A Strategy for Higher Education in the late 1990s and Beyond*[5] stresses that a major concern in the development of higher education over the next decade:

> must be to ensure that the standards of student achievement and learning experience are maintained. The maintenance of access, the introduction of more flexible entry requirements, and the use of alternative teaching strategies, will all be of little value if the effect is to undermine quality.

As this publication seeks to demonstrate, special access strategies need not undermine quality and may, indeed, enhance it. Based on some available evidence it is possible to demonstrate that non-traditional entrants achieve better results at final degree level than those who enter by the more traditional routes. Part of a long-term study of the Council for National Academic Awards graduates shows that 42 per cent of non-standard entry students gained an upper second or first class degrees as distinct from 31 per cent of traditional 'A' level entrants. In 1985 came *Academic Validation in Public Sector Higher Education: The Report of the Committee of Enquiry into the Academic Validation of Degree Courses in Public Sector Higher Education* (the Lindop Report).[6] The *Report* asks institutions of higher education to bear in mind the dangers of their being involved in organising or helping to organise such courses because:

> Arrangements of this kind can result in the formation of relationships and understanding which lead to students from the access courses being accepted for degree courses even if they lack the ability to reach degree standards.

But these relationships and understandings can be greatly beneficial and assure an appropriate scrutiny of standards. The report of the Lindop Committee unfortunately does not seek to emphasise the benefits of new links between agencies of adult, further and higher education, and neither, sadly, does it offer evidence on which to evaluate its misgivings.

I believe that the professionals involved in this development are taking great care to ensure the maintenance of standards. Access studies have brought about new links between further and higher education institutions and staffs. I have seen the benefits of these new links in the context of the Council for National Academic Awards validation exercises, and whilst chairing the Open College of South London Access Studies Panel – which has itself been cited by Ken Millins as a valuable example of inter-institutional cooperation.[7] Such links seem to me to be a most exciting aspect of the development of access courses and are entirely necessary to their operation.

Although the development of access courses inevitably involves the planning of courses in a further education setting, there needs also to be a specific contribution to both the planning and the delivery of such courses from a partner institution of higher education. Not only that, there are direct implications for courses in the receiving institutions of higher education. As the Further Education Unit has indicated in the conclusion of a paper entitled *Access to Further and Higher Education*,[8] a curriculum response from higher education generally to the contribution made by non-traditional students will benefit all partners in the access initiative. Receiving courses may well find that access students necessitate a review of counselling procedures, the curriculum and particularly the subject content and delivery of material, teaching methods and key professional concerns. Access courses, in short, propound and necessitate new relationships and understandings.

In its report *Access to Higher Education*,[9] the Inner London Education Authority demonstrated that the establishment and maintenance of close relationships between the providers of access courses and the receiving institutions of higher education is one key to success. Where such relationships were either casual or defective, an access course was unlikely to reach its full educational potential or to serve its students as well as it might. The converse was equally apparent. Good, caring collaboration between institutions was frequently seen by students as a valuable part of their preparation for higher education courses. I know from my own experience of Brixton College students coming to the Polytechnic of the South Bank that this is the case.[10] Even such relatively undemanding activities as occasional visits to the polytechnic for discussion about the courses, or the use of its libraries or resource centres, or to meet former access students, play an important part in reassuring students of the integrity of the access course. At a curricular level it is apparent that only constant identification of higher education staff with an access course can ensure that the curriculum is an adequate preparation for the diverse requirements of the higher education courses the students are aiming for.

It becomes clear that the access partnership can be an agent impelling rather than impeding a scrutiny of course content and standards. Such partnerships have most often brought about a greater awareness of institutional constraints, of academic objectives and methodological innovations, and of the needs of students as learners who can be active participants in, rather than passive recipients of, their further and higher education. In operating across traditional boundaries access studies can be perceived as signifying a move 'from patronage to partnership' in terms of facilitating non-traditional entry to higher education.[11]

The development of collaboration and new institutional links is further explored in the Department of Education and Science Evaluation Project *Access Studies to Higher Education*. Here cooperation between institutions of further and higher education is viewed as 'both the keystone in the development of access studies and a fresh, invigorating principle in the English education system'. This idea is pursued in the section of the report describing institutional developments:

> The encouraging fact is that virtually every Higher Education Institution concerned in the Initiative readily accepted joint responsibility with the providing college for the promotion of these courses. It would be true to say that this responsibility has usually been shouldered by a small number of staff, acting on behalf of their departments and/or faculties. In a few instances they have represented their institution. Sometimes they have felt themselves to be perched near the tip of a green branch, whose strength was as yet untried. But ... they have reported a growth of understanding and participation among their colleagues.

Perhaps even greater courage and commitment has been demanded of access students themselves. In the preamble to *Access Studies to Higher Education* a course tutor describes a woman student of Caribbean origin. In her mid thirties with two children, she has now entered higher education:

> As well as pursuing very diverse occupations over the years she has been busy bringing up her family and 'looking after' her husband, a chronic alcoholic – a fact which became apparent during her second term. At various times during the year she found herself doing battle with the DHSS, the psychiatric hospital at which her husband was a voluntary patient and the local council to whom the family owed £700 in rent. Her husband regularly took money from her purse, frequently spent the Benefit on drink. At one stage he was admitted to hospital as a weekly patient and sent home for the weekend, which was the only time she had for housework, shopping and catching up with College work. This proved a great strain, particularly when she had to produce an extended essay during the second term. Then her husband would become violent and the police had to be called. She nevertheless completed her essay, and it was particularly praised by the outside moderator.

This mixture of courage, perseverance and talent has a familiar ring to those who teach access studies. Also familiar to course tutors is the emphasis put on the group as a source of support and strength. This is summed up, in the same source, by a group of black British students at the end of their access year:

> A major feature of the course has been the way in which we have all stuck together in times of crisis. A lesson to be learned for future years is that, if an Access Course is to succeed, group commitment is vital.

Apart from the thrill of achievement it is valuable, in this and the many other similar examples, to notice the understanding which access students generate of the process they are going through. Most urban courses deliberately focus recruitment on certain ethnic groups and particularly on Asian and Afro/Caribbean communities. Commitment to social, ethnic and gender priorities varies from course to course, but it is certain that successful students will create a more balanced constituency in at least some of the professions they enter subsequently, which must surely be an ambition of all educators today.

The developments which have taken place in less than a decade have brought about a rethinking of access which is bound to have implications for receiving institutions of higher education and beyond. Reflecting on the achievements so far and anticipating those to come, one is drawn inevitably to the next question. Access to what? Rethinking notions of access inevitably generates a questioning of what people are to gain access to and that is just as important as questioning who is going to gain that access and how. I pointed out at the beginning of this chapter that a number of major educational agencies have in recent years issued statements about access to further and higher education. These are an indication not only of the interest and efforts of policy- makers, but also that broader and more comprehensive policies are still at a formative stage. As chairman of the Open College of South London Access Studies Panel and in other contexts, I have seen evidence of real commitment to access, to quality control, to counselling and to part-time students, and perhaps most of all to social, ethnic and gender issues relating to opportunity. This commitment must not be allowed to disintegrate into the fragments of individual enterprise; it must be integrated within a more comprehensive policy in the service of access.

Notes and references

1 Thomas Hardy, *Jude The Obscure*, Macmillan, p. 121.

2 P K C Millins, *Access Studies to Higher Education: A Report*, London: Roehampton Institute of Higher Education, 1984.

3 Articles describing such schemes can be found in *Teaching At A Distance* (ed. D Grugeon). The Open University: No 11, 'An experiment in Group Admission to the Open University' by Robin Fielder and Mike Redmond; No 12, 'New Opportunities for Women: a Group Entry Project at Newcastle upon Tyne' by Geraldine Peacock, M Susan Hurley and Jonathan F Brown; No 26, 'An East End Group Joins the Open University' by Ray Kennard.

4 For instance, I have recently been involved in the development of a TVEI Extension Programme at Bedford College of Higher Education. One component aims to aid access to further education vocational courses for black 16–18 year olds. There are countless other examples.

5 National Advisory Body, *A Strategy for Higher Education in the late 1980s and Beyond*, London: NAB, 1984.

6 DES, *Academic Validation in Public Sector Higher Education: The Report of the Committee of Enquiry into the Academic Validation of Degree Courses in Public Sector Higher Education*, London: HMSO, 1985.

7 Ken Millins, 'Quality Control of Access Studies to Higher Education: the Role of the Moderator' in *Journal of Access Studies*, Vol 1, No 1, 1986.

8 *Access to Further and Higher Education*, draft paper (9/10/86), FEU: London.

9 ILEA, *Access to Higher Education: A Report of Review of Access Courses at the Authority's Maintained Colleges of Further and Higher Education*, HMI: London: ILEA, 1984.

10 From 1979–1986 I was responsible for liaison between Brixton College of Further Education and the Polytechnic of the South Bank with regard to aspects of access studies.

11 Gareth Parry, 'From patronage to partnership' in *Journal of Access Studies*, Vol 1, No 1, 1986.

11 Women in technology

Ailsa Swarbrick

Introduction

Since 1982 Women in Technology has run as a positive action project within the conventional open access provision of the Open University (OU). More recently national bodies such as the Women's National Commission (WNC, 1984)[1] and the Equal Opportunities Commission (EOC, 1986)[2] have emphasised the ineffectiveness for women of simply providing opportunities in education and training and declaring them open to both sexes. This apparently reasonable policy ignores the barriers of previous educational experience, social pressures and cultural expectations which inhibit women from gaining equal benefit. By the late 1970s the results of open access policy for the OU were that although it had been more successful in recruiting women students than conventional universities (44 per cent in 1978 rising to 50 per cent in 1985) it had not proved capable of attracting them into the non-traditional subject areas, particularly technology.

The implications here for women are both vocational and educational. On the one hand expansion continues of jobs in information technology requiring new skills which few women have – under 5 per cent in electronics, 10 per cent in software – (Connor and Pearson, 1986),[3] and on the other, deskilling and a decline in jobs where women are mainly employed, for example office work and banking (Huws, 1982).[4]

Women students are also less likely to have either an informed awareness of scientific and technological developments and their potential effects on society, or the basic knowledge and skills to function independently of men (Kelly, 1978).[5] They relate to technology mainly as passive consumers (Griffiths, 1985).[6] There are implications too for the OU. The near absence (until recently) of women students in the Technology Faculty helps to maintain its male orientation, where the majority of part-time tutor–consellors and tutors are men, most of the students are men, and where study materials have been written and produced almost entirely from a male perspective.

Origins of the WIT project[7]

Women in Technology began as an updating or retraining programme for women engineers not currently in paid employment for family reasons. It aimed to help them prepare to bridge the career break while still at home by studying a relevant higher-level OU technology course. The aim was also to encourage more women generally to study technology courses. A career survey (Chivers, 1977)[8] had revealed that women engineers found it difficult to combine family commitments with a career. If they left engineering they rarely returned later. Lack of contact with their profession usually meant the loss of expertise and self-confidence, so that they eventually ceased to regard themselves as engineers. The retraining needs of such a group had to take into account existing domestic commitments, and the geographical spread of a small group with a wide range of specialisms. Distance learning methods seemed to offer a solution. During the same period, internal OU research had demonstrated (Swarbrick, 1978, 1979)[9,10] that home-based distance-learning had many advantages for women who wished to improve their qualifications and possibly career prospects while at home with young families. However, very few women studied higher-level technology courses (see Figure 11.1).

The vast majority of technology students were men, updating or improving their vocational qualifications while at work, and often sponsored by their employers. The project target group of women already qualified in engineering and technology could have benefitted similarly. The reasons why they did could not include the loss of personal and professional self-confidence, well-documented among women students by adult educators (Bould and Manifold, 1985)[11] and the fact that at a time when family budgets are most stretched, payment of OU course fees is usually out of the question. This research defined an unfilled gap in the career structure of women engineers and suggested a means to overcome it.

The co-founders from the OU's Yorkshire Region and the University of Loughborough therefore planned a project of positive action which would need extra cash resources. The provision of non-means-tested bursaries was seen as essential since it would give women the option to study independent of family income, financial priorities or pressures. With the support of the Engineering Industry Training Board (EITB) and the Women's Engineering Society

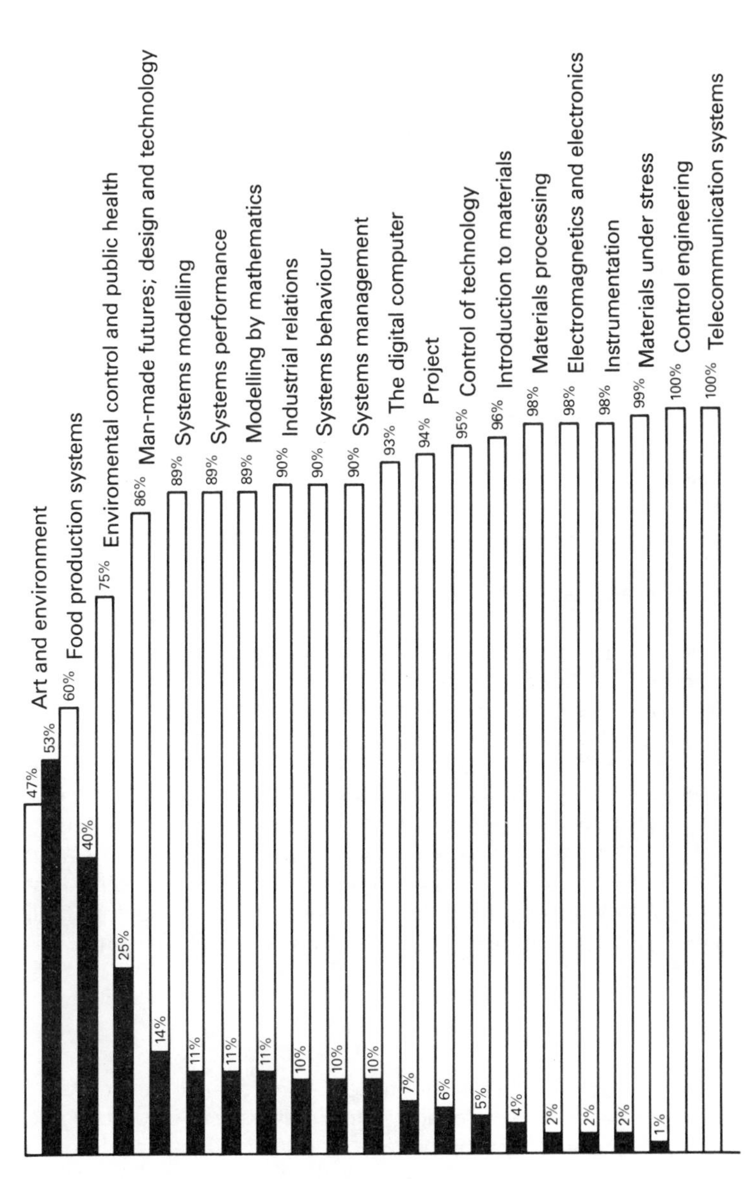

Figure 11.1 Technology Faculty: population of post-foundation courses, 1979

(WES), the Training Services of the Manpower Services Commission (MSC) agreed to provide funding from their small budget for women returners. This initial pilot project ran for three years and was then expanded to include a two year conversion option for women new to technology. It will enter its sixth year in 1987.

Positive action – the WIT project

The immediate aims of the WIT project in 1981 were to develop a publicity approach appealing directly to women; to build up confidence and a strong sense of group identity before the WIT students started their courses; and to provide a network to support them through their year of study. The two main methods were to set up an all-women WIT office to run the specialised publicity and support services, and to provide a residential weekend preparatory course at the Centre for Extension Studies, at the University of Loughborough.

The WIT project in effect provides additional support for 'its' students as an add-on to those regularly available to all students, and focussed specifically on the now well-documented needs of women in technology.

The Sex Discrimination Act 1975 recognised the disadvantages women start from by providing for positive action in areas of education and employment where women traditionally have been severely underepresented. Such elements as a women-only staff, individual personal pre-course counselling by women, and establishing group solidarity, have all been used successfully by women-only information technology centres (East Leeds, 1981–5;[12] Sweet Street, 1985).[13] Their achievements in recruiting and sustaining students through to course completion contrast favourably with traditional open-access courses in conventional institutions. It is possible for the WIT scheme to add these elements on to the regular provision of the external funding which provides for project staff to undertake, for example, labour-intensive telephone monitoring, and an amount of autonomy within the scheme which allows for an all-women staff at the project office and the residential weekends.

The WIT office

The project's centre was based in Leeds. For a small project with a minority target group operating within a university of 65 000 degree-level students, we felt it important to establish a woman-friendly identity. The project staff consists of the project coordinator, two technologist advisers and one secretary/administrator. All are women and combine a range of family and other professional responsibilities in a cooperative and flexible way, thereby demonstrating one of the project's goals in action. Publicity is aimed specifically at women. Leaflets and posters emphasise *who* the scheme is for rather than the courses and the institutions. The contact person is a named individual woman rather than a job title, and although the packages of information and application forms contain a standard letter, the enquirer's name has always been inserted – even before the advent of word processors. In the early years, with the cooperation of all UK universities and polytechnics, women qualifying in technological subjects in the 1950s and later, were written to individually, inviting them to apply. Help was also provided by the Equal Opportunities Commission, the Trades Union Congress, the Confederation of British Industries, the Women's Engineering Society and many professional engineering institutions. Now women's information networks help publicise the project. The response has expanded rapidly in the five years of the project's life as Figure 11.2 shows.

Individual telephone advice and counselling begins from the project office. At first many women are diffident or need reassurance on their eligibility – 'It sounds ideal for me, but I think perhaps I'm too old'. Some write of their interest, explaining why circumstances

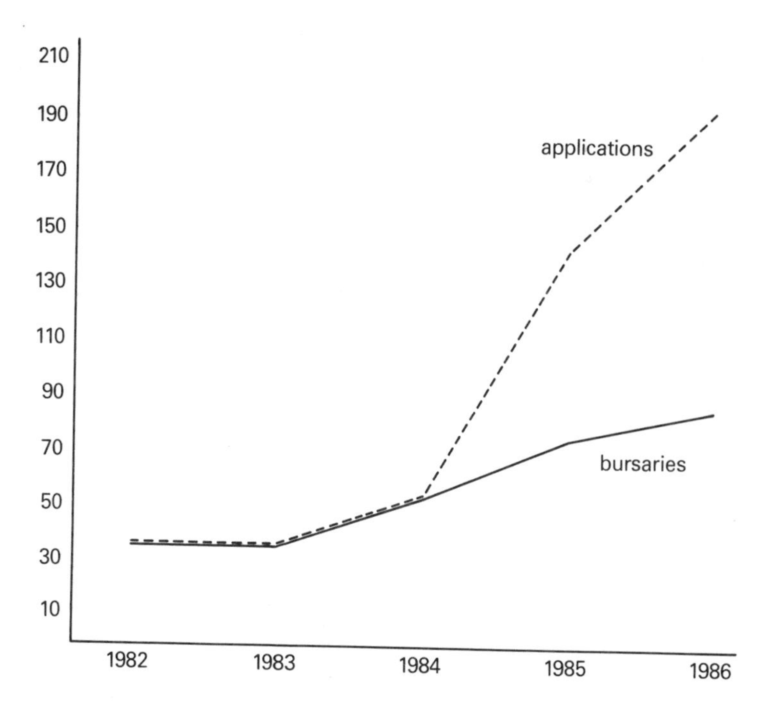

Figure 11.2 Expanding WIT

prevent them applying yet. Other courses of action or sources of grant are suggested for unsuccessful applicants. The approach is supportive, with realistic advice given in an informal manner.

The residential weekend courses

All women are required to attend a preparatory weekend course at the University of Loughborough. They work in small groups with a group leader, all of whom are women who have been through the scheme successfully and are now either in jobs or related activities, or continuing their studies. They freely discuss their own experiences and coping strategies, contributing to the rapid growth of self-confidence observed at every weekend so far held (Chivers and Marshall, 1982).[14] Confidence-building modules are now an important part of any course aimed at women returners (Thompson, 1983).[15] For a minority group of women technologists who may have spent years actually *concealing* their previous careers, it is essential. They move from arriving exhausted after organising detailed household or family maintenance during their absence, to the re-awakening of self-esteem – 'I'd forgotten there were other women like me!' and 'I thought I was completely inadequate', but now I can face the world again'.

The course also refreshes skills needed to study and work in technology, and introduces the OU system of study. Women are encouraged to keep in touch with each other, since once on the course they have chosen, they are likely to be very much in a minority in study groups populated mainly by men. The WIT network can be particularly useful in such practical ways as alerting the project office to the need for extra tutorial help on a specific academic problem, or helping to arrange group attendance at a technology summer school. Throughout the course the project staff monitor progress by the continuous assessment sheet and personal telephone call. An informal chat can often reassure or sort out a difficulty that the student felt was too trivial to bother the tutor with, or felt reluctant to expose in the study centre group.

Women technologist returners

The arguments which secured MSC funding were that the target group of qualified experienced women technologists represented a wasted investment, lost to the national economy after only a few years' work. The project could recoup this loss in an area of rapidly growing skill shortages, particularly in new technology.

During the planning stage we encountered sceptical views – that there were no women engineers who wanted to return; that they would be difficult to find; that it would not be worth the effort. Figure 11.2 provides evidence that the need for such a scheme does exist.

To be eligible for a bursary applicants had to be women who had left work for family reasons, have technological qualifications at higher technician or degree level with previous working experience in technology and plan to return to work within three years. Information on students' backgrounds confirmed that the WIT students are well-qualified and experienced technologists (see Table 11.1).

Table 11.1 WIT students – technologist returners: previous qualifications 1982–5

Qualifications	Number
Technical qualifications	33
First degree	115
Higher degree	19
Chartered Engineer	8
Professional institutions	18
Other related professional qualifications	50

On average returners had had 7.5 years previous working experience in areas like aerospace, electronics, civil engineering, mechanical engineering, atomic research, technical/scientific research and development, programming, systems analysis for employers such as CEGB, GEC, ICI, ICL, EMI, Shell, Plessey, Marconi, British Airways, British Rail, British Steel, GKN, Mather & Platt, British Leyland and all branches of local and central government.

But the fact that they were also *women* meant that their career patterns did not always follow the expectations aroused by their qualifications. Marriage and having a family had usually meant breaking off a career by dropping out of the professional mainstream. At first it was sometimes possible to work part-time, or on a consultancy basis for the previous employer. These remaining professional contacts could be broken by a husband's job change, as could family support networks. Sometimes part-time or supply teaching of maths and physics had kept alive basic skills. Not surprisingly, since their previous jobs had been highly specialised, many had begun to feel out of date. The key factors which attracted them to the scheme were the bursaries, the possibility of career development through technical updating closely linked with the stage of their children's progress towards independence.

WIT students have tended to choose OU courses in 'new technology' areas even though few were previously qualified in computing, microprocessing or electronics. This is an area which has developed rapidly during the period the women have been away from their profession. During the life of the scheme this trend has increased and is due to a combination of effects, from media publicity about the industrial demand for skills in these areas, to advice from staff. In general students are satisfied, with their OU courses although a few have found that they under-estimated their abilities and chose a course of too low a standard. Distance learning and independent study are seen as both the strengths and weaknesses of the WIT scheme. Those in rural areas particularly appreciate that distance learning schemes offer the only realistic possibility for study at an appropriate technical level in a specialised field. Students enjoy being in control of the pace and style of their learning. On the other hand, relative lack of contact with their tutor and other students on their OU course was seen as the major disadvantage.

Of the 31 students in 1982 taking assessed degree-level courses, 29 achieved a course credit, 9 with distinction. Two withdrew for family reasons, and a further 7 successfully completed a differently assessed microprocessor project package. Since then students have begun seeking work earlier, during the year of the course. When they are successful, the additional pressure can sometimes cause them to drop behind in course work and fail to complete. However, the MSC who funds the scheme is primarily interested in the return of students to appropriate paid employment. There is an annual follow-up by questionnaire. The most recent figures are given in Table 11.2

Table 11.2 WIT outcomes: technologist returners

A	3 years later	%
38	Worked since course	72
	Further study/training	14
	Not yet returned/unknown	14
B	2 years later	%
30	Worked since course	64
	Further study/training	20
	Not yet returned/unknown	16
C	1 year later	%
54	Worked since course	50
	Further study/training	27
	Not yet returned/unknown	23
D	3 months later	%
Option 2	Worked since course	34
44	Further study/training	32
	Applying	16
	Not yet returned/unknown	18

In the present employment situation women are more likely to find part-time, short-term, freelance or self-generated jobs than a permanent full-time post with a large employer in manufacturing industry.

A brief selection of the kinds of job secured includes the following:

- Project Planning Engineer;
- Medical Computer Officer;
- Head Process Engineer;
- Technical Supervisor;
- Software Quality Assurance Engineer;
- Senior Microwave Engineer;
- Civil Engineering Technician;
- Electronic Engineer;
- Ecologist and Horticultural Supervisor;
- British Telecom Executive Engineer;
- Chair of Environmental Pressure Group;
- Marketing Executive in Software;
- County Councillor (Education and Training Spokesperson);
- ICL Support Programmer;
- International Trainee Project Manager;
- Road Design and Drainage Engineer;
- Research Posts in Building;
Metals;
Water;
Transport and Roads;
X-ray Interferometry;
- Teaching engineering, computing, electronics, maths, science, in school, college, polytechnic, university or skill centre

Participation in the project has a positive effect on students in other ways. If finding work is not an immediate possibility, WIT women do not allow their newly refurbished skills to lapse again. They pursue further training or research, become involved in community or pressure group work, or in freelance home-based consultancy work. Women are learning the necessity of sheer persistence in seeking employment. Jobs are now much less available to them than before their career break, although they are well-qualified in the areas identified for expansion to meet skill shortages (Senker, 1983).[16] For those who live in isolated rural areas or where levels of unemployment and the contraction of industry are high, this may be inevitable. There are exceptions even here though, as one such woman was taken on by a regional hospital to use her updated skills in computer-aided diagnosis. Elsewhere there is evidence that conservatism of employers militates against them. There are reports of suspicion towards their gender and lack of recent experience, together with the absence of either state or workplace crèche provision, job-sharing or flexitime.

Four years on, career development patterns are beginning to

emerge. WIT women make long-term plans to take account of their family circumstances. Those who began with part-time work in technical education are now beginning to find jobs in industry having successfully negotiated flexible hours to make this feasible. As the project becomes more widely known, employers are beginning to notify us of vacancies. It seems easier to obtain employment in technical and higher education, and training, where facilities and working arrangements are more compatible. In itself this must benefit the education and training system where role models for girls studying in the technology area are rare. For women engineers it can also be a useful way of exercising updated knowledge (one woman was offered part-time work at a local college in order to teach her new expertise in engineering applications of the microprocessor); of establishing outside professional contacts (another part-time tutor was invited to carry out a modelling study on a consultancy basis for a local engineering company); and for an applied physicist now working in a women's skill centre a chance to fulfil a different kind of social responsibility: 'I am lucky because I had a *second* chance, but these women have had no chance. I think every human being has the intelligence to learn something, and if that person is given a chance she or he for that matter will do it. But 'he' has a lot of chances already'.

Women entering technology

Up to 1984 it had been possible to make awards to a small but increasing number of women without previous experience of study or work in technology. Their success in study and in finding work subsequently showed the potential of WIT as a conversion course. As a result, in addition to the bursaries for women engineer returners, from 1985 two-year bursaries have been offered to non-technologists, enabling women to study the Open University's Technology foundation course in year one, followed in the second year by a higher-level more specialised course. This also corresponded well with the aims of WISE Year (Women into Science and Engineering, 1984) to encourage girls and women into science and engineering.

Broadening the base inevitably made the project more complex. With a choice of two options for applicants, the demands on pre-course and in-course counselling sharply increased, requiring an expansion of staff. Two experienced women technologists now run this extra service. More enquirers need to discuss which option best suits their needs and to be encouraged, once studying, to make full use of their *regional* support services (see Chapters 3 & 23 for a fuller account of regional services).

It cannot be emphasised strongly enough that for students in an obvious minority – sometimes the only woman in a study centre group

– it can seem easier to keep quiet about a study difficulty rather than run the (not always imaginary) risk of ridicule; and consequently easier to fall behind and drop out rather than expose one's ignorance. The WIT telephone monitoring aims to pick those students up *before* elaborate rescue operations become necessary, and continues to show the importance of regular encouragement from women technologists, additional to the support from a (usually male) tutor–counsellor. Calls are made at the time of the first assignment, before summer school and the examination, and whenever assignment records suggest a difficulty.

The first intake of 30 students began their two-year study period in January 1985 (Kirkup and Swarbrick, 1986).[17] Their personal background was very similar to that of the women technologist returners. Most were in their 30s with two or three children mainly under 12, and five were single parents. Their previous educational background covered a wide range of qualifications. Nine had first degrees in non-technological subjects with some post-graduate qualifications in, for example, education, management or banking. Two had HNCs in chemistry and one had a librarianship qualification. The remainder ranged from no qualifications up to 'A' levels. Their previous working experience reflects that of women in general, with only two at higher levels of responsibility. The others had been low scale teachers, laboratory technicians, or clerks, with one librarian and one stage manager.

Although all the women had been thinking for some time about retraining and returning to work, a few had only very vague notions about what to do. Seeing the WIT advertisement had started a completely new train of ideas. The main reasons for choosing technology were concerned with perceived job opportunities and interesting work, and the majority had been looking for at least a year for a way of entering technical training. They all felt that distance learning would suit them because of their circumstances – lack of mobility, and of child-care facilities. For one, the OU was 'not just a good way' of retraining, it was 'the only way'.

Those students with a previous professional career tended to see their study of technology as a way of enhancing their earlier qualifications and experience. The personnel manager wanted to move into industrial management, the librarian into technical librarianship and the accountant wanted to acquire competency in new technology. Those who had previously been teachers in non-technological subjects thought that future job openings would be more likely in technology-based subject areas. Others were aware of structural employment changes and felt the only openings would be in electronics and computing.

Of the 30 who began in 1985, 25 successfully completed the continuous assessment, and were eligible for bursaries in 1986. For these students, as for most women students, their adult responsibilities centred largely on the family. Since many families are used to the near-total availability of the wife/mother, it can be difficult to make a new start and establish the right to some private time and space without interruptions. Of the 25 who completed continuous assessment, 3 were single parents, 2 of whom had very supportive parents, anxious to help their daughters improve their prospects. Eight said their husbands were actively supportive. Five said their husbands 'didn't mind', but did nothing of practical help. One said her husband found it amusing and another's husband was continually telling her how disorganised she was. Children's reactions ranged from intense interest and pride in their mother's new activity, to loud groans whenever technology was mentioned.

A small number experienced major setbacks, but nevertheless managed to complete the course successfully. Two students experienced close family bereavement. One student, whose family lived overseas, experienced continuing anxiety because of an unstable political situation. One was responsible for a disabled parent and another had chronically ill twins, needing occasional emergency hospitalisation. That these women succeeded in spite of abnormal demands on their time, attention and concentration is extremely creditable. The withdrawals have been mainly for serious health or family reasons.

Of the original 30 who started, 20 are near to completing their second, higher-level technology course. About half of these plan to continue for a technology degree as well as look for work. Eighteen months ago after the first assignment, their attitude tended to be one of disbelief and anxiety arising from their uncertain confidence.

> It's an enormous change and I have no background at all. I've managed the calculations but am not sure whether I really understand the block as a whole.
>
> I wondered if my grade (100 per cent) was a mistake or perhaps my tutor was just being kind.

To have come so far is a real achievement. But as well as the tangible results of the project – opening up a completely new area of study for a group traditionally excluded from it, and enabling qualified women to re-enter the labour market – there are other results concerned with individual growth and development. Some have found a new use for their abilities while others have widened their interests as well as their employment prospects.

> Since completing the course I have found that I'm now interested in all sorts of topics that I previously thought boring, nothing to do with me, or beyond my scope. I've thoroughly enjoyed the maths and the challenge of tackling scientific problems.

For many women, starting a family still means a clear break in paid employment. But the period at home can be used as an opportunity to develop new interests or change direction vocationally as the experience of the Open University and the proliferation of New Opportunities for Women courses have shown. Open learning systems offer a way of overcoming such obstables as lack of mobility or child-care, although open-access courses often fail to recognise the range of responsibilities, the continual distractions and the sense of isolation borne primarily by women. These are recognised by NOW courses and women-only projects, where a supportive group solidarity is seen as essential for individual student progress. Women in Technology is one attempt to combine the advantages of both open learning and a women-only scheme.

References

1 WNC, *The Other Half of Our Future*, Report of the Women's National Commission on training opportunities for women, 1984.

2 EOC, 'Response of the EOC to the Green Paper *A Development of higher education in the 1990s*', Equal Opportunities Commission, 1986.

3 H Connor and R Pearson, *Information Technology Manpower* (sic) *into the 1990s*, Institute of Manpower Studies (sic), 1986.

4 U Huws, *New Technology and Women's Employment: Case Studies from West Yorkshire*, Equal Opportunities Commission, 1982.

5 A Kelly, *Feminism and Research*, 1978.

6 D Griffiths, 'The Exclusion of Women from Technology' in W Faulkner and E Arnold (eds), *Smothered by Invention: Technology in Women's Lives*, Pluto Press, 1985.

7 A Swarbrick, *Women in Technology*. A report to the Training Division of the Manpower Services Commission on the retraining programme for qualified experienced women technologists, 1984.

8 G E Chivers, *Women Engineers: A Career Opinion Survey*, internal report, Centre for Extension Studies, University of Loughborough, 1977.

9 A Swarbrick, 'Backgrounds, Developments, Futures – a Study of OU Women Graduates in *Studies in Adult Education*, Vol 10, No 2, 1978.

10 A Swarbrick, *A Tinier Minority: Women Electronics and Instrumentation Students*, internal report, Open University, 1979.

11 P Bould and C Manifold, 'New Opportunities for women – Setting up a course – A personal View' in M Hughes and M Kennedy, *New futures: changing Women's Education*, Routledge, Kegan Paul, 1985.

12 East Leeds 1981–5, *East Leeds Women's Workshops Ltd*, European Social Fund Report, 1985.

13 Sweet Street Report, *Women's Courses in Electronics and Computing*, Sweet Street High Technology Training Centre, 1985.
14 G E Chivers and P Marshall, *A Report on the Residential Preparatory Courses held at Loughborough University of Technology for the WIT scheme*, 1982.
15 J Thompson, *Learning Liberation – Women's Response to Men's Education*, Croom Helm, 1983.
16 P Senker, Technical Change and Women's Engineering Jobs, in EOC Research Bulletin, *Women in Engineering*, No 7, 1983.
17 G Kirkup and A Swarbrick, *The Women in Technology Scheme: Women entering Technology*, unpublished report, Open University/Manpower Services Commission, 1986.

Further reading

D Griffiths, 'The exclusion of Women from Technology' in W Faulkner and E Arnold (eds), *Smothered by Invention: Technology in Women's Lives*, Pluto Press, 1985. Discusses women in relation to many aspects of modern technology – reproduction, housework, paid employment – where men are in control.
P Bould and C Manifold, 'New Opportunities for Women – Setting up a Course – A Personal View' in M Hughes and M Kennedy, *New Futures: Changing Women's Education*, 1985. Explores how adult education can offer women an opportunity to break away from traditional moulds, with innovatory case studies from contemporary adult education.
WNC, *The Other Half of Our Future*, Report of the Women's National Commission on training opportunities for women, 1984. An establishment indictment of women's education and training opportunities.

12 Meeting community needs – Community Education at the Open University

Angie Ballard

Introduction

Since 1977 there have been over half a million users of Community Education materials generated by the Open University (OU); there have been over 83 000 course registrations, 37 000 discussion packs distributed and over 135 000 course book sales. We know the majority of course purchasers discuss material and often share material with others. Less conservative claims of a million plus are made if one includes those watching TV programmes on video or via CEEFAX and those receiving material in much adapted form via serialisations in newspapers and women's magazines.

The OU is now well known for its undergraduate programme but since its inception it has recognised a responsibility to provide for the wider community as this extract from the Charter shows.

> The objects of the University shall be . . . to provide education of University and professional standards for its students, and to promote the educational well-being of the community generally. (Open University, 1969)[1]

Thus in 1977 a new department of Community Education was formally established within the OU, to provide non-degree level courses aimed to meet the functional needs of adults at various ages and life stages. This incorporated the experimental work being funded within the University by the Health Education Council on new material for parents.

But how does a university distance teaching institution make such provision, and how does it establish that it is meeting community needs? Producing the range of materials and reaching new learners has not been a smooth process. Community Education has had its failures as well as its successes, and the needs of its participants can cause problems operating in a system designed for undergraduate studies. Today it is part of the Continuing Education area of the University along with five other programme areas:

Health and Social Welfare Open Business School Personal and Cultural Education	directly located in the centre for continuing education at the OU;
Scientific and Technological Up-dating Professional Development in Education	located within the relevant faculties.

This structure has an impact on what is provided to collaborative projects such as the Strathclyde Open Learning Experiment (SOLE) outlined in chapter 13, which are able to draw on a very wide range of materials, differing in content and level.

Present aims

Today the overall aims of the Community Education programme are briefly:
1 To meet the learning needs of individuals at various stages in their lives: in their roles as parents, consumers, employees and citizens, in the context of their family, workplace and community . . .
2 To reach as wide a range of learners as possible regardless of prior educational achievements, through appropriate learning materials and support for their learning.
3 To collaborate with national and local organisations in defining needs, developing learning materials, sharing resources, publicising and promoting learning opportunities organising support for learners and in evaluating the provision.
4 To finance this work, within the rules laid down by the University, from student fees, external grants and other sources of income. (At present the financial policy of the University is that Community Education should be self-financing, although at the end of 1986 a case was being prepared for some baseline funding.)

(Community Education Academic Plan, 1986)[2]

Note within these aims the use of the terms *learner* rather than student, *learning materials* rather than courses, and the emphasis on collaboration with national and local organisations.

The analysis of diversity

The individual independent learner has always been seen as the main end user of materials, but it was hoped material would be adapted and used by others. The adaptation and use by professionals and community workers was much more than anticipated (Calder *et al.*, 1980),[3] and chapter 5 in this volume takes up this issue.

Feedback on the take up and use of material revealed a diversity of use with learners from a variety of contexts with a range of orientations and approaches to learning. There was also an unexpectedly high use of material by professional and community workers (illustrated in Figure 12.1).

In 1986, to help clarify the situation for prospective material users, two separate catalogues and guides were produced for those two audiences.

Changes over time

Increased provision

In 1977 two courses were available in Community Education: *The First Years of Life* and *The Pre-School Child*. By 1986 there were some 12 courses and 15 study packs ranging in price from £1.25 for the individual theme packs from the *In and Out of Unemployment* material to £30 for a study pack and assessment pack bought together. Presently courses and packs are concentrated in the parent and health area, reflecting the predominance of the collaborative programme established with the Health Education Council. There is material relating to wider issues and roles within the community with packs on *Racism*, *School Governors* and *Energy in the Home*, but such provision concerned with change and development within the community is in the minority. However, within the parent and health material there is emphasis on group and collective action as well as on individual change and action.

Today, the five main areas for materials development within Community Education are: Parent Education, Health Education, Consumer Education, Employment and Consumer Roles. Most material is specially written but there is also adaptation of material from other sources, most notably Build Your Own Rainbow, based on Hopson and Scally's work on counselling and decision-making, a pack aimed at the general public.

Figure 12.1 Users and uses of Community Education materials

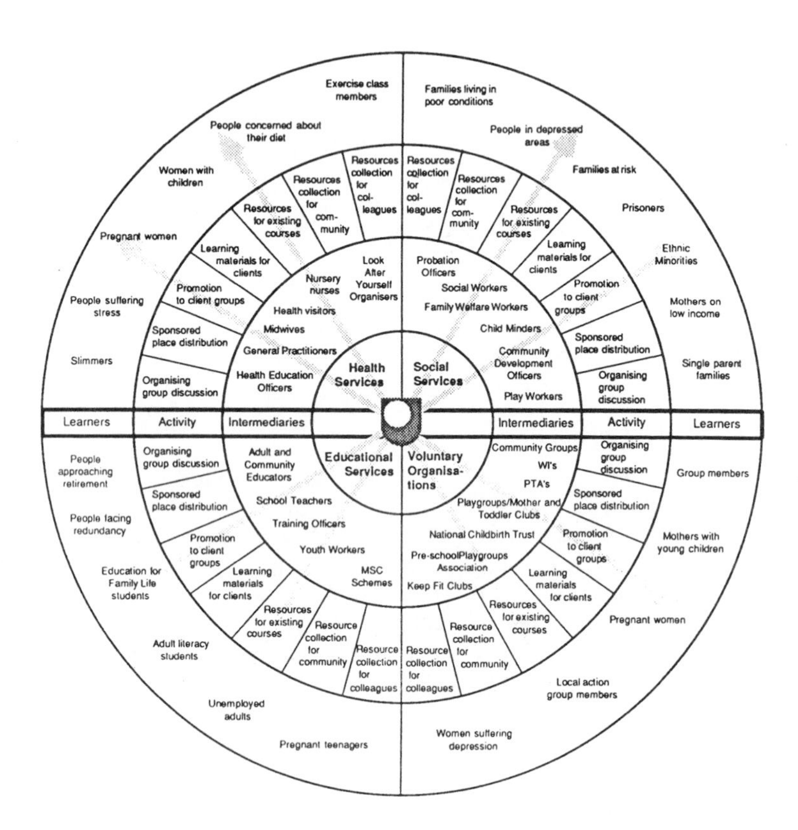

(Source: Farnes *et al.*, 1986)[4]

Increased flexibility

Not only is there now a greater variety of material available: it is also available in a variety of formats: as a study pack, as a course consisting of a study pack and an assessment pack, and as a discussion pack based on a selection of the material. To take the example of one of the first courses in the programme, the *First Years of Life*:

- 1977 – produced as a course – 8 booklets, 2/3 pages per topic;
- 1978 – selected offprints used by Health Visitors in their work (Calder *et al.*, 1979);[5]
- 1978 – course made available to a wider audience through sponsorship (provided by the Health Education Council);
- 1979–81 – used in a research and development project funded by the Van Leer Foundation – underpinned production of a pack of materials: *Women and Young Children* (Lambers and Griffiths, 1983);[6]
- 1979–81 – made available as two discussion packs – with material from other parent courses: *The Developing Child and Family Relationships*;
- 1986 – superseded by three new study packs, with optional assessment.

This diversification of provision came about as it became evident very quickly that recipients were a more diverse group with different needs than originally envisaged. Some wanted to study for a recognised certificate, others wanted material as resource material or to browse through at their leisure, whilst others were using the material in their work. This diversity of needs and goals among those taking the parent courses has been found in other areas of Community Education. By 1984 courses had been replaced by flexible learning materials; all material is now available either as study packs or as discussion packs. The former are the equivalent of the old 'course' without the assessment, whilst the latter are smaller units of material that have been found particularly beneficial in group discussion. The commitment to two and three page spreads for topics has facilitated such multiple harvesting of material. The optional assessment pack allows those that seek some form of accreditation to submit Computer Marked Assignments. It is only at this point that Community Education purchasers come into contact with the registration systems set up for other areas of the University. More importantly, the optional assessment enables those sharing study packs to register for their own assessment packs to receive certification in their own right. Developments within the Strathclyde Open Learning Experiment with the increasing demand for such a system were instrumental in making these changes.

More flexibility has been built in with rolling mailings; applicants now receive material usually within three weeks of application in contrast to open and closed periods for applicants in the early years, which were a direct transfer of the system operating in the undergraduate area. Assignments are also available on a rolling basis, allowing more flexibility in study patterns.

Material Development

Collaboration with other agencies is a key feature of material production, both for deciding the broad areas and providing consultants to write specialist materials. Early attempts to develop material directly from community work with local groups met with only limited success but, as Lambers and Griffiths show in their 1983 paper,[6] it did clarify the boundaries of what was feasible for a distance learning organisation like the OU. However, using collaborative projects in the developmental testing materials has worked well.

Jack details in chapter 13 the complexities in establishing collaborative community projects, describing SOLE as 'a sextuple collaborative system'. The SOLE experiment has been very much a two-way process. Materials from Community Education have gone out into the community, but this community has provided valuable input to the development of new courses, particularly *Parents and Teenagers* and *Healthy Eating*. Use and comments by the groups have not only fed into the material directly, but also provided the basis for detailed group guides. Working with SOLE allowed course teams to refine material so that it was meeting needs and seen as relevant in a wide variety of settings.

Increasing accessibility – experiments in reaching people

Community Education provides a wide range of materials in a variety of formats but to reach the wider audience envisaged by Venables in 1976[7] and to extend the audience, demands awareness of provision, accessible material, relevance to learners' needs, and support – both from the material and others and outcomes of value to the learner (Ballard, in press).[8] The SOLE project shows how, in spite of its 'University' labels, disadvantaged learners will use material if they find it accessible and relevant. With the support provided by peers and community workers they usually benefit from the material but more importantly, they gain confidence to go onto other things (see also Lever and Munro, 1983).[9]

The idea of sponsorship developed from early experiments by

Health Education departments and local education departments when the courses were first presented in 1977, and groups were provided with material. Funded courses made available to disadvantaged learners also overcame the problem of finance: the courses were £9 in 1977, £30 for the equivalent today. Thus in 1978 Health Education Council (HEC) provided funding for a pilot scheme to provide sponsored places. The success of this scheme, especially in demonstrating that the materials were accessible to a wide ability range, led to the extension of the scheme to other HEC courses (see Calder and Ballard, 1981 for more details).[10] Since 1977, 31 000 sponsored places have been provided by the HEC. In addition, the Scottish Health Education Group provides funding for sponsorship, and since its inception SOLE has also provided sponsored places. Further to this provision, an increasing number of learners are supported via OU funded schemes.

As well as these formal sponsorship schemes run through the OU centrally, many intermediaries using the material with others, and several individual students using the material themselves, are funded indirectly since their employing agencies pay for the materials they use.

The five-year funded programme provided by the HEC came to an end in 1986, but the provision for sponsored places is to continue. However, it is now restricted to the material predominantly related to health issues and participants will be required to make a contribution to the cost (as is already the case with the University scheme) for unemployed students.

The provision of sponsored places has definitely widened the audience for these materials. On the first two courses the proportion of users who had left school with no formal qualifications was less than 10 per cent, whilst in the latest figures for sponsored places in 1983 the proportion was over 60 per cent. Most of both fee-paying and sponsored-place students had not done any other OU courses: the proportions for the first scheme were 99 per cent for sponsored students and 88 per cent for fee-paying students. A greater contrast was shown in the proportions not knowing anyone who had done OU courses, which was over half of the sponsored-place students at 57 per cent, and just under a quarter of fee-paying students at 23 per cent.

Learner support

With the presentation of the first two courses two networks of voluntary coordinators were established since it was recognised that peer support allowing a sharing of experiences would provide additional benefit to learners, just as the tutorial support and self- help groups provided for undergraduate students.

The networks for these came from the Pre-School Playgroups Association, who were collaborating with the production of *The Pre-school Child*, and Health Education Officers via the collaboration with the HEC. The self-financing prerequisite for Community Education prevented the establishment of any formal scheme but many regional colleagues within the University nevertheless provided active support and encouragement to the scheme. With the presentation of new courses, new networks were included and by 1981 there were 550 voluntary coordinators who facilitated access to the material, as well as 200 sponsored-place organisers, to encourage and support sponsored-place students who were seen as more vulnerable learners. The system needed some rationalisation and additionally in 1982 the University provided funds for dedicated regional support at each of its 13 regional offices. This devolution of support to a local and regional basis was seen as an encouraging development, especially as collaborative projects with other agencies had begun to take shape – most notably in Strathclyde. However, changes in the economic environment and drastic cuts to the University budget resulted in withdrawal of dedicated funds from this area, and the situation today is in a state of flux. There are now regional contacts for the whole of the Continuing Education area, but regional colleagues have to juggle limited funds as most appropriate for their circumstances across the whole range of non-graduate provision. Feedback from their work and from recent studies of pack purchasers shows how the outside audience perceive OU provision as a single entity, and therefore pick and choose material from across the range of non-degree programmes on offer.

Collaborative projects

Locally based collaborative projects, fostered through local contacts with regional offices, seem to be a productive and efficient way of reaching as wide an audience as possible and taking the material out into the community. SOLE, described in detail in chapter 13, is one shining success, especially as the agencies provided funding to match the OU input. Other collaborative projects which involved Community Education directly have included work with local education authorities and health authorities in Peterborough, Buckinghamshire, Northamptonshire and Kensington and Chelsea, and these have all been reported on separately (Runnacles, 1984;[11] Flynn and Annett, 1984;[12] Spratley, 1982;[13] Rodmell and Smart, 1982).[14]

The most notable other longterm project with similarities to SOLE has been developed by regional colleagues in the South East working with the Manpower Services Commission. During the period

1983–5 over 130 Community Development Officers each provided learning opportunities for an average 40 learners (Dolley, 1984;[15] Woodley *et al.*, 1984;[16] Burd and Burmeister, 1985).[17] In 1986 the scheme was expanded and developed to a national agency scheme with potentially 400 Community Development Officers, which, if it has a similar level of uptake as the earlier scheme, will provide contact and opportunities for some 16 000 learners.

Conclusions

One of the main features to emerge from our several studies is how often the material acts as a catalyst, boosting people's confidence to go on to other things, which includes taking other courses locally, or indeed, taking further OU courses, The value of Community Education is much more than just the number of registered students or numbers purchasing material. In addition, Community Education has made an impact on the University as a whole, especially through the new experience it has brought in such as:

- the format of material and the production of that material with other agencies;
- using intermediaries to reach a much wider audience than that prepared to sign on individually;
- adapting material for diverse settings and for professional users in updating programmes.

References

1 *The Open University Charter*, 1969, paragraph 3.

2 *Community Education Academic Plan*. Internal paper, 1986.

3 J Calder, J Shields and A Lilley, *Topic Leaflets*, CEEG Paper No 10, Milton Keynes, IET, The Open University, 1980.

4 N Farnes, A Ballard, M Jones and S Baines, *A review of a Collaborative Health Education Programme 1976–1986*, Milton Keynes, Community Education, The Open University, 1986.

5 J Calder, A Lilley, W Williams and S Baines, *Informal and Alternative Uses of 'The First Years of Life' and 'The Pre-School Child' Course Materials*, CEEG Paper No 7, Milton Keynes, IET, The Open University, 1979.

6 K Lambers and M Griffiths, 'Adapting Materials for Informal Learning Groups' in *Teaching at a Distance*, No 23, pp 30–39, 1983.

7 *Venables Report 1976*, Report of the Committee on Continuing Education, Milton Keynes, The Open University, 1976, p 14 paragraph 1.

8 A Ballard, 'Potential and Limits of Openness: Community Education at the Open University; a Case Study', Chapter 12 in *Beyond Distance Teaching: Towards Open Learning*, V E Hodgson, S J Mannas and R Snell (eds), (in press).

9 M Lever and H Munro, *Health Education in Areas of Multiple Deprivation*, Milton Keynes, Community Education, The Open University, 1983.

10 J Calder and A Ballard, The Sponsored Places Pilot Scheme, CEEG Paper No 13, Milton Keynes, IET, The Open University, 1981.

11 M Runnacles, *Support Models for Community Education*, Collaborative Projects: the Peterborough project, IET, The Open University, 1984.

12 R Flynn and J Annett, *The Bucks Foxcombe Hall Project*, Milton Keynes, Community Education, The Open University, 1984.

13 J Spratley, *Northamptonshire Area Health Authority and The Open University Corby Health Choices programme*, CEREG Paper No 8, Milton Keynes, The Open University, 1982.

14 S Rodmell and L Smart, *Pregnant at Work: the Experiences of Women*, Open University and Kensington, Chelsea and Westminster AHA, Community Education, The Open University, 1982.

15 J Dolley, *Open University and Manpower Services Commission Community Project August 1983–July 1984 Interim evaluation of a collaborative project*, Milton Keynes, IET, The Open University, 1984.

16 F Woodley, A Ballard and B Sayer, *Support Models for Community Education*, Summary report, Part 2 Collaborative Projects, CEREG Paper No 20, Milton Keynes, IET, The Open University, 1984.

17 J Burd and C Burmeister, *Evaluation of East Sussex Project 1984–1985*, Milton Keynes, Community Education, The Open University, 1985.

13 SOLE – the Strathclyde Open Learning Experiment

Marion Jack

'What did you learn from taking these courses?'
'We learned we're not as stupid as they made out we were at school.'

(Conversational exchange among participants of SOLE)

The Strathclyde Open Learning Experiment is a venture in working partnership between two major institutions: the local authority and the Open University (OU).

The project was inspired by the prospect of advantages to each in the collaborative pursuit of common objectives: to make community-based learning experiences more readily available to adults; and more generally to promote developments in the concept and practice of open learning. Established in 1981 after several years of exploratory work in Strathclyde with the OU's Community Education packs, its initial objectives were concerned with cooperation in improving learner support systems and in the development of flexible use of the material to suit varying needs. Originally a formal system of bringing together the key departments and personnel in Strathclyde and in the OU in order to share experience and expertise, it settled after three or four years into a looser network of relationships embedded in the normal working pattern of both these bodies, becoming an effective means of continued liaison and development.

Liaison was, indeed, not only desirable but necessary. Although Strathclyde's community educators had noted the potential of this new learning material, they felt this potential could not be fully realised without mutual attention to several new policy, management and educational issues which its use had brought to the surface.

Among these issues lay the need for negotiation over costs, and the coordination of financial procedures; the development of learner support systems including the use of sponsored places and the training of local staff; promotion of new informal uses of the materials; and educational evaluation including the nature and function of student assessment. A further issue was the wish for involvement on the parts of the local Social Work Department and Health Boards, which had independently become engaged in using the same material with similar kinds of learner groups; the objectives of both these departments could be furthered by cooperation with Community Education, through developing community awareness of the themes treated in the OU learning packs – principally *Health Choices*, *The First Years of Life*, *The Pre-School Child* and *Childhood 5–10*. The Scottish Health Education Group also had an interest – not least through its investment in the production of certain of the materials and subsequent sponsorship of student places. All these agencies could both profit and contribute through collaboration, and the small advisory group eventually formed to guide the SOLE project included representatives of each.

This group facilitated liaison at management level, participating in certain OU policy discussions and working locally through a specifically dedicated executive post within the Strathclyde Community Education establishment. A secondment from either of the principal bodies to the other might have been equally workable, but consideration of possible communication difficulties caused by distance suggested this particular decision might be more practicable. Responsibilities associated with the post included the promotion of open learning in general terms, initially using the OU Community Education packs as the principal vehicle; identification of procedural problems in bulk supply of materials; the creation of a local resource base for materials, information, advice and support; the development of new uses of the material to suit particular local needs; the training of learner group leaders, and the formation and support of new learner groups. On its part, the OU agreed to make appropriate changes in administrative procedures, offered price concessions, permitted the adaptation of its materials without copyright restrictions, collaborated on new developments initiated locally, and invited involvement in its developing Community Education operation.

The first task of the advisory group was to consider the appointment to this post – the SOLE project organiser – and one benefit of the pooling of experience was immediately apparent: the advantage of appointing someone already familiar with the OU system at both undergraduate and Community Education level, and who as a seasoned OU tutor–counsellor on a foundation course, was likely to have a sensitive understanding of the needs of inexperienced students. Such an appointment could also enable day-to-day liaison with the OU regional operation, facilitating exchange of information and combination of effort.

But why was open learning such an important issue? The reasons may lie in the nature of the community itself, and in the previous educational experience of its people.

The community

In the mid 1970s Strathclyde Regional Council adopted a policy of investing special resources in areas of greatest social need, and 45 of these were designated APTS (Areas of Priority Treatment). Six years later this number was more than doubled.

Despite the delights of some of the finest art collections, architecture, music, open spaces and sports facilities to be found anywhere in Britain, the Glasgow conurbation has been likened to the upas tree: it flourished, but much that lay beneath it was blighted. An inheritance of now obsolete patterns of employment and poor social conditions for many has caused any social or economic development the greatest difficulty in taking root (Checkland, 1981).[1] The same is true of many of the dozen or so towns throughout the region of Strathclyde, and of its many smaller rural communities where geographical remoteness compounds the problems by increasing the costs of communication.

Alongside many more affluent middle-class districts, pockets of intense multiple social deprivation exist, characterised by high rates of longterm unemployment, low wages, overcrowded and elderly housing, poor health and adverse family circumstances. Strathclyde is no different from many other areas in this respect, save perhaps that with its population of 2.25m the scale of the problem is immense: in 1983, more than 600 000 people lived in households eligible for supplementary benefit (Strathclyde Regional Council, 1983*a*).[2] Associated with such poverty, health statistics pointed to the perinatal death rate as high overall, but in one district it was until recently the highest in Europe; again the death rate in Glasgow for men under the age of 65 was in 1982 the highest in the western world. In the same year over 30 per cent of the mothers in some areas were under the age of 20, with large numbers of them unmarried – as many as 41 per cent in one district (SRC, 1983*b*).[3] Two-thirds of the children taken into care in areas of multiple deprivation came from households where the head was unemployed and/or a single parent, and these children had very much less chance of being received into foster-homes (Butt and Gordon, 1984).[4]

The intention of creating the APTs was to tackle the prevalent air of depression by concentrating resources and intensified effort on general community development, with special emphasis on the needs of particular categories like single parents, pre-school children, the unemployed, and on health and continuing education.

Identifying educational needs

Surveys of attitudes towards continuing education in the APTs revealed little that was new. Take-up was low. People said they did not know what, if anything, was available; they couldn't afford the fees, or the bus fares/leave children/find the time or the energy/see the point; or that they were too old; it wouldn't lead to a job; there was no subject that appealed to them and little sense in turning back the clock. Clearly echoing within their replies were memories of school-days, of authoritarian officials, immutable timetables, externally-imposed rules, of rigidly traditional curricula, and of 'failure'; the institutionalised flavour of the whole experience had left them with a sense of alienation such that 'Education' was not for them – neither enjoying it nor influencing its direction. They were, in short, not impressed.

This was no surprise: the socially selective barriers to access inherent within the educational system itself are well documented. Funding tends to drift away from the customers, often finding its way to the providers instead; administration-based decisions, dominated by particular groups, can determine everything from the timing and pacing of study to the values implied by the subjects offered and the final award; and these decisions can often be geared more to the needs of officials than to those of the customers – for example, to the working hours of janitors and caretakers. Such tendencies inevitably affect the quality of post-compulsory education anywhere, but in the bleak APT communities it was of critical importance that policy should take account of this: unless the realities of adult life – the values, responsibilities, the anxieties and the potential – became and remained the pivot of a genuinely new approach, the barriers would remain unbreached. Outreach needed to take account of adult autonomy, to allow a measure of control to the learners, to de-professionalise and de-mystify – that is, to go some way along the road towards 'de-schooling'.

Officials noted with interest at the same time the learner response to experimental work already begun in one or two of the APTs. Almost paradoxically, it seemed, in this context of formidable social and educational problems, something was happening which might be built on: small numbers of young women who had never since leaving school shown any interest in learning were now studying with evident enjoyment, and were asking for more. They were engaged in a form of open learning, using the new OU Community Education packs.

The discovery of open learning

The immediate appeal of these learning packs seemed to lie not only in the themes of close personal concern, but also in the novelty of the presentation, designed to please. In layout and design, the books resembled the familiar commercial magazines rather than textbooks, and were complemented by updateable leaflets and fact-sheets to which learners could add their own. Audio-tapes and optional videotapes allowed individual choice of media, especially interesting for those with reading or language difficulty. But for most people, the ready accessibility of the style, based on a reading age of 12 and constantly invoking an active response to quizzes, attitude probes and suggestions for home activities, seemed to be removing one of the main barriers to adult learning – the memory of school learning as a passive process. The initial scepticism caused by the word 'University' on the front covers was soon conquered by curiosity, and nowadays the local term 'open uni' has acquired its own connotations, being bandied about with familiarity and affection in the APTs where it has achieved some recognition as part of their way of life.

To possess one of these glossy articles in one's own home lent status to the idea of study in the eyes of the family, and since about 90% of those interested were women, this has a particular significance. Furthermore, children and others at home were known to dip into them, asking questions about the contents and often showing curiosity about the pages dealing with their own relationships within the family (perhaps being especially interested in the pages dealing with the human reproductive processes!). In a sense, the attitudes of family and friends were supportive to the learners for these reasons – somewhat to their own surprise.

But the deeper appeal, in the view of these learners, lay in the departure from the traditional authoritarian approach, the invitation to assess one's own personal experience, and the immediate applications to intensely personal interests. The non-prescriptive and non-judgemental style of the text paid respect to the learners' wish to make their own decisions as to how they would respond. Interesting illustrations included their own adaptations to, for example, references to assumed family behaviour which they thought unrealistic, or 'middle class':

> In our house, there's never the time to watch the kids the way they seem to think in the book – it would be all right if you were rich and didn't need to go out to work – but you've always just got to change it to suit yourself.

Or again,

> Our group just couldn't take that bit about letting wee ones help in the kitchen – four is far too young to be using a knife like that, our

> Christine thinks she's left-handed too, so we just talked about it ourselves and made a cassette, then we listened to it again about a month later to see if we would have said anything different.

Thus learners were developing a confidence in the legitimacy of challenging a printed text; and were also learning to enjoy the success which comes with supporting an argument with evidence and new information. And the ease with which they could internalise the ideas, where they chose to, opened up a new way of assessing their own capacity to learn, contributing substantially to a change in their view of education for adults. From *The Pre-School Child*, most would proceed to *Health Choices*, then *Childhood 5–10*. The urgent question then became, What can we do next?

The SOLE project

The learners' enthusiasm communicated itself to the workers organising group study of these packs, and it now seems clear that it was the developing commitment of these workers which put the packs to their best use. They incorporated them into their own normal work, encouraged by the SOLE project.

Group leaders

These workers, the group leaders, derived great satisfaction from the improved relationships they could establish with their learners, whose sense of achievement became manifest in their new confidence in themselves and in their ability to learn. Little difficulty was met in establishing study groups because of the learners' need to talk about their response; indeed, many who had demonstrated an already existing need for group contact (sometimes amounting almost to a need for counselling support) by joining mother-and-toddler, nursery-school parents, church or other community groups, fell naturally into group study. Occasionlly some who joined study groups had been referred by social or health workers, a further source of satisfaction to the workers, albeit often offering a much greater challenge.

The group leaders' training was based mainly on methods of forming new groups and sustaining learner motivation, on group discussion techniques, and also on adaptations of practice for specific purposes. For example, certain pages or videotapes could be selected specially for learners with reading or language difficulties, or for those who wanted perhaps one day's study only; relevant parts of several packs could be combined, in one instance to form a composite for the use of foster-parents; print material could be recorded on audio-tape for the blind; methods were even adapted (in a companion project) for men and women about to be released from prison.

Selection was equally important as training. Those with more formal qualifications could sometimes be at a positive disadvantage, since the somewhat authoritarian approach often associated with qualifications was found to be counter-productive; a 'teacher' was not wanted. The 'right' personality – personally supportive and completely reliable – was often the best qualification, and this remains of critical importance.

Study groups

The SOLE project organiser initially spent much of her time with study groups, in order to obtain experience and then to demonstrate good practice to trainee group leaders. More flexible ways of organising group study were then encouraged: discussion might concentrate on one or two topics only; might focus more on either reflection on personal experience or on the act of learning, according to need, and might spread over weeks or months depending on what the group decided. This measure of control exerted by the learners could be critical in their decision to join, or to continue.

Groups met when and where they found convenient – community centres, community flats, Women's Aid centres, homes, playgroup premises, schools – or the lounge of the King's Arms Hotel, the weekly meeting-place of one group of young mothers in a depressed rural district who were stealthily inveigled into study by a determined group leader deliberately starting a loud argument about bringing up children ... (one need not always be so devious!). Initiating new study groups was often a matter of displaying the packs, perhaps open at a page about children fighting, about eating well, or talking to your doctor – whatever might be of immediate concern to the potential learners, along with an invitation to come and join a discussion group. Any spark of interest needed to be fuelled immediately; the packs had to be to hand, the venue agreed, the hour decided upon – quickly, before potential learners felt a sense of being 'let down' from which they might take a long time to recover. For some, however, interest did not lead to immediate action, and even years might pass before the seed once sown might take root. Patience was necessary, but the community 'grapevine' effect seemed to provide one of the strongest incentives to join: after a comparatively slow growth in the first three years, the number of study groups increased by about a hundred each successive year throughout the region.

The award – open assessment?

Perhaps most interesting of all was the attitude of the learners towards assessment at the end of a course. Assessment was an option, not a requirement; yet it came to be sought by the large majority. Based on Computer Marked Assignments, it suited those who were wary of committing sentences to paper, but usefully stretched those nervous of official forms. It offered a ratio of about one question in five which demanded more than a very simple process to find the answer, but the award was a proper official Certificate. This Certificate proved one of the most significant elements in the welcome the project received in the APTs, throwing a fresh light on the frequently-stated view that 'a piece of paper' is a mere and often misleading formality. In this instance, the piece of paper was likely to be the first-ever award presented to the recipient for educational success. It had no standing whatsoever in the formal educational system, only in the eyes of the holder and in the community itself; but its effect in building morale and self-confidence was seen to be incalculable, and and was one of the greatest rewards to all associated with the SOLE project.

With a new-found temerity, some of the learners asked whether a more searching test could be devised by the OU's computer. They were also dissatisfied by the form of the OU Certificate, which they found disappointingly unimpressive in appearance. The SOLE project organiser herself carried out their wishes on both counts, organising her own independent assessment schemes and her own new and smarter Certificate. This Certificate now bears two logos – that of Strathclyde along side that of the Open University. Presentation ceremonies can sometimes be elaborate affairs, graced by the presence of Regional Council members and senior officials, and on one major occasion by the OU Vice-Chancellor himself. Smaller local presentations, however, are also favoured as carrying more of the community flavour, and are often reported in the local press.

Most of those achieving a Certificate now decide to tackle another course of the same kind, and often then proceed further by trying perhaps an 'O' Grade course in English, secretarial studies or some other school or vocational subject, sometimes doing so in a local secondary school where as more confident adults they find the experience quite different from what they remember from the past. Many, however, continue to prefer open forms of learning. But academic study is not necessarily the goal; some simply feel better-equipped as parents, and many choose to become involved in voltuntary work, perhaps learning how to run committees, initiate neighbourhood action, or organise some activity rather than merely participate – like forming a Women's Health Group, or acting as group leader for the next cohort of OU pack users. Some will apply to become foster-parents or childminders, and two groups derived particular satisfaction from being invited to test and comment critically on drafts of a new OU course on Childminding.

Funding

The decision not to impose even a token charge on the learners is seen as essential if that particular barrier to learning – be it financial or psychological – is to be removed. The costs are evaluated in terms of the policy of positive discrimination in the APTs, and in terms of the educational response. Packs once purchased are deposited in a resource library, and used by at least three successive learners. Mainstream funding is supplemented from other sources: the OU offers discounts on bulk purchases, and provides basic materials gratis where it sponsors complementary MSC-supported projects; greatly reduced prices are available for individuals who receive any form of state benefit, or who are on YTS schemes, while the Scottish Health Education Group (in England, the Health Education Council) offers sponsorship to innovatory projects. Other external sources available to local authorities are still being vigorously pursued.

Community development

The policy of concentrating effort to saturation point in target areas exerts an effect not only on general attitudes to adult education, but also on the development of a stronger community awareness. One example is the Adult Education Group formed by the residents themselves in one of the APTs, which determines its own policy. Community Education staff offer encouragement and practical assistance. When OU regional staff approached this Group with a suggestion to support its activity by sponsoring an MSC-funded project, it formally minuted approval but stipulated that the Group itself would direct all operations, that the employees would be members of the local community and would be selected by its Executive. It made the further decision that a follow-up MSC project should be sponsored by the Group itself. The Secretary of the Group holds Certificates for *The Pre-School Child*, *Childhood 5–10*, and *Health Choices*, which she then followed with an FE course in history. Several members of the Group are similarly qualified, one also holding a Pass in the Foundation Course in Social Sciences.

Since the establishment of SOLE, almost 8000 people in the APTs have studied at least one of these courses, and obtained a Certificate for doing so. But the story is not without its frustrations. One is the reluctance of men to participate; men seem to be interested mainly where some form of professional training might be enhanced, as for example youth and community workers. This is an old problem, but new objectives have developed, among them a concern to generalise the lessons learned by taking the impetus from SOLE work into other areas of post-compulsory provision, including those where men might already be more involved – that is, by offering students at other levels a greater control over their learning through the use of a more open approach.

Further reading

Implementing Open Learning in Local Authority Institutions, published in 1986 by the Further Education Unit and the Open Tech Unit of the Manpower Services Commission. A detailed explication of the administrative and management issues involved in open learning systems, with a close analysis of resourcing, costing and pricing and resource deployment, along with a useful bibliography. Most of the recommendations are applicable in Scotland, but the important differences are noted in a Scottish supplement published by the Scottish Commission on Open Learning and the Scottish Council for Educational Technology, 74 Victoria Crescent Road, Glasgow G12 9JN.

Jeanette Best, *SOLE Report*, 1983 . An evaluative account of the issues, problems and *modus operandi* of the first three years of the SOLE project, published internally and available from the OU in Scotland, 2 Park Gardens, Glasgow G3 7YE.

M Lever and H Munro, 'Health Education in Areas of Multiple Deprivation' in *Journal of Community Education*, Vol 5, No 2, 1986. A description of the SOLE approach and methods of working within the context of community health education, by the SOLE Project Organiser and the Education Officer (Continuing Education), Strathclyde, respectively.

Leading a Group, available from the Learning Materials Service, the Open University, PO Box 180, Milton Keynes MK7 6DH at £4.50, a useful booklet for those about to form study groups and act as group leaders. A range of material useful for training in post-compulsory education is available from the same address, including *On the Line*, which deals with methods of telephone contact with learners who are unable to attend group meetings, for example those in rural districts. The OU intends to develop further its training facilities for users of Community Education packs in the future.

References

1 S G Checkland, *The Upas Tree*, University of Glasgow, Glasgow, 1981.

2 Strathclyde Regional Council, *Dependence on Supplementary Benefit in Strathclyde: an analysis of recent statistics*; Committee Report by Chief Executive and Director of Social Work, 1983a.

3 Strathclyde Regional Council, *Demographic indicators of deprivation – 1978–1980*, an internal report, the third in a series of studies based on the register of births, 1983b.

4 J Butt and G Gordon, *Strathclyde: Changing Horizons.* Scottish Academic Press, 1985.

14 Skills training and responsive management

Roy Webberley and Ian Haffenden

Introduction

Open learning has come to play a strategic role in the national training policies of the UK and other countries. At the same time attention has been drawn to the high level of initial investment required and the consequent value-for-money debate which has arisen in some quarters. The authors contend that success and failure in open learning projects is associated with the management models employed and that the production of open learning materials, especially for disadvantaged or less receptive target audiences, suggests that some management models are preferable to others. It is further suggested that a successful example of such a model exists in the OPTIS Open Tech Project: the Oxfordshire Project for the Training of Instructors and Supervisors.

Management and design in open learning projects

There exists no universally-agreed, adequate and comprehensive definition of open learning. At least, if such a definition exists, it has yet to become a baseline for management decisions regarding open learning, certainly in the educational and training subcultures of the UK. Thus it is important to define what is meant by open learning in the context of this discussion. The definition is operational in character and as such expressed in terms of behaviours and outcomes rather than concepts. Thus open learning systems should enable participants to:

1 Study wherever it is convenient, whether at home or at work.
2 Enrol at anytime, without having to worry about previous qualifications.
3 Study at a pace which suits the learner.
4 Leave the system in a manner which suits the learner.
5 Have access at his or her own discretion to tutorial support and guidance.

The above criteria can be met by a variety of different projects, all of which have been described as 'open learning'. For example:

- a distance-teaching pack of text materials, written by a trainer at head office and intended purely for self-study, with no further tutorial support or feedback;
- a 'training resource pack' intended to supplement a face-to-face programme with self-study materials;
- a package involving some distance-learning, self-study components originated by head office but with learner support groups among the trainees;
- a video package with 'trigger' sequences, designed to provoke discussion and allowing a great deal of local interpretation and follow-up;
- a 'learning by appointments' scheme, where release for training or college attendance is negotiated on an individual basis according to that individual's needs;
- a 'drop in centre', where structured learning materials are available within a flexible pattern of hours, alongside advice and optional tutorial support;
- a fully-accredited, enrolment-based system, using enquirer support, applicant support, tutorial support, distance-teaching and exit guidance.

This list is not exhaustive, but has been drawn from actual schemes which have been developed based on the criteria described above. A considerable emphasis is placed upon accessibility and structured learning materials. It will also be evident to practitioners of training and education that there is no distinct cut-off between open learning and traditional methodology: it is more a matter of ethos and emphasis. We would argue that there are, nonetheless, identifiable implications for management practice that arise through the use of open learning, particularly as a result of its arrival in the domain of skills training.

This is important because open learning is rapidly becoming a major instrument in the implementation of education and training policies, as evidenced in the recent advent of the Open College in the UK. The further education sector, for so long the bastion of localism, has received increasingly direct encouragement to involve itself in open learning, both in the provision of support networks, for the

Open College and in the operation of its own projects. In a recent address to FE practitioners,[1] Geoffrey Holland, Director of the Manpower Services Commission, made it clear that open learning was almost the only means whereby the UK could make the quantum-leap in training and educational provision that is now necessary. When faced with such compelling reasons for open learning as an instrument of national policy, it becomes equally compelling to manage it properly.

What does proper management consist of and what is it that is to be managed? We contend that what has to be managed is the participative, learner-centred ethos of open learning and that 'good management' consists of the optimum handling of the involvement of both the development team and the target audience. But this is not easily achievable. One intangible, but nonetheless critical characteristic of open learning projects is that their development involves forms of educational and training ethos that do not always blend easily together. One element in this blend is the increased acceptance, at least in certain areas of industry, of more facilitative, less directive styles of management, education and training. Within the MSC, whose *A New Training Initiative*[2] has been such an important feature of recent developments, there was not merely an impetus given to open learning through the Open Tech Programme but, in its execution, a general stress laid upon learner-centredness, which many would claim to be a foundation-stone of any open learning system. Within the Youth Training Scheme, for example, the Modular Training Objectives of 1983[3] were designed to hinge upon the concept of 'trainee-centred learning'.[4] Similar emphases could be identified, no doubt, in the Adult Training Strategy.[5] It is within this framework that the open learning features of accessibility, flexibility of time, pace and place, have been able to flourish.

Alongside this liberal aspect, other features of open learning are considerably more hard-nosed and pragmatic. They relate to the production priorities of open learning materials and the structuring of an open learning programme. Because of the emphasis upon distance-teaching, learner-centredness and flexibility of access, open learning is a form of benign subversion of teacher-centredness, rigid timetables and learning in a fixed place. Its role is to de-institutionalise educational and training provision in an organised way. It can only work effectively if the structures of institutions are modified or replaced: it cannot work without any structure whatever. New practitioners of open learning also often have to learn the strange and unforgiving disciplines of print and audio-visual production, marketing and distance learner support. The impact of these upon traditional trainers or educators can be very hard indeed. The Evaluation Reports on the Open Tech Programme published by the Tavistock Institute,[6] underline the fact that many project managers underestimated the above tasks at first, particularly as regards the time-constraints of print and video production. In a number of cases, it appeared that projects were delayed because of the need to re-train staff in the attendant open learning disciplines. Subject expertise was not enough.

The challenge to managers of open learning projects thus becomes one of balancing the liberal and facilitative elements of open learning with the tough and sometimes ruthless methodologies of its development, production and marketing. To illustrate these points, we examine below an Open Tech project, the Oxfordshire Project for the Training of Instructors and Supervisors (OPTIS) which, through problems of time and target audience, had to face this challenge in a particularly acute form.

The nature of the OPTIS Project

The Oxfordshire Project for the Training of Instructors and Supervisors began operations in 1984 as an Open Tech Project with a brief to produce open learning materials for instructors and supervisors in the Youth Training Scheme. Its brief was a national one involving a potential target audience of over 40 000 and spanning a huge range of abilities, attitudes and experience. Target audience research showed that a considerable percentage of the potential clients would be inexperienced, unconfident and frequently reluctant learners. The timescale for producing materials was approximately 19 months from April 1984. Within that deadline OPTIS had to develop a project which could be researched, produced and marketed successfully, for the deadline marked the end of its funding lifespan of £268 000. The tangible product was to be a system of eight text modules and three videos with the following titles:

Text

1 Instructor Skills
2 Developing Effective Learners
3 Working with Young People
4 Planning Training Programmes
5 Induction of Young Trainees
6 Assessment and Reviewing
7 Guidance and Support
8 Trainee-Centred Learning

Video

0 An Introduction to the OPTIS System
1 Trainee-Centre Learning
2 Instructor Skills
3 Guiding and Supporting Young People

In addition, it was decided at an early stage to produce an audiotape for use with the *Instructor Skills* text. Text modules were envisaged as being in a looseleaf format, with relatively short sub-units, often no more than three to four printed pages in length. By the same token videos were to consist of short, 'trigger' sequences separated by text-referenced pause points for discussion. The target reading age was to be no more than 14. A more detailed account of format and design issues is given in Webberley (1986).[7]

Towards a new style of management

It is not surprising to find that, within such temporal and fiscal constraints, the OPTIS directors were to consider the top-down style of management (with ownership and control vested in the hands of the directors) as inappropriate for the development of the type of materials that seemed to be required. To produce materials that met the required training needs, yet were acceptable and saleable to the client group within the defined time span, the directorate needed to unify and utilise the expertise possessed by both those with training knowledge and 'know-how' and those with practical experience – the working supervisors. A style of management was required that would foster the participation of such groups.

To this end, the directors of OPTIS were to develop a style of management that would enhance the participation and involvement of both those expert in the field of training (who were to become module co-ordinators) and the client group, consisting of YTS supervisors and instructors. The aim was to develop a relationship between these two groups, which would empower each of them to participate cooperatively and constructively in the development of the modules. Thus, instead of the writers writing and the supervisors approving the drafts, the wish was to reverse the process: the supervisors would set out their needs, deeds and work-ethos to the writers, conveying it in its raw form, on flipcharts, in cartoons or as anecdotes of supervision in the workplace. A style of management was thus required that would enable and encourage the valued participation of each group, in the sense just described, while avoiding barriers to the participation of either.

As OPTIS was a new organisation the structure of participation had to be created. Unlike many other Open Tech projects OPTIS was not linked to a large organisation and as such the 'meta-structure' for OPTIS had to be set up afresh. Thus as the project developed, new norms had to be created and then maintained. A fresh set of social relations between the directors, trainers and supervisors was needed – a set of relationships that could maximise the project's success. Obtaining the funds had been one thing; effectively managing them to fruition would be yet another.

The organisational structure that emerged contained three distinct elements: writing clusters, client workshops and a coordinators' committee. Each was designed to provide a forum in which the required participation, consultation and developments would take place. For example, the eight writing clusters (one for each module of text) were set up to bring together a range of expertise and perspectives. Each writing cluster consisted of: a module co-ordinator (an expert in the particular field of the module, recruited by invitation to tender); a consultant writer; various combinations of instructors and supervisors; a strategic advisor and editorial support. Furthermore, through the involvement of experts in the field of open learning, previously-researched principles for quality could be incorporated.

While the writing clusters could ensure the participation of the supervisors/instructors, they could not on their own ensure that the content and the approach adopted within the text would be properly contextualised, related and generally acceptable to their peer group. Research had shown that this was a group which frequently led a dichotomous existence, mediating between, on the one hand, the cultural needs and rhetoric of management and on the other, the often competing culture and language of the shop floor (Webberley, 1986).[8] It was to maximise the active involvement and influence of this wider audience of supervisors and instructors in the writing clusters that the second element of the organisational structure, the client workshop, were ingeniously devised and incorporated into the contracted agreement, which was given added strength by being phased. The payment for each phase was to be made only following the successful completion of the former phase. Those who spy a misplaced liberalism in this 'bottom-up' strategy should note that some clear 'top-down' leadership was required to bring the policy into effect!

Thus the coordinators of each writing cluster were contracted to hold two client workshops prior to the final drafting of module texts for which they were responsible. In each workshop an invited group of instructors and supervisors were asked to share anecdotes of their experiences, both good and bad, prior to the generation of a draft. Thus an 'anecdote bank' was set up. The intention was that this could be offered to writers as a basis for their first draft. Thus through the workshops it was possible to develop modules which were grounded in the everyday life and experiences of the workplace.

Finally, OPTIS held regular coordinators' meetings, not only to enable the sharing of information and ideas but to ensure the active participation of contracted coordinators in the decision-making process.

To summarise: to develop open learning materials within the constraints outlined earlier, the OPTIS directors were led into adopting what could be called a 'process-centred' model of management. This emerged as a participatory model where the role of the directors was essentially the maintenance of a set of devolved elements in which the production work was carried out. Thus, through the creation and servicing of the writing clusters, client workshops and coordinators meetings, the OPTIS directorate were able to manage the internal participation (Haffenden, 1986)[9] of the desired groups, while the contractual agreement ensured the management of involvement extrinsically within a specified period of time.

Managing the dynamics of achievement

But how was the structure outlined above to be put into operation? What were the managerial decisions and actions that had to be taken in order to activate the model of management by involvement? The essentials seemed to be the following:

1 In any management structure that is closely concerned with facilitation activities, one of the essential decisions is to determine the balance between facilitation and control. The OPTIS directorate, while devolving day-to-day control of the writing clusters to the module coordinators, chose to participate actively in the clusters, partly to maximise participation of individuals.

2 The module coordinators met regularly to ensure inter-group communication.

3 The directorate participated directly in the writers' workshops.

4 Module coordinators were selected not merely for their subject expertise but also for their capacities as group facilitators.

5 Writers were selected as much by their ability to listen as by their ability to write. It became important that they should, at least in some measure, subscribe to the pattern of values implied by a participatory management model. They needed to allow themselves to be shaped by the anecdotes and experiences of the supervisors before writing.

6 It also followed that the group itself, consisting of module coordinator, writer(s) and members of the target audience, needed to possess certain characteristics if it were to provide an appropriate environment for the individuals it contained. Features such as strong mutual support, the ability to brainstorm (suspend critical judgement on ideas) and adopting flexible and mutually-agreed group-management practices were critical to the success of these sessions.

Before going on to examine the OPTIS product in terms of its success in the marketplace, it is important to add that the above management model had very real, concrete implications for the design of the eventual product. Because there was an insistence upon target audience participation in both verbal and visual modes, the design team became more actively involved than would otherwise have been the case in a more centralised model of production. Editorial participation was also both earlier and more vigorous. The proportion of graphics to text, the role of checklists and activities, the actual length of modules and sub-units, even the titles, were frequently altered by target audience input. But it should also be noted that such a strategy has very real implications also for the phasing of resources and associated decisions.

How were the materials received?

The general record of acceptability and application of OPTIS materials is a good one. Some results have been reported elsewhere (Webberley, 1985[10] and 1986,[11] Webberley and Drowley, 1986).[12] Here we would like to recapitulate on the general findings of the independent evaluators (University of Surrey) that, based on a questionnaire survey, addressed the following areas:

- the materials' readability;
- the materials' presentation;
- the materials' effectiveness;
- the mode of use;
- their use as a support;
- the usefulness of the materials;
- suggestions on modules not covered.

The conclusions were:

> . . . the OPTIS modules evaluated in depth proved to be readable, acceptable, well-presented and effective in the opinion of the YTS supervisors. Though constructive criticisms were made over a wide variety of aspects, roughly 90 per cent of the respondents said that they would use materials of this sort if they were made available to them. In addition to this, a surprisingly high number of respondents to both modules stated that they would actually change their approach as a result of reading the module. (Haffenden *et al.*, 1985)[13]

The questions that were asked were of a qualitative nature which led the respondents on to personalised statements of opinion that were both critical and instructive. Furthermore, since this evaluation took place during the piloting phase of the materials it enabled valuable client feedback prior to going to press.

For example, the following extract taken from the evaluation report (Haffenden *et al.*, 1985)[13] demonstrates the point with respect to the module format:

> *Layout*
> Comment here ranges from favourable:
> '. . . liked the "simple layout"; "very well laid out"; "initial reaction – rather daunting (but) once started I found it easier than expected"; "very easy to read, which means that even if you

> haven't got long to consult it, the relevant part can be found and understood quickly"; "logical"; "the use of coloured printing and shaded boxing makes the format attractive and readable"; "the drawings were well done, they made me realise how often I have been in those situations".'
> through to ambivalent:
> "... because the design/layout is visually stimulating it does tend to distract the reader away from points/ideas outlined in the text"; "a substantial improvement on previous attempts that I've seen but I think that the design/layout is just too visual";
> and lukewarm:
> "supervisors with no formal training may have some difficulty"; "has the appearance of being put together in a rush"; "easy to read but layout could have been better (no examples given"; "easy to read; boring, repetitive";
> to specifically, and possibly, therefore, more helpfully, critical of the layout:
> "... not easy to read"; "at times it was a little messy ... I was inclined to look all over the page"; "relative paragraphs of information dotted round randomly were off-putting, I tended to skip some of them – and then have to backtrack"; "gaps and margins not definite enough"; "I would prefer the information set down in broad block rather than in columns".

However, 99 per cent found no problems with the vocabulary and 90 per cent recorded that the module was easy to read. Since the above data were gathered at a pre-publication stage (though in the case of one of the modules, this involved a two-colour, typeset production), a positive response was made to the criticisms in the final edition.

In summary, OPTIS found that as a result of such feedback and through adopting the management model described above, the end product was to have a high level of street credibility. As stated by one of the respondents:

> It isn't stuffed shirt or jargonese; it's plain and deals with real issues.

As Webberley (1986)[14] points out, the street-credible nature of the OPTIS materials led to considerably greater market success than might otherwise have been the case. As the product was designed by the marketplace, it could reasonably be expected to do well in it.

Conclusions

In view of the growing size of the general open learning enterprise, issues related to its management require careful consideration. It seems clear from the case study that the effective management of its production requires specific skills. Furthermore, since open learning materials are not cheap to produce or to buy, value for money is an essential consideration in the development of an open learning management strategy. To this end, it has been argued that active involvement of the client group in the production process needs to be the rule rather than the exception. OPTIS exemplifies this principle. The successful production of the OPTIS materials was a direct result of the qualitative elements of the package being determined by supervisors rather than by management-oriented colleagues. Had the project proceeded 'top-down', via a traditional committee structure, which tends to ration or restrict involvement or to encourage the adept committee-manipulator, the OPTIS directorate could not have emphasised the management of participation and the full involvement of members of the target audience in materials creation. The outcome was a credible, user-designed and ultimately profitable open learning enterprise that, at the time of writing, has become self-supporting.

References

1 G Holland, Address given at launch of *Implementing Open Learning in FE*, FEU Publications, Connaught Rooms, London, 24th June 1986.

2 Manpower Services Commission, *A New Training Initiative*, HMSO, 1982.

3 Manpower Services Commission (reprograph), April, 1983.

4 Manpower Services Commission, *ibid.*, 1982.

5 *Ibid.*

6 Tavistock Institute, London, 1984, 1985.

7 R Webberley, 'OPTIS: Involving the Target Audience in Open Learning' in *Media in Education and Development*, March 1986.

8 R Webberley, 'The Loneliness of the Long-Distance Learner' in *Personnel Management*, June 1986.

9 I Haffenden, 'Issues in the Development of Open Learning: a Case Study', *Proceedings*, the American Adult Education Research Conference, University of Syracuse, May 1986.

10 R Webberley, 'Designing for Open Learning: a Grass Roots Approach', in *Training and Development*, July 1985.

11 R Webberley, June 1986, *ibid.*

12 R Webberley and B Drowley, 'Applying Street Wisdom to Open Learning' in *Transition*, April 1986.

13 I Haffenden, *et al.*, 'OPTIS Final Evaluation Report' (reprograph), University of Surrey, 1985.

14 R Webberley, May 1986, *ibid.*

PART III LEARNING TO LEARN

15 Returning to study

Andy Northedge

Introduction

Taking up serious study in adult life can be an exciting experience. The sense of taking hold of the reins of understanding for the first time, after a lifetime of being led by the nose by the media, parents, schoolteachers and the rest, can give an intense satisfaction, as forbidden questions are at last asked and cunningly manufactured nonsense is reconstructed as sense. It is this thrill of intellectual self-development which surely provides the primary thrust behind the drive to adult studenthood (as opposed, say, to enhancement of career prospects). However, there is also, of course, a negative side. Studying is always a difficult process with pains and disappointments as well as achievements. And while teachers and teaching institutions act wisely when they capitalise on the enthusiasms and self-discoveries of newly-begun studies, they also act foolishly when they neglect the many difficulties through which new students need to be helped. This chapter is concerned with those difficulties (particularly as they apply to beginners in the social sciences in the Open University (OU), though hopefully with relevance to all adult beginners). But I am anxious not to create the impression, that newly-begun studies resemble some form of acute illness in which suffering blots out all other sensations and grim-faced survival is the only goal. The thrill and inspiration must always be a more important focus, since without them the impetus to study soon withers away.

Learning how to make 'meaning' happen

Some of the most pressing problems for students beginning to study again are also disarmingly mundane. The task of reading, for example, often raises the humdrum problem of becoming bored very quickly and inspires the intensely felt attraction towards making a cup of tea, tidying the shelves, watching a TV programme or whatever, after only a couple of paragraphs of reading. Although teachers tend to regard the reading of a chapter as a relatively straightforward assignment, new students may find even the first page a tremendous obstacle. The problem is that though the students may be thirsting for knowledge, what they want is to extend the knowledge and understanding they *already have*. However, what is on the page tends to be a very different kind of knowledge, which makes hardly any sense in terms of what is already known. Unfamiliar words may be part of the problem, but far more fundamental is the fact that even familiar words are used for concocting quite unexpected and unfamiliar meanings. This is very frustrating. One knows that the writing is about the subject one wishes to study, but one cannot *make* the writing '*make sense*'. One re-reads a paragraph several times and still the mental gears will not mesh. The motor of one's mind stays in neutral and the words stay stubbornly 'out there' on the page.

Now think of the opposite – say reading a novel. One is scarcely aware of the printed words. One's eyes seem to drink meaning thirstily from the page. How? Because the places, characters and action that the words refer to have become powerfully 'internalised' as a set of dynamic images which work apparently spontaneously. The external words on the page mobilise this vigorous inner experience, not in the sense that each word triggers off a separate unit of meaning but through well established patternings of the flow of words – characteristic phrases, the style of the writing, conventions of character and plot. Indeed, when one 'gets into' a particular genre of novel one can construct the internal version of the story so effectively and rapidly that one takes in the sequences of external words in very large gulps. As one turns the page one already knows what the other half of the sentence is going to be. In other words, there is a very close fit between internal processes and external symbols.

On the other hand, with educational texts, instead of images of people and events, one is working with more abstract internalisations, such as conceptions of the economy or the role of the Health Visitor. And as a beginner one finds it difficult to produce internal operations upon these concepts which correspond to developments within the external sequences of printed words. In fact, unless one has the beginnings of the relevant train of thought already available at the forefront of one's attention there is little the words on the page can trigger off. This is the problem for 'beginning' students. Until they have become launched into the system of discourse within a given field of study, sequences of words may mean very little. (This applies also to lectures and seminars.) A system of discourse involves concepts, ideas and conventions of explanation. These accumulate round any collective 'expert' analysis of a subject, be it gardening, football tactics, physics or literary criticism. In every such 'expert' discourse the newcomer is likely to be baffled as to why particular issues are the focus of debate, why one factor is seen to be related to another, why a distinction is made here and why a causal connection is assumed there. Ironically, much of what is absolutely central is often missing from the discussion, precisely because it is so fundamental that 'insiders' to the discourse take it for granted.

As an 'outsider' to an 'expert' discourse the struggle through even a page or two of a text may represent an intense burst of learning. One's initial wrestlings to gain a first purchase on *what* is being said and *why* constitute a fundamental stage in entering the discourse. To succeed at this point one needs strategies which help bridge the gap between the sense one habitually makes in everyday discourses and the sense one needs to be able to make in order to 'read' the text.

One strategy is to 'hunt for clues' in a fairly open-minded 'investigative' way, taking a rather flighty approach to a text in the first instance. Instead of ploughing into page one, one dips in here and there, looking ahead to the conclusion, glancing back to the contents list or the dust cover 'blurb', scanning pictures, figures and tables, to try to get a sense of what sort of issues the text deals with, how and why. Another strategy is to engage with the text very actively; underlining words, taking notes, attempting to summarise a section in a sentence or two, etc. An active approach of this kind emphasises the *making* of sense and helps offset feelings of impotence and passive defeat. The gritty chiselling-out of small nuggets of self-constructed sense produces a gradual accumulation of written notes, which stand as a symbol of work done and of progress made. More importantly, it helps to provide a makeshift mental platform of provisional meanings from which one can launch oneself further into the discourse. A third strategy is to discuss the text with fellow students. The exchange of approximate versions of the 'expert' discourse again helps in the process of throwing up a temporary frame of workable concepts which assists subsequent progress in reading the texts.

To the extent that strategies such as these assist in the making of sense they will also help students resist the urge to stop studying to do something else. This urge to escape the study process is a sign of the deep discomfort caused to us when we cannot 'make sense' of something. We are beings whose entire lives revolve around and are dependent upon meanings, so that situations where meanings elude us are experienced as undermining and repellent. Because by its nature studying involves dismantling old meanings and constructing new, it arouses powerful and ambivalent feelings – hostility as the familiar is undermined and satisfaction as the new is constructed. (Teachers, texts, assignments and teaching institutions all become targets for these ambiguous reactions.) *New* students necessarily have more to lose and to gain in the dismantling and reconstruction of meaning and may therefore suffer more dramatic emotional fluctuations in their studies. They also have less experience of coping with the feelings, so the urge to escape from study may arise frequently and intensely. Consequently it is of immense value to them to discover or invent ways of forcing texts to yield up sense in however small a measure. In this way they can protect themselves against the threat of being immersed in a paralysing mystery. Instead they can develop confidence that they have the power and the skill to *make* meaning happen. (Note, that although we have concentrated on the reading process, much the same can be said about listening to lectures and participating in discussions. Here lapses of attention, daydreaming and loss of the 'thread' are prevailing problems for similar reasons.)

Understanding the process of learning

If we look at studying, then, as essentially a process of becoming initiated into a particular system of 'expert' discourse, there are important consequences for how students should approach their studies. They need, for example, to recognise that 'experts' are those who can both *read* 'expert' texts and *produce arguments* which carry weight within the relevant system of discourse. This may be in contrast with 'taken-for-granted' models of learning, picked up from school or from the general culture (e.g. films portraying student life, or programmes like Mastermind), in which learning is taken to be the storing of vast quantities of information in the memory. But intelligent learning is not 'memorising' as such, as it is not primarily the number of pages covered that counts. It is the time spent engaging actively and purposefully with constructing meanings out of unfamiliar material. As those meanings become established and consolidated the text eventually, in retrospect, seems more or less transparent, even commonplace. When that has happened it has been 'learned'. In other words 'learning' a text is a process of coming to understand it, with sheer 'memory' of the content an incidental accompaniment.

To look at learning this way leads to quite different strategies of action, some of which I have already mentioned. However, one strategy of more general significance is that of *reflecting* on and *questioning* of the results of studying. Whereas it is relatively straightforward to check whether one has 'memorised' something, it takes a rather more subtle insight to judge whether one is making useful progress in 'understanding' something. Because understanding proceeds unevenly (at some times assisted by sticking with a difficult point, at others by moving on rapidly over a range of related material) students cannot develop routine habits which will invariably work. Instead they need to develop a *flexibility* of approach based on experiment and reflection on results. They need to acquire an ability to recognise when their understanding has advanced and when not, so that they can direct energy into those activities which are productive. Otherwise there is the danger that they will become acclimatised to incomprehension and will develop habits either of work-avoidance or of 'busy work' (such as re-writing notes in neat) which eases feelings of guilt and inadequacy. Honest reflection on one's own learning processes is not easy, partly because of the difficulty of identifying and assessing developments, but also because of the intense hopes and fears bound up in adult study. Nevertheless, a habit of self-monitoring is virtually essential if the aim of studying is development of the intellect rather than the memory.

Another consequence of shifting from a model of learning as acquiring information to a model of learning as developing the ability to understand and 'speak' within an 'expert' discourse, is a shift in the *status* of 'knowledge'. Instead of accepting as 'fact' what authority presents, students must take on responsibility for assessing the claims of competing accounts of 'the truth'. They must seek out and grapple with 'knowledge' as it is relevant to their current understanding, rather than wait to be fed pre-processed capsules. Such a switch from an assumption of passive, deferential receptivity to one of active, critical constructivity is likely to be at once alarming and difficult for new students and they may need help in the early weeks if they are not to retreat into rigid, defensive 'coping' tactics. To develop broad strategies adequate to the task of genuine rather than perfunctory study they must develop an adequate understanding of the study process.

Understanding the writing proces

A critically important consequence of viewing studying as a process of becoming initiated into a discourse is that assignment writing becomes far more than a necessary evil, serving the purposes of assessment. Writing is the other half of learning. On the one hand one learns to listen, or to read, within an 'expert' discourse and on the other one learns to speak or write within it. It is in the process of writing that one *discovers* what one knows. Indeed in writing one is re-constructing and in a sense *creating* what one knows. Thus writing (or its equivalent in subjects using algebraic or other languages) whether in the form of jotted notes or carefully polished essays, is fundamental to studying.

But writing is a difficult process fraught with crises as even the most prolific of professional writers testify, partly because it involves us in grappling with unresolved frames of meaning; experiencing the discomfort of inadequate, unstable and often evaporating meanings. What new students have to come to terms with is that the writing component of a course will often be very time consuming and accompanied by emotional troughs and peaks. The important thing is to develop ways of coming at writing tasks constructively; recognising an essay as the product of a complex process of construction involving a number of different states, requiring craftwork and skill. To attempt it as a single, continuous effort, beginning on line one, is to head straight into difficulties and eventual disappointment. To begin with there is the stage of thinking one's way into the title set (which may take a day or two). Then certain of the various loosely formed ideas floating across one's mind have to be snatched, 'externalised' and 'concretised' as jottings. After this some knocking into shape has to be done to work out a preliminary structure and some points may have to be developed in sentence form to see how they look. Sections may come to be written out of sequence; but eventually, with re-jigging of plans and cobbling, cutting and re-working, a first draft can be assembled. After which one probably needs to re-examine the title set to see how far the answer has drifted from the point. Finally, a polished-up version can be produced.

This is perhaps a somewhat sketchy account, but the point remains that *because* writing is that half of the process of *learning* through which one acquires use of the language and ideas of the 'expert' discourse, it cannot be a simple or easy process. Students need to take a strategic approach to it, breaking the process into stages and experimenting and reflecting on ways of tackling each stage. Otherwise there is a danger that students will experience the difficulties of writing as personal failings rather than as universal and intrinsic problems to be worked at and overcome. They may then seek to avoid writing, or keep putting it off so that they never have time to work constructively at it. Or they may seek escape into plagiarism. If instead they accept writing as a lengthy and rather bitty process of jotting, drafting, re-drafting and polishing, their progress is likely to be steadier and more satisfying.

Putting structure into studying

On both the reading and writing side of the learning process I have emphasised the fragmented and uneven nature of studying. And indeed when adults take up studying, the general messiness of life tends to move up several notches, with new demands on time and energy in a life which is already full. OU students writing advice to new students, in the University newspaper *Sesame*, frequently assert that the first requirement of successful studying is that of creating order within the general chaos. Decisions have to be made about when to read, how long to work at a stretch, which books to start on, to what depth to read, whether to take notes, how long to persevere with the same task and so on. Habits and strategies have to be developed. The student has to set up a place to work, arrange materials and a filing system, discover how to get hold of books, make arrangements to be left undisturbed, draw up a calendar of deadlines, etc.

To create order and put some overall structure into studying, students have to be able to stand back from the course and identify the major components and requirements, assigning priorities and planning their distribution of time and energy. But this does not simply involve identifying the *demands of the course* (quite a difficult task in itself for beginners); it also involves identifying their *own goals* with respect to the course.

Placing oneself in relation to the institution

Taking on the role of 'student' is quite an adventure for some adult students. A lot may be at stake for students whose studies in effect set them apart from the interests and aspirations of friends, or withdraw them from the family. As a result it may take time to set newly begun studies into a workable relationship with the rest of life. Is one to feel perpetual anguish and inadequacy about impossible-seeming reading tasks? Is family life to go by the board each time an assignment is due? Is one going to attempt to be a smarty pants in the classroom or keep quiet? How is one to cope with demands to 'criticise' and 'assess' the sacred printed word? Questions such as these force students to examine the extent to which taking on a student role involves also taking on a general shift of self-image and a shift of social identity in the eyes of others. How far are the expectations imposed by studenthood to carry over into other areas of life? How far would that be desirable? Is change in oneself part of the attraction of becoming a student? The other side of the issue is how hard to push back against the demands of the course. How tough and independent can one be in staking out one's *own* aims and commitments as a student?

After the driven studies of childhood, pursued because state, school and family demanded it, it can be hard to switch to a frame of mind where one is consciously studying *for oneself*. Nevertheless it is important that students come to see themselves as 'consumers' of the education service – not *ruled by* the teaching institution but *using it* to extend their own lives. If adult students are to succeed over an extended period it becomes essential that they periodically re-examine their goals, considering the impact of study on the rest of life and weighing up what is being gained. It is easy to set study targets which are over idealistic and to continue pursuing them in spite of failure and of damage to other areas of life. Studying involves a constant tension between on the one hand one's high ideals and the demands set by the course and on the other the reality of fitful progress and competing demands from elsewhere.

Advising students on study techniques

Out of all this arises the question as to what help students can be given in approaching early obstacles to studying. Certainly there seems to have been a rapid rise in the level of recognition of students' needs for advice if one is to go by the expansion in 'How to Study' publications in recent years. But perhaps the very proliferation of advice also suggests that no universally effective approach has been discovered. (Unless one simply concludes that in an area of high anxiety there is a compulsion to keep buying advice regardless of repetitiveness – as for instance with beauty hints and slimming guides.)

The problem with trying to offer 'handy hints' is that the process of studying is too variable to be neatly encapsulated in formulae for success. Genuine learning is not a repetitive, systematic process. It is a struggle to construct sense and it demands an intense focussing of attention on key issues within the subject matter. As soon as the study process is subjected to a routinising technique one's attention tends to become diluted as the repetitive rhythm of the technique hypnotises and anaesthetises. In fact the technique itself may become the dominant focus of attention as students monitor their application of it. Moreover, the way techniques are presented in guides to study often implies that studying can be made virtually painless and that those suffering and struggling are merely ignorant of the appropriate techniques. Consider, for example, the wording of this advertisement in the OU student newspaper:

> Develop your memory. You can! It's easy with the '...' method. Discover how you can develop a powerful memory, acute powers of observation and a laser-sharp mind. Develop a super grasp of facts, figures and faces – Fast! Pass exams ... learn languages ... recall complicated numbers.
>
> *Sesame*, p 12, December 1986

It would appear from this that the problems of study have been solved (though prudently the answers are not revealed to all and sundry). Those who can afford the price of easy training for a laser-sharp mind can, one might suppose, confidently anticipate a first-class degree and a PhD in record time. Or can they? Advice on 'speed reading', for example, tends to make such claims as that to read just the first line of every paragraph, or to search out just the key words, not only makes 'reading' very fast but also enhances comprehension. (If this were true an enormous saving in education costs could be achieved by only printing the first lines of paragraphs or listing key words – and you would not be reading this suggestion, since it is not the first sentence of the paragraph.)

Clearly what is implied by such an approach is that learning, far from being a process of grappling with ideas and struggling to construct sense around them, is a matter of acquainting oneself with a sample of the words in the set texts. Interestingly a major line of recent research in University education has focussed on the distinction between 'deep' and 'surface' learning styles (Marton and Saljo, 1984).[1] The studies identify some students as tending to read for the underlying meaning of the text and others as skimming the surface perfunctorily. The findings are that the 'deep processors' are the more likely to *enjoy* their studies and to *succeed*. Yet much advice on reading positively advocates the superficial approach.

Another example is the popular advice for constructing elaborate 'mnemonic' devices to aid in the retention of information. Drawing parallels with remembering shopping lists and the like, the implication is made that what is to be remembered by a student is essentially a set of arbitrary and disconnected items. In fact the opposite is the case. The student should be at work constructing frames of meaning within which items of information are embedded as intrinsic elements. When a conceptual and theoretical frame has become fairly well established the facts and figures come with it. The need for memorising by rote should then be very limited.

Techniques such as speed reading and mnemonics provide a diversion for students – an opportunity to avoid facing the genuine intellectual effort of trying to understand something. The somewhat prosaic truth is that real studying is tough but enjoyable in the way that, say, mountain climbing is. If students are to persist with adult studies it is very important that they hold onto a sense of pleasure in the accomplishment of understanding. Techniques which promise to routinise the difficulties immediately threaten to depersonalise study and turn it from an internal process to an external set of dutiful exercises. Rather than generalised recipes students need advice which accompanies and is *intrinsic* to studying the subject matter they are working on – advice which helps them *reflect* on the learning processes they are currently experiencing, helps in *setting targets* and helps in *exploring alternative practices* and *strategies*. Very little advice on *specific* practices suits everyone and all circumstances. In the end individual students have to be able to guide themselves by trial and error and reflection on experience. This is not easy, particularly for beginners. But advice should press in the direction of that *exploration* and *self-reflection*, not offer to shoulder the burden for the student by supplying foolproof and painless remedies.

Practical applications

The point of studying by means of a course, rather than by personal inquiry, is the fruitful tension achieved by placing a turbulent experience of the development of new ideas within the frame of a formal set of tasks and requirements. In other words the function of a teaching institution is to supply source material, experiences and demands such as to create a structure within which the rather inexact, fitful and mysterious processes of intellectual development will be stimulated and sustained. In the last part of this chapter I will try to illustrate how the foregoing analysis can be translated into practice by describing some aspects of the current OU Foundation course in the Social Sciences: D102 (The Open University, 1982).[2]

Learning to make meaning happen

Because the subject matter of the social science is, in certain senses, already familiar to students, an obvious approach to teaching beginners is to select everyday issues and invite students to bring their everyday ideas to discussing them, whilst gradually drawing in more academic ideas. However, dangers lurk within this very appealing approach. In fact the very familiarity of the subject matter may make the distinction between everyday frames of meaning and academic ones difficult to grasp. Correspondingly the task of *bridging* the gulf between the two may become confused because students do not perceive the gulf at all. It may 'sound' as though what is being said in the text is to all intents and purposes identical with 'common sense'. Similarly, efforts to reassure students that academic ideas are not impossibly distant from everyday ideas may lead them to a complacent reaffirmation of current thinking. In fact the teacher has the somewhat contradictory task of *emphasising differences* between the understanding students bring and 'what the books say' and at the same time *building bridges* between the two.

A second problem is that a course shaped around the world of everyday experience may lack intellectual coherence. When theories are brought in piecemeal as they apply to specific everyday problems the *underlying rationale* behind each theory, the *kind* of theory it is and its *relation* to other theories is *never revealed systematically*, only glimpsed in incoherent flashes. Thus, although the strategy of *putting immediate, everyday social experience at the centre* of a course for beginners and *illuminating it through theory* might seem the obvious thing to do, in fact our experience had been that students became frustrated and irritated when each week brought new fragments of theories but produced little advance in terms of coherent understanding. The students observed the theories in use by the teacher/author but could not 'take on' the theories for themselves and try them out in a way that produced cumulative gain from one week to the next.

To tackle this second problem the D102 course team set out to construct a central theoretical debate which runs throughout the course. Two basic theoretical positions are presented, in order that students can come to understand the nature of each in the light of the contrast with the other. Through the eight months of the course the students see the debate worked out in terms of the economy, politics, social structure and so on and they become sufficiently versed in the two theoretical positions to be able to move across from their everyday frames of reference to first one and then the other theoretical orientation in gradually more demanding contexts. Having constructed this broad frame the course writers *then* chose examples from everyday life which would serve to introduce aspects of the theoretical debate. Thus as students work through the 'real life' issues they repeatedly find themselves moving into a familiar frame of reference, gradually absorbing more and more of the nature and implications of two broad positions. In this way the course strategy reverses the previous priorities by placing a *theoretical debate at the centre* of the course and *bringing in 'real life' to illuminate the theory*; setting it up and breathing life into it. This switch of tactics has been a great success, taking raw beginners in the social sciences at a steady pace towards a firm grasp of two broad conceptions of the nature of British society and of the issues around which theoretical debates have turned.

To illustrate these principles it is instructive to compare two superficially similar 'units' (one week's work) from the present course and its predecessor. The second unit of the earlier course was on the subject of *crime*, while the first unit of the present course is on *vandalism*. On the face of it both might be seen as no more than opportunistic forays into 'tabloid' territory to exploit popular preoccupations. However, the impact of the two is quite different. The former deals with 'crime in general', dwelling with imaginative eclecticism on a wide range of issues and drawing in an assortment of briefly sketched theories. Undoubtedly the unit stimulated interest and thought but it left students with bits and pieces of ideas and no clear directions ahead. It also left the dividing line between common sense and social science very blurred.

By contrast, vandalism is a much narrower subject of study: simpler to graps and to discuss. To place it in very sharp focus it is even defined visually in the unit by means of an extended exercise using photographs. Students have to decide wich ones show instances of vandalism. This capitalises on the potential for making this kind of topic immediately accessible and it draws everyday ideas forcefully into the action. However, the exercise includes difficult cases which challenge everyday ideas and the subsequent discussion of each case deliberately highlights the boundaries between commonsense assumptions and more careful analysis. In this way *personal* everyday understanding is brought into play but at the same time its foundations are loosened.

The unit then draws in a range of everyday explanations of the causes of vandalism taken from newspapers, grouping them together and indicating general characteristics. Thus the ground of public 'common sense' is clearly marked out. After this, explanations representing one of the main theoretical perspectives of the course are sketched out and similarly grouped together. Finally, explanations representing the other perspective are presented. Although this three-part structure is carefully set out, culminating in a table displaying it explicitly, in fact the moves are made in easy stages using everyday language, so that the structure emerges gradually and apparently naturally. By starting with an immediate familiar and concrete phenomenon and using photographs and newspaper cuttings the students have no initial difficulty in 'making meaning happen' as they work on the text. But as the context gradually shifts while they continue to 'make meaning happen' they are eventually, and largely unknowingly, making it happen along lines parallel to subsequent discussions in the course. It is in this way that the unit gives priority to theoretical structure and uses everyday life to illuminate it rather than the other way round.

Another aspect of the design of the unit on vandalism concerns the level of perceived difficulty of the text. It is inevitably very tricky pitching an introductory text at a suitable level for a wide range of students. The danger of *boring* students with trivial-seeming *simplicities* is as great as that of *mystifying* them with *complexity*. The strategy of the unit on vandalism is to begin at a very 'chatty' level, moving gradually into more formal and analytical language and content until in the last fifth of the text there are some rather demanding arguments. The idea is that while every student ought to be able to make substantial progress in mastering, say, three-quarters of the text, at the same time because the 'difficulty gradient' increases more and more sharply towards the end most students will run into something which they find quite challenging and thought provoking.

Understanding the process of learning

At the end of the vandalism unit the students are directed to exercises and discussions designed to help them reflect on the first week of studying. These are largely in the form of a popular magazine 'quiz', where students are invited to pick the answers which reflect their own study practices and turn to a later page to find comments on those practices. This format is chosen because it reflects a familiar form of amusement within popular culture, whereas study advice can be forbiddingly proper. Past experience was that, although students would say that study advice was a good idea, they tended to avoid reading it and seldom made practical use of what they did read. This may be because people cherish their own study habits as expressions of their own accommodation to life, their own intellectual organisation and their own personality. It may also be because the proffered images of perfection of practice contrast so unflatteringly with real-life inefficiency and pragmatism. In any case the course team took it as essential to present the study advice in a form which is highly accessible, engaging and immediate; encouraging students to recognise their taken-for-granted habits, as revealed in studies just completed, and to reflect upon them. The quiz answers, in effect, contain all that would have been written in a straightforward chapter of advice, but not presented as solid prose.

Elsewhere in the course other tactics are also used, including exercises involving audio-cassettes to 'talk the students through' study processes such as note-taking, essay writing and reading tables and graphs. These exercises on study techniques occur weekly to begin with and then at intervals of about a month throughout the course, concluding with quizzes and an audio-cassette giving very specific help with preparing for the examination.

Understanding the writing process

To help the students see writing as a process of communicating an *argument* in response to the title, (rather than simply as an opportunity to display items of information) they are asked to act as 'tutor' in reading three short essays on the topic of vandalism. That is to say, before writing an essay themselves they assess the quality of three pieces of writing and to note down advice they would offer the writers. This helps students understand the role of their tutors in relation to their own essays, and in particular to understand them as the silent 'other half' of a written dialogue (– silent, that is, until they write comments back to the students). The aim is to develop the 'sense of audience' stressed in the research of James Britton and his colleagues into the development of writing ability (Britton *et al.*, 1975).[3] It also helps students to see that the criteria of good writing are not mysterious, but relate to such obvious matters as clarity of expression, convincingness of argument and coherence of organisation. The exercise is embellished by an audio-cassette in which a tutor takes the students point by point through the first essay pointing to difficulties and suggesting alternative ways of saying things. After this the students are directed to a re-worked version of the essay containing the same points as the original but better organised and expressed. The other two essays are also discussed and re-worked, in rather less detail. The broad aim of all this is to make public the normally very private and personal process of producing written work; highlighting the very common problems of communicating ideas effectively and suggesting strategies for setting about solving them.

This detailed attention to *real essays* on a topic the students have just studied holds a very different significance from broad recommendations about essays in general. Students can identify with the processes that have led to the production of the sample essays and can also identify with the problems of tutors having to assess and advise them. This kind of detailed and concrete analysis is much more likely to achieve a practical impact on writing strategies than well meant homilies about 'getting your thinking straight before you start writing' and such like.

Apart from the direct offering of advice, *the way the written assignments are set* is also aimed towards the gradual development of writing ability. Writing ability is not taken to be a set of separate technical skills which can be added one by one to the students' repertoire. Rather writing is seen holistically as an effort at producing a meaningful statement within a specified context. Past experiments with 'fragmented' writing tasks (such as writing a precis) indicated that the tasks alienated students from their own writing, because they denied them the opportunity to '*speak*' through the written word. Instead the early D102 assignments are 'whole essays' but made short and simple. The task is brought within the beginner's capability by being set on a restricted topic, with a concerete, practical element to provide a focus, and drawing on easy readings. Playing with these parameters (scope, abstractness, difficulty of sources, length) gives plenty of opportunity for adjusting difficulty levels without breaking out of the essay format. Thus although the assignment is on a small scale the student is nevertheless engaged in trying to *say* something which *makes sense* as an *argued response* to the *title*. If this broad frame of meaning is abandoned, in the interest of focussing on some more specific task, the students are deprived of their most effective asset – the ability to make sense.

Putting structure into studying

All OU courses go a long way in helping students to structure their studies. The work is divided into weekly 'units' of study, with an assignment to be submitted every few weeks. This 'pacing' is emphasised in D102 (as in other foundation level courses) by weekly TV programmes, fortnightly radio programmes and regular meetings at local study centres. The structuring goes further in that each week's work is set out in the form of a table indicating the appropriate allocation of 12 study hours to various tasks. And within the printed 'course units' the content is itself structured into sections broken by summaries and by 'student activities' to encourage students towards active involvement in checking their progress. Although all this 'spoonfeeding' might seem like a recipe for longterm dependency, in fact by launching students quickly into active and effective study practices, they are able to begin to 'model' the various processes involved (through practice and reflection). At the same time their studies develop a momentum which carries them on under their own management as the supports are gradually removed – the 'water wings and instruction' method as opposed to the traditional 'in at the deep end and sink or swim'.

Placing oneself in relation to the institution

The various quizzes in the D102 course text invite students to reflect on their own study aims and the competing pressures from elsewhere. OU tutor-counsellors are also encouraged to discuss these issues with students individually and collectively. However, the main help available is probably that of talking to fellow students at study centre sessions and at summer school. In addition the course has a newspaper, the *Grassroot*, through which students can get a sense of how other students are responding to the course and what their aims and interests are; and there is a monthly radio 'magazine' programme 'Grapevine', which links the course debates to current events and offers advice on forthcoming assignments.

Conclusion

Adults returning to study almost always find the going exhilarating but tough in the early stages. This can be understood by recognising that they are, in effect, travellers entering a foreign culture with its own language and customs and that they suffer the difficulties of communication and the dislocations of personal identity to which newcomers are always exposed. However, I have tried to show that, by recognising these problems of entry into an unfamiliar 'expert' discourse, one can both equip students themselves for more effective engagement with the obstacles and one can design courses which provide support in the crucial areas. I have given rather detailed attention to certain aspects of the OU Social Science Foundation Course: D102, by way of illustration of the analysis presented. But in case my account seemed too fulsome I should add that at the time of writing, a new course team is forming for the production of D103. No doubt in a few years time the solutions I have outlined will have been consigned to history and replaced by better approaches not yet thought of. On the other hand the problems they will be addressing will surely be the same.

References

1 F Marton and R Säljö, 'Approaches to Learning' in F Marton, D Hounsell and N entwistle (eds), *The Experience of Learning*, Edinburgh, Scottish Academic Press, 1984.

2 *D102: Social Sciences – A Foundation Course*, The Open University, 1982.

3 J Britton, T Burgess, N Martin, A McLeod and H Rosen, *The Development of Writing Abilities*, London, Methuen/Schools Council, 1975.

16 Learning from television

A W Bates

Television: essential or extravagant?

Perhaps of all the media available for open learning, television is the least understood and most neglected by designers and tutors of open learning. Firstly, it is generally considered to be an expensive use of resources, and when it is used in open learning, it is often used very badly. However, television can be an extremely valuable resource, when used selectively and with care.

Secondly, television as a medium is subject to considerable change. New technology is both extending its range of uses, and helping to eliminate some of the weaknesses previously associated with its ephemerality. New organisations and methods of delivery (Open Tech, Open College, Open University, video-cassette, video-disc, cable and satellite) are developing, which are leading to greater diversity in the use of television. This diversity also makes generalisation difficult, but even so, a good deal is now known about how to use television successfully in open learning. I shall refer to a number of organisations in what follows, and addresses are listed at the end of the chapter.

The different uses of television

It is important to be clear about the different kinds of television available for open learning. There are three main parameters: the method of distribution, the method of utilisation, and the type of production.

Distribution

The most common form of distribution is by *terrestrial broadcasting* through the BBC or IBA transmission network in Britain, i.e. radiated from a ground transmitter, with programmes often relayed between different transmitters to form a network perhaps covering the whole country. Other forms of broadcast distribution which are becoming increasingly important are by *cable* or *satellite* transmission. Another way of distributing television is by *cassette* or *disc*, mailed directly to students or purchased or hired.

Utilisation

Television can be used in several forms. Perhaps the most common is the uninterrupted programme, seen straight through, once only. This is the way an unrecorded broadcast *must* be used; however, it is not uncommon for television to be used in this way, even when recorded on cassette.

Once recorded onto cassette or disc, though, television can be used quite differently from viewing a broadcast. The cassette or disc can be stopped, some parts can be selected for use, and not others, and the same television material can be used as many times as required.

Television can stand independently, as a broadcast programme on its own, or it can be integrated with other media, such as print or audio-cassettes. The print may just back up a programme (as with many adult education broadcasts), or may (as at the Open University) be the main medium, with television as another component of the course.

Computer control can be added to either a cassette or disc, so that the student is guided to work through different parts of the television material, with activities or tests of learning built in.

Lastly, programmes may be used by an individual student, or in a group, with or without a tutor. Again, the material is likely to be used differently, according to the context.

Production

The different types of television production vary enormously, but one major difference is whether television is being used primarily to distribute illustrated classroom lectures to a wider audience, or whether it is being used deliberately to exploit the unique visual characteristics of television. In the relayed classroom lecture, the emphasis is not so much on the unique *presentational* characteristics of television (discussed in this next section of this chapter), but more on its *distributional* characteristics.

Programmes made by broadcasting organisations are generally

meant to stand on their own, in that they have a unity of their own. *Broadcasts* tend to adopt a continuous flow, deliberately being constructed to hold the viewer's attention right through the programme, and often provide material not otherwise available to the viewer or teacher, thus exploiting the unique presentational characteristics of the medium.

Television, though, while concentrating on its unique presentational characteristics, can be structured quite differently from a broadcast programme, particularly if it is intended to exploit some of the utilisation characteristics of the *cassette* or *disc*. Thus television material may be made in short independent segments, with clear stopping points and explicit directions for activities or questions for discussion. (Similar points on the use of audio-cassettes are made in more detail in Chapter 17). These directions may be either on the cassette itself, or in computer software controlling the cassette or disc. A cassette style can be adopted, whether or not the programmes are broadcast. For instance, most secondary schools, further education and adult education colleges record broadcasts on cassette for later viewing (time-shift recording). If that is the main use, there is no technical reason why broadcast programmes could not be produced in a cassette style, particularly if transmitted at times when few are likely to watch, such as the middle of the night; broadcasting may be just the most economical means by which cassette format programmes could be distributed to large numbers. However, in general, broadcasting organisations have not made many programmes in cassette style for broadcasting, although the numbers are increasing.

Lastly, programmes may be either completely pre-recorded, or include a *live* element, including feedback or questioning from students, or exchange of materials from different sites. There is no technical reason why live, interactive programming cannot be done using terrestrial broadcasting, but due primarily to scarcity of time on terrestrial networks, such use has tended to be confined to cable or satellite broadcasting.

These different characteristics of educational television are very important for open learning. Television is not a homogeneous medium, but can be used in many different ways, according to the learning context and the teaching aims.

Unique characteristics of television

Before going any further, we should ask *why* we should use television in open learning. What can it do that can't be done by other methods, such as print or face-to-face tutorials? This means looking at the unique educational characteristics of television. As well as the ability of television to *deliver* learning material to large numbers of students, there are two main *presentational* characteristics of television.

The first is television's ability to bring to open learning students material not otherwise available, such as experiments requiring expensive laboratory equipment, case-study material of social and technological events, field-visits, dynamic presentation of ideas through animation and graphics. Many more examples could be given (see Bates, 1984a, pp 244–7, for a list of such functions found appropriate in the Open University context).[1]

The second is television's ability to help the learning process in unique ways. Television can provide concrete examples or models of abstract principles, can model processes, and through the combination of picture (usually providing the example) and commentary, relate example to principle. In other words, for many students there are often times when words are not enough; they need to be able to see to understand, and television is one way – in an open learning situation often the only way – in which this can be done.

If it is accepted then that television can in principle be useful in open learning, how can it be practically and economically harnessed?

Using existing material

Broadcasts

Even before the Open College gets going, there over 1000 educational programmes a year aimed at adults broadcast in the UK (BBC, ITV companies on the IBA network, Channel 4, and the Open University). Each organisation has a publication giving brief details of all the series to be broadcast each year. All of this material is available to educational users free of charge, if used as a live broadcast. There are constraints, though, on recording broadcast material, depending on the broadcasting organisation. BBC and ITV schools and continuing education material may be recorded free for educational purposes, but must not be kept beyond a certain period of time, nor used for commercial gain. In the case of Channel 4 and the Open University, a licence is required to make recordings. At the time of writing, it is still illegal to record non-educational broadcasts, but the whole question of recording material for educational use is being discussed by parliament. It is likely to become easier rather than more difficult to record broadcast material free of charge for educational purposes, partly because policing is difficult, and partly because broadcasting organisations want their educational materials to be widely and flexibly used. If you want to incorporate broadcast material into open learning packages, however, it is essential to get clearance first.

The standard way of using educational broadcasts is to play them through, either on transmission or on cassette, with some brief pre-programme preparation, and then have questions or discussion afterwards, or some individual work. This mode of utilisation is encouraged both by the style of production, and by the notes accompanying the broadcasts. While there are occasions where this might be helpful to a tutor looking for material to support an open learning package, this is not likely to be the best way to use television for open learning. There are several other strategies.

One way is to build an open learning package around a television series. This enables broadcasters to exploit the full range of televisual techniques and the presentational characteristics of television, and can draw in large audiences to further study around the series. The National Extension College, for instance, has designed several courses around educational television series (e.g. the BBC's *The Computer Programme*). This appears to be one of the major uses proposed for the forthcoming Open College. Broadcasters will make television series (in this case in the technical and vocational area) and it is expected that other agencies will run courses around them. There are two ways in which this could be done. One is to have a series of lectures or tutorials which coincide with the broadcast series (either showing the programmes followed by discussion, or students watching programmes on their own at home, with lectures or tutorials running independently). The other is to prepare independent study materials, in the form of printed material, to accompany the programmes. In other words, students watch and study primarily at home. The first method has the advantage of being relatively simple to organise and does not need much advanced preparation on the tutors' part; it has the disadvantage though of requiring students to attend regularly at local centres. Both methods of course can be combined.

One practical problem of preparing special print support material is co-ordinating the production of the print with the television material. Broadcasters have their own production schedules, and scripts and programme material may not be available until quite close to transmission. This can mean lengthy negotiation with the broadcasting organisation, and knowing well in advance what they are planning. It may be better to run the open learning course for the first year *after* television presentation. Another disadvantage of this strategy is that the television series may not cover the subject matter in the depth or the way that your open learners need.

One way round the problem of the broadcast material dictating the curricular approach is to *select* from a range of broadcast material those elements which will best fit into the open learning package you are intending to develop. In this way, only that television material which is directly relevant to your teaching is included. This may mean using quite short clips, and accumulating them on to a cassette, which students access as and when they need to. While this is simple to do technically, there are major practical difficulties. First of all, you will need to know which programmes are likely to be useful, and have them available in a recorded version of good enough quality for reproduction. (This will require recording on at least a ¾″ master, if many ½″ copies are to be made. There are plenty of companies, however, who will do the copying from the master tape, relatively cheaply.) The major problem is that you will need permission from the broadcasting organisation to use their material in this way, and it may not be forthcoming, particularly if you intend to market the open learning packages. Clearing copyright can be expensive and time-consuming, particularly if the programmes contain secondary rights (in other words, the production used material, such as the music in the programme, whose rights were owned by someone other than the broadcasting organisation). Nevertheless, it may be worth the trouble of seeking clearance. Some programmes, when made by broadcasting organisations, have all rights cleared, and it may well be possible to use such material for a relatively small fee to the broadcasting organisation. There are also plenty of hard-bitten educators around, though, whose view is that it's not worth the effort to try to get clearance to use broadcast material in this way, because of the costs and the difficulties.

It can be seen that despite the availability of a great deal of high quality broadcast television material, it is not a simple matter to incorporate it into open learning material.

Non-broadcast material

In Britain, there are over 200 educational establishments with their own production facilities, ranging from full broadcast-standard facilities at places like the University of Leeds, to small ½″ recorders and a camera in some schools. The great majority of these production centres belong to the Educational Television Association. Many of these centres have high-quality materials already made and available for sale. Many of these are listed in the catalogue of another association, the British Universities Film and Video Council. In addition, there are another 200 commercial video and film companies making training and promotional material for industry and commerce. Many of these belong to the International Television Association (ITVA – no connection with ITVC, which is a representative organisation of independent broadcasting companies in Britain). As its name suggests, the ITVA has branches in many countries, and the non-broadcast production centres is usually much easier for secondary use, and certainly much cheaper in most cases, than from the broadcasting organisations.

However, one needs to be very careful in using this material. It can be very patchy in quality, and tracking down just the right example or insert will in most cases be extremely time-consuming. In many cases, the material may not exist in the form required.

It is not surprising then that in most cases, people generally end up wanting to make their own materials for a particular open learning package.

Making your own programmes

Making your own television materials for an open learning package is never going to be a cheap option, but it may cost a lot less than you think. Before embarking though on making your own programmes, it is important to be clear about what you want the television programmes to do.

Defining your needs

This is certainly the most important, and perhaps the most difficult, step to take, and one where professional advice is likely to be essential. *Why* is television to be used, and for what *teaching purposes*? It may be that the aim is to take advantage of the *distribution* characteristics of television, by recording and distributing illustrated classroom lectures. If that is the intention, though, questions need to be asked as to whether or not this might be done more cheaply and effectively by print, or a combination of print and audio cassette. If on the other hand the aim is to exploit the unique *presentational* characteristics of television, then three kinds of expertise are required. The first is knowledge of what television can do, related to the subject matter to be taught. This is important, because a skilled television producer may be able to suggest ways of using television which would never occur to a teacher without any experience of using television. The second is knowledge of the subject matter, and valid and effective ways to teach that subject matter. The third is expertise in instructional design, how to integrate the television material with the other teaching material, and how to help learners get the most from the television material. These three kinds of expertise rarely exist in one person; therefore a team approach is required, where those with different expertise work together to create the whole package. Exploiting the presentational characteristics of television can be particularly valuable when learners lack a basic understanding or grounding in a subject, or where the ideas in print tend to be abstract and difficult, because television can provide concrete or real-life examples of the ideas and concepts being discussed.

The team approach, however, takes time, and costs money. Speed and cost may be of the essence. If the main purpose is to get the latest information on new developments out as quickly as possible, or to update those with already a good grounding and basic understanding of a subject, then the illustrated lecture may be the best approach, since the television production time is less, and it needs less preparation time for the subject experts, for whom this may be an important consideration. This assumes, though, that the alternative of audio-cassette or print production has been considered and dismissed.

In-house or external production?

There are basically two ways to make your own television material. The first is to use the in-house production facilities of your own institution, if they exist. In most cases, this will mean you will have to pay only marginal costs, i.e. the actual costs involved in making the programme (film, commissioned graphics, actors, etc.) but not the overheads (salaries of production staff, studios and equipment), because the facility already exists. The disadvantage is that your in-house production facility may not have the skills or facilities to do just what you need. It is important to define your needs before committing yourself to in-house production.

If you do not have in-house production facilities, it would not be justifiable to invest in them for open learning purposes, unless it is planned to produce enormous quantities of television material (over 200 programmes a year). There is already a wide range of educational production facilities, and plenty of spare production capacity. Many production centres are willing to charge just marginal costs, or only a small amount for overheads, in order to maximise their facilities and bring in extra revenue. Care is needed in choosing the right production agency for your needs, but production may cost far less than might be expected, depending on your needs. Simple programmes, requiring recording of events or simple studio work, can cost as little as £2000. The BBC/Open University Production Centre, which is probably the best equipped educational production facility in Europe, if not the world, can charge as little as £8500 for a 25 minute, high quality programme in the Continuing Education area, at marginal cost rates. On the other hand, a 25 minute programme requiring expensive computer animation, overseas filming, actors or musicians, or expensive special effects, can cost anywhere between £20 000 and £100 000. As always, one tends to get what one pays for, but for open learning purposes, relatively low-cost production may often be quite adequate.

Distribution and format

In most cases, open learning material will best be distributed on cassette. In 1986 approximately 50% of all homes in Britain had a video recorder. Unless you go through the Open University or Channel 4, it will be difficult to get access to broadcasting, and unless you are primarily concerned with just recruitment or raising awareness, the material will be more effective on cassettes. The Open University has found it cheaper to distribute material on cassette than to pay transmission charges when there are less than 350 students on a course per annum.

Computer-controlled video-discs are attracting a good deal of attention in the industrial training area. These can be valuable, where there is a specific training need involving complex skills or subject matter, a fixed and invariant way of doing things, and many individual points of training (e.g. the training of bank cashiers). However, computer-controlled video disc production is extremely time-consuming, complex and expensive, and can only be justified where alternative training methods are equally costly. Cassettes, in fact, with suitable built-in activities, for either individual or group work, can be a much more flexible training medium than computer-controlled discs.

Learning from television

In the end, though, what do learners get from television? Do they learn just as well as from, say, print or face-to-face lectures? Yes, students can learn just as well, if not better, from television, but *what* they learn, and how effectively, depends on how the programmes are designed.

There is a good deal of research evidence which suggests that content may be learned just as well through television as through print (see for instance Schramm, 1974, for a good summary of this research).[2] However, media differ in the kinds of learning they encourage. Thus in general, print is best for teaching in a condensed way, dealing with abstract principles, where knowledge of detailed facts or principles is important, and where knowledge is clearly defined. Television, on the other hand, is much better for dealing with complex or ambiguous situations, for providing concrete examples to illustrate abstract ideas or principles, and for encouraging students to make their own interpretations and to apply what they have learned in an abstract way to new situations (see for instance Trenaman, 1967;[3] Salomon, 1979;[4] Bates, 1983;[5] Bates, 1984).[6]

The extent to which television is successful in doing this depends on how programmes are made. Television is rarely best used as the prime medium for delivering large quantities of information: instead, it is much more valuable for providing deeper understanding and for developing skills of analysis and application of ideas presented through other media, particularly print. If the programme is designed to give concrete examples of abstract ideas, it is necessary to make the relationship explicit. Open-ended documentary style programmes, bringing in case-study material for analysis by the student, can help develop students' skills at applying and interpreting what they have learned (see Bates and Gallagher, 1987).[7].

Because television is such a familiar medium, it tends to be taken for granted that students will know how to learn from it. This is not the case. There is evidence (Bates and Gallagher, 1987)[7] that students need help and guidance to use television, particularly where comprehension is not the main purpose. Most students approach television as if it were a lecture, unless the programme is made in such a way as to encourage them to question and analyse what is being presented to them. This may mean building in stopping points for discussion, direct questions on the commentary, replaying sequences with different interpretations, etc. Television can be a very passive medium. For individual learners, this can be avoided by designing the programmes to encourage frequent interaction with the material through relevant activities (see Durbridge, 1985).[8] The most effective way to get the most out of television material, though, when interpretation and application are the main aims, is through group discussion, guided by relevant questions for discussion. This is one reason why live, interactive programming, even for rather straight television lectures, is so important.

A question of quality

Despite the difficulties and the extra costs incurred, there is no doubt in my mind that television has an important and valuable role to play in open learning. As well as being highly motivating, adding interest to a course, it can help students with difficulties in comprehension, and even more so can enable students to develop the high level skills of analysis, interpretation, evaluation, and application. Many of the weaknesses of ephemeral broadcasts can be avoided by recording material in a permanent form, and by designing material to encourage interaction and active learning from the students. A well-designed television component can not only help reduce drop-out and increase comprehension, it can also assist the development of higher-order learning skills. In other words, television can increase the *quality* of open learning.

Useful addresses

BBC Education
The Broadway
Ealing
London W5

IBA
London
SW3 1EY

Channel 4
60 Charlotte Street
London W1

The Open University
Walton Hall
Milton Keynes
MK7 6AA

Educational Television Association
The King's Manor
Exhibition Square
York YO1 2EP

British Universities Film and Video Council
55 Greek Street
London W1

International Television Association
Gt Queen Street
London WC2

References

1 A W Bates, *Broadcasting in Education: An Evaluation*, Constables, 1984*a*.
2 W Schramm, *Big Media, Little Media*, London, Sage, 1974.
3 J Trenaman, *Communication and Comprehension*, London, Longmans, 1967.
4 G Salomon, *Interaction of Media Cognition and Learning*, Jossey-Bass, 1979.
5 A W Bates, 'Adults Learning from Educational Television: the Open University Experience' in M Howe (ed.), *Learning from Television*, London, Academic Press, 1983.
6 A W Bates (ed.), *The Role of Technology in Distance Education*, Croom Helm, 1984*b*.
7 A W Bates and M Gallagher, 'Improving the effectiveness of Open University Television Case Studies and Documentaries' in O Boyd-Barrett *et al.*, *Media, Knowledge and Power*, Croom Helm/Open University Press, 1987.
8 N Durbridge, *Design Implications of Audio and Video Cassettes*, Open University, IET (mimeo), 1985.

Further reading

A W Bates, 'Some Unique Characteristics of Television and Some Implications for Teaching and Learning', in *Journal of Educational Television*, Vol 7, No 3, 1981.

17 Using audio-tape in course production

Nicola Durbridge

Introduction

Perhaps the best way to gain insight into the potential of audio-tape for teaching and learning is to begin at the learning end. There is good evidence that the medium is effective, that it lends itself to the teaching of a wide range of subject matter, and that most people find it a convenient, attractive and helpful way of learning. But why? What is special about the medium, and how can such 'specialness' be exploited?

Learning with audio-tape

The experience of learning with audio-tape has been explored through a series of interviews and case-studies at the Open University (OU), and it is clear that it is a popular medium. OU students offer a number of explanations ranging from the practical to the psychological. Audio-tape is described as an easy medium to work with – the technology is simple and thus it does not inhibit or intrude upon the learning process itself. It is a convenient medium for studying, since it allows learners to choose where and when they listen to their audio-tapes so as to fit in with individual domestic circumstances. Perhaps more tellingly, learners can choose to listen at times which match their own learning pace, – the speed with which they cover and digest other course components such as text-books. This control learners have over audio-tape study extends to the way they work with the material; the medium is very flexible and, as with the study of a written text, this means learners can use it in ways which meet their own preferred learning styles and strategies. It is clear that individual *control* is one feature of audio-tape usage which helps learners to learn.

But audio-tape has a number of features which it does not share with a written text, and these can be very telling when carefully exploited. Take the seemingly obvious point that the teaching is heard and not read. The human voice, unlike a written text, can be modulated. Stress and inflection enhance meaning: they can clear up verbal ambiguities, or touches of humour, for example, which in a written text are potential stumbling blocks unless they are sensitively interpreted. The modulated human voice also helps to convey a strong sense of the speaker, and the importance of this should not be underrated. For example, a teacher's enthusiasm for his or her subject matter is motivating and this can stimulate a flagging or a passive learner. But perhaps even more significant is the way this can lead to a simulated sense of personal involvement. Learner and teacher are linked, as it were, directly – such is the immediacy of the sound of the human voice. At their 'best' then, audio-tapes can appear to be offering the learner individual attention, and a personalised, private lesson. Incidentally, the word 'private' is not without relevance when thinking about helping adult learners to learn. Audio-tapes which are designed for individual rather than group work do protect the less confident. Such students can hear and re-hear the material as they feel the need, and in a constructive frame of mind, that is, without the potential constraint or fear of appearing 'slow' to others.

Teaching with audio-tape

The positive features of tape-study just described – learner control, the sense of individual contact, personalised and private study – are those to exploit. This suggests that the medium is not best used to present a lecture, a public genre which allows for little sense of personal involvement or interaction. The sorts of learning strategy which suit the medium are those which engage the learner in active work, in which they, so to speak, participate in a cooperative enterprise. In order to facilitate this, and to enhance the 'personal' link between teacher and learner, it is advisable to prepare a series of visual references which both parties use as a common reference point. Visual material might consist of texts *or* artefacts (maps, charts, photographs, scientific apparatus), in sum a wide range of materials relevant to the discipline or topic being taught and which constitute part of the course subject matter. On the other hand, visual material can be specially prepared to provide a sequence of reference points. They might be used, for example, to illustrate abstract concepts and this can be particularly helpful in disciplines such as pure mathematics, physics, chemistry, and accounting. The OU practice is illuminating here for the Mathematics Faculty pioneered – very successfully – the use of the audio-visual in their teaching. They adopt a visual style which complements a direct and informal or personal style of speech, and use hand drawn, concrete images to represent the concepts being introduced. Such visual material provides a good framework for an audio-tape lesson. It helps to overcome the ephemeracy of 'sound' alone, helps the learner to concentrate on the spoken word and can provide the basis for a range of teaching strategies.

Visuals may be used to simulate the sense of cooperative learning merely because the speaker's voice acts like a guiding eye through images or texts. Thus audio-tape can very usefully teach by 'live' example and in this way helps students to develop or to practise skills such as verbal, visual or aural analysis. Visuals may also be used in a more obviously interactive way. They can present questions, for example, questions which the learners stop the tape and tackle on their own before listening on to the tutor's own answers. Visuals may consist of a series of questions or instructions, referred to and replicated on the sound track; they may consist of images, texts, or artefacts, or they may be a mixture of the two – it will depend on the teaching strategy employed. In any event it is this visual material which tends to ensure that learners are actively involved. They are either simultaneously looking and listening or carrying out some practical task. Cassette technology – the stop/start facility – lends itself to structured interruptions (and a spoken 'stop now' can be rather compelling, particularly if followed by a tone signal of some sort). These may be used to present short exercises, such as calculations or plotting a graph, or involve the learner in taking longer breaks while they set up special equipment perhaps, or carry out some small project (e.g. an interview), or analyse a text to discern its arguments. These are just a few examples; obviously the range is very wide indeed.

The stop/start facility of audio-cassette players lends itself to another invaluable teaching strategy, particularly relevant to developing problem-solving skills. The problem can be broken down into easy stages – each stage involving the learner in some practical work which is then discussed by the teacher. From the teacher perspective, then, the medium is very flexible but a combination of sound and vision used in a variety of ways is particularly effective for the direct teaching of course material. It is particularly valuable for communicating the meaning of abstract concepts, for guiding students through practical procedures relevant to a wide range of disciplines, and for presenting a series of practical exercises or questions, the answers to which are withheld from the learner's eager eye but spoken later on the sound track.

The personal, individual nature of audio-tape work, previously discussed, certainly supports the learning process. Indeed a further use of audio involves exploiting this potential further. Audio-tape lessons can focus directly upon the studying process, and be used to help students develop learning skills such as note-taking, essay-writing, revision and preparing for examinations. Again, this kind of work is best explored and explained by involving learners in practical examples, where teachers both demonstrate the processes involved and set learners exercises that they work upon themselves, before hearing their tutor's own comments.

All the points about audio-tape study made so far assume that learners are using the material on their own, and it has been argued that this exploits the characteristics of the medium well. However, an audio-tape might be used to encourage and facilitate group work too. In this context the design of the material will probably be rather different. Basically what would be needed would be a short spoken text, focussing upon a controversial issue relevant to the discipline being studied, followed by a question to open up a group debate. Open-ended questions on the whole work much better in the group situation, where learners have been provided with an emotional trigger or catalyst, but where others are present to help them sort out their instinctive responses.

It is perhaps worth noting that audio-tapes can serve another useful function, and that's to store certain kinds of course materials. Obviously this only applies to subjects where sound itself is of the essence. Music is a good example, but so are some kinds of speech, for example, particular dialects, primary source material in oral history, 'live' recordings of social interactions – all these are the sorts of resources to which tape gives learners ready access.

Preparing the material

The production process of audio-tapes has various stages. First of all teachers will probably want to work on their text and tape at home with their own recorder. If they are going to use visual materials these will need to be prepared and collected together before a full script can be drafted. This is because sound and vision need to be carefully coordinated to be effective. Sound should be used to lead a listener's eye through the sequence of any visual references, and instructions need to be clear. As a general rule, questions that are heard should be replicated precisely in writing. It is important, too, to remember that scripts are to be spoken and not read and that this affects style. When preparing a draft it can be helpful to imagine that the listener, one person, is there in the room. But much of this requires commonsense, rather than a professional hand. A useful, probably essential, test of any draft tape is to try it out on someone else, and ask them to comment on such things as clarity, pace and spoken style. A professional speaker is rarely needed or even to be recommended – far better that learners hear the enthusiasm, and gain a sense of a person who really understands the subject being taught. Expert help comes into its own at the recording stage where appropriate facilities can ensure good sound quality.

Conclusion

This chapter has concentrated on examples of teaching with sound and vision, and this is undoubtedly an effective and appropriate way to capitalise on the potential of the medium. Many examples given envisage students actually doing something as they listen – that 'something' being directly related to the learning involved. In other instances students' hands are free to carry out quite unrelated tasks – driving the car and domestic chores are possible examples. Students are likely to appreciate this economy of being able to 'study' at the same time as doing other things, and it is, of course, quite feasible to prepare useful material with this in mind. What will work in such contexts will be very different from the highly structured teaching described so far. Perhaps the best ideas can be garnered from general radio broadcasts – the lively debate, the inspiring 'talk' (by a well-known name on occasion), or the challenging interview. Such presentations enrich teaching rather than directly instruct – but it is important, nevertheless, that students see their relevance to the course they are taking. This kind of audio material is particularly valuable at the start of a course, or at some other time when there are ideas, concepts, themes or controversial issues to introduce. It can make for a motivating opening. Alternatively these sorts of talks are also useful at the end of a course; they can be designed so as to help students think round, consolidate and re-assess the ideas they have met with during their studies.

Further reading

N Durbridge, *Audio-Cassettes in Higher Education*, Milton Keynes, The Open University (mimeo), 1982.

N Durbridge, *Designing Audio-Cassettes – A Self-Instructional Package*, Milton Keynes, The Open University, 1969.

P Groves, *Series of Audio-Cassettes and Workbooks*, Hertfordshire, The Royal society of Chemistry, Letchworth, 1981.

J G Maiagn, *Effective Speaking*, London, Harrap, 1962.

F Marton, D Hounsell and N Entwistle (eds), *The Experience of Learning*, Edinburgh, Scottish Academic Press, 1984.

N Postletwaite, *The Audio-Tutorial Approach to Learning*, Minneapolis, USA, Burgess Publishing Company, 1969.

D G Ryans, *Characteristics of Teachers: their Description, Comparison and Appraisal*, Washington, USA, American Council on Education, 1960.

18 Using audio-tape to support the learner

Steve Ryan

What are tutor tapes?

In this chapter I shall be outlining the use of audio-tapes to provide tutorial support in a distance learning system and extracting points of practical relevance to their use in open learning systems generally.

The Open University (OU) uses tutor tapes alongside other forms of student support where there is a demand from students and tutors during course presentation. By tutor tape I mean an audio-tape recorded by a tutor (or equivalent figure) to provide teaching, guidance and support to the group of students they are teaching at the time. These tapes do not form part of the formal package of learning materials (unlike the use of audio-tapes explored in the previous chapter). They are not designed during course production but are produced at intervals by the tutor and are designed to support, help and assist a particular student and/or student group through study of the course.

The recent growth in open learning systems is reflected in the number of students studying at a distance. Woodley has recently reported that: 'At any one time there are probably over half a million people studying at a distance in the United Kingdom' (Woodley, 1986).[1] With numbers on such a scale there is, of course, a great variety of student needs, and, as face-to-face tuition is unlikely to be available for many students, it is important to explore other methods of providing support and advice.

The scope and possibilities for tutor/student dialogue within open learning systems varies considerably. On the one hand, there is the OU with its developed regional structure, offering tutorial support and counselling to all its students, and on the other, there are now a variety of open learning packages offering little or no support to learners, outside that embedded within the course materials. But even within the most sophisticated open learning systems, the possibilities for direct tutor/ student contact are usually limited.

In addition, a considerable number of students are not able to take full advantage of the tuition and counselling facilities that are available, and it was as a response to the need to explore alternatives to face-to-face tuition for students that the OU began to explore the possibilities of tutor tapes.

Using audio-tapes to support the distance learner

At first glance it may seem mistaken to distinguish between tutor tapes and other uses of audio-tapes. Surely all the course materials and all related activities such as tuition are directed towards the same end, that of teaching the learner? This is, of course, the case but there are important differences. For example, an audio-tape made by the course team for an arts course might contain a discussion between two academics on the nineteenth-century novel. On a science course it might be part of an audio-visual presentation describing an experiment. In contrast, a tutor tape for either of these two courses would be produced by a tutor in response to the needs of students currently studying the course and might contain a discussion of assignments produced by their students on the nineteenth-century novel or provide feedback or follow-up advice on carrying out calculations based on the experiment.

Tutor tapes, then, are essentially a means of providing teaching and support to the learner. They can be used to underpin, reinforce and clarify the materials, to personalise the learning process and to provide morale-boosting support. There may also be unforeseen benefits; for example, a student commented that a tutor tape had demonstrated incidentally the correct pronounciation of scientific terms.

Why use tutor tapes?

A number of advantages in using audio-tapes have been identified (Kelly and Ryan, 1983*a*).[2] These include:

Cost and convenience

Cassettes are comparatively cheap to produce and the cost of producing multiple copies from a master tape is small. Audio-tapes can thus be produced cheaply for ten, a hundred or thousands of students (Lewis and Meed, 1986).[3] Ownership of or access to cassette recorders is widespread. Most students will have a cassette recorder either at home or work.

User control

Audio-tapes enable a high degree of user control. Students can listen at a time they find convenient. Tapes can be stopped and started at will and particular sections replayed as often as required.

'Personal contact'

Audio-tapes can help humanise the relation between the institution and the student. A voice on tape can sound less formal and more 'personal' than the printed word.

Tutor tapes can build on and exploit these features. They can be produced quickly and relatively cheaply because they do not aspire to 'broadcast quality'. Unlike face-to-face tuition the problems of inconvenient location or scheduling of meetings do not arise.

The user control enables the student to play or replay the tape at the most appropriate time. Advice from a tutor on writing assignments can be listened to when the student is ready to produce the assignment. Tips on exam technique can be played again and again during revision time.

The element of personal contact can be particularly important in maintaining morale. The tutor who may know individual students through correspondence teaching or possibly personal contact, can build upon this knowledge when making tapes.

In an evaluation of tutor tapes in the OU comments such as '(Tutor tapes) reduce isolation in courses with only a thin student population' and 'Being an overseas student they are the only real contact with the tutor' were made (Bell *et al.*, 1983).[4]

Outside the context of the OU other uses may be more appropriate. For example, some open learning 'delivery systems' provide tuition yet are separate from the originators of the open learning package. In these cases tutors who develop a sensitivity for student problems and have an awareness of particular study difficulties or omissions within the package, may be able to produce tapes which utilise this knowledge and can thus help learners overcome study problems.

In open learning systems without fixed start dates or where students are working through the materials at differing rates a tutor tape adopting a 'magazine' style format covering a range of different items, could provide timely advice and support to a range of students.

Limitations of tutor tapes

There are a number of important limitations with this form of support. Firstly, these tapes are not interactive: students and tutors cannot respond immediately to each other and tutor tapes are not really suitable for dealing with important or pressing queries. Unless tapes are being made for one individual student, only issues of a general nature can be dealt with and specific help cannot be given to any one person.

Secondly, not all tutors feel comfortable making tapes. A tutor who feels at home in the lecture theatre or who is adept at correspondence teaching may feel uneasy talking into a microphone. While these tapes do not need to be of a professional quality (the evaluation of tutor tapes found most students to be pretty tolerant towards background noise, etc.), if the person recording the tape is tense, or unhappy with the medium, this can quickly be communicated to the listener.

A third important limitation is that some students may not find audio-tape a particularly useful study aid. They may prefer written communication, or if it is available, telephone contact. A small number of students have commented that they found tutor tapes of no help at all.

How tutor tapes can be used

Arising from the OU experience, a number of suggestions can be made on how these tapes can best be used. A survey of students showed that the most popular use was for advice and comments relating to assignments. In the OU system where the tutor is responsible for marking assignments, students valued advice both on assignment preparation, and then general comments on their performance after the assignment had been marked. Other favoured uses mentioned included help and advice with exam revision: dealing with issues raised by students; and the provision of contact when tutorials are few.

The survey also pinpointed one or two potential difficulties. Tutors need to be careful not to add to the course material. At its extreme this leads to the possibility that tutors will use the tapes to produce an 'alternative course', that is, cover topics in the way they would have done if they had been on the original course team. As one student put it '(The tapes) tended to confuse because the ideas in them differed from the text'.

By and large students do not want a 'taped lecture' but rather seek advice, help, hints and clarification: the kind of help that a tutor can provide for students they know individually.

A good format to use is that of a magazine or notice-board style whereby a number of short items are covered on the tape. A total run time of something like 30 minutes is appropriate. A tape could consist of the following:

- introduction, welcome, non-urgent news, general supportive comments on studying the material (5 minutes);
- discussion of common problems arising out of the last assignment (5–10 minutres);
- dealing with an area of the course the tutor knows from past experience can cause difficulty or treatment of a topic that has been requested by students (10 minutes);
- preparation for the next assignment or forthcoming exam (10 minutes).

The above can, of course, be adapted for different circumstances but it does indicate the type of approach that has worked well within the OU.

Making tutor tapes

Tutor tapes are not part of the 'permanent' package of course materials but are rather produced to provide support at appropriate times. They do not need to be of professional quality. Satisfactory recordings have been made using good quality domestic equipment, although care needs to be taken with the recording to reduce extraneous noise. If studio facilities or an acoustic booth for voice recording are available, so much the better.

If more than a very few copies are to be made then a fast copying facility will be required. Further information will be found in the handbook *Making Tutor Tapes: a Guide for Tutors*, Kelly and Ryan (1983*b*).[5]

Conclusion

In many open learning systems student support facilities are very limited and in some cases virtually non-existent. Even where correspondence teaching remains the main avenue of student support, there appears to be a need for other cheap and easily accessible means of facilitating tutor–student communication. One such means is through the use of audio-tapes. The OU experiments with tutor tapes do indicate their potential and it is likely that other open learning systems could adapt this approach to provide student support appropriate for their own circumstances.

References

1 A Woodley, 'Distance Students in the United Kingdom' in *Open Learning*, No 2, pp 11, 1986.

2 P Kelly and S Ryan, 'Using Tutor Tapes to Support the Distance Learner', in *ICDE Bulletin*, No 3, pp 19–23, 1983*a*.

3 R Lewis and J Meed, *How to Manage the Production Process, Open Learning Guide 7*, Council for Educational Technology, pp 93–6, (Provides some indications of costings for tapes), 1986.

4 M Bell, R Fergusson, P Kelly and S Ryan, 'Tutor Tapes for Tutorial Support' in *Teaching at a Distance*, No 23, pp 59–62, 1983.

5 P Kelly and S Ryan, *Making Tutor Tapes: a Guide for Tutors*, Milton Keynes, Regional Academic Services, The Open University, 1983*b*.

19 Computer conferencing and electronic mail

Tony Kaye

Introduction

Although distance education methods have now come of age, and are seen as being successful in the adult education and training fields in a wide range of contexts, it would be foolish to ignore the real problems associated with these pedagogies. These are particularly evident in the national and regional large-scale distance teaching systems of the 'Open University type', which have been established in many countries during the last two decades (although they also appear amongst the more traditional and longer established correspondence education institutions catering for large student enrolments). Some of these problems are linked to the shift of the major cost elements in distance education, as opposed to face-to-face education, from student-related, recurrent, teaching costs to course-related materials development and infrastructure costs; they include:

- the limited opportunities for dialogue and group interaction amongst students, and between students and tutors, within what is predominantly a one-way communication system catering for geographically widely dispersed populations;
- the expense of updating and modifying mass-produced print and audio-visual materials: in many cases, a course life of 5–8 years seems to be considered as necessary to amortise materials development costs, (although the use of desktop publishing technologies is certainly changing the economics of *print* production);
- the relative inflexibility of many distance education systems in responding to individual student's needs, interests, and experiences.

Some of these problems can become particularly acute when a system originally designed for handling very large population introductory courses is required to deliver a wide range of higher-level, low-population courses, in response both to the diversity of student interests and to expectations of what constitutes a comprehensive curriculum. In 1985, for example, 44 out of 129 post-Foundation Level Open University undergraduate courses had less than 200 enrolments; a further 21 had between 200 and 300 students. Given that these students are spread all over the country, the opportunities for face-to-face contact are minimal.

In the design of any distance education project now, in the late 1980s, attention should be paid to the ways in which developments in information and communication technologies could produce flexible systems with more scope for two-way communication, for updating of course materials, and for 'customising' of courses, than in the more traditional distance and correspondence education institutions. This need not necessarily imply greatly increased running costs, even if it does imply a shift away from an emphasis on front-end costs. In the not too distant future, even in the Open University, course presentation costs might even be reduced if every tutor and student were supplied on registration with a micro-computer with communications facilities. This could lead to reductions in the costs of some elements of tutorial provision, in the costs of mailing and processing a proportion of the written and printed materials, and in the areas of student and course administration (e.g. through on-line access to databases containing relevant information, on-line registration facilities, etc.). But, above all, it would help overcome the problem of isolation of students and tutors in distance education programmes, by providing access to electronic mail and computer conferencing facilities, thus making the system more interactive and convivial.

Electronic mail can permit almost instantaneous turn-round times on text communications between a student and tutor. Computer conferencing, much more interestingly, opens up the possibility of group communication and collaborative work, regardless of space and time constraints. In both cases, we have an example of a computer technology with a strong potential 'humanising' element – able to provide opportunities for discussion, negotiation, and interaction within educational systems which are often singularly lacking in such features.

Electronic mail

There exists a wide range of 'store and collect' electronic mail software packages, adapted both to particular makes of mainframe computer and to specific user needs. They all have a number of structural features in common, although the particular commands used and the design of the user interface in general vary from one package to another.

The basic unit of an electronic mail system is a 'message' – a discrete item of text produced by a sender and addressed to one or more named readers. Messages can vary in length from a few words to very many pages of text, although, in practice, many electronic mail systems impose an upper limit on the size of an individual message. In most systems, the text of each message is accompanied by a 'header' containing information about the message (sender, addressee/s, time and date sent, title or key words, message size expressed in number of characters or number of lines, and status – e.g. new, unread, read, answered, etc.). Messages are routed by the system to the addressee's mailbox (which is, of course, a computer file) on the central computer, and wait there to be read the next time the addressee logs in to the system. At this point, the latter can then read the message, reply to it, leave it in his or her mailbox for later attention, delete it, forward it to someone else, and/or file it.

Most electronic mail systems allow users to search for messages according to a number of parameters – including information held both in the message 'header' and in the text of the message. Thus a user can ask to view all messages in his or her mailbox from a particular person, or sent since a specific date, or containing a particular word or sequence of words in either the message title or text. Some systems include a 'recorded delivery' feature, where the sender of a message is automatically notified when the recipient has accessed it.

Group communication – as opposed to messaging between individuals – can be achieved in two ways in electronic mail systems. A circulation list can be set up for sending a message to a named list of individuals, but this becomes cumbersome if it involves more than a few people, and replies copied to everyone else on the list by each person get mixed up with all one's other mail. The alternative is for the system operator to set up a bulletin board on a particular topic (effectively, a mailbox for that topic) to which all concerned send their messages, which are then available to all members registered on the particular bulletin board. A bulletin board editor is then needed, with responsibility for deleting old and unwanted messages, editing messages, and providing summaries and progress reports of the information and discussions on the board.

Computer conferencing

Computer conferencing systems, although based on electronic mail, offer, in addition to person-to-person messaging, more sophisticated group communication facilities than topic-based bulleting boards. Individual users can join 'conferences' on specific subjects of interest. A given user may be a member of several such conferences – each conference containing the cumulative total of messages sent to it by the various conference members. As in electronic mail, conferencing on such a system is asynchronous – it does not require that all members be present and active at the same moment. Unlike face-to-face conferencing, or telephone or video-conferencing, participants are not put 'on the spot' to respond immediately to questions and to other participants' intervention. These can be read and reflected on at ease, and one's own contribution sent in when it is ready and at a time which is convenient. The conference transcript becomes a valuable record which can be consulted at leisure, and even edited and used as a basis for a subsequent report, as all contributions to a conference are automatically stored on the system.

The more sophisticated systems offer a range of facilities to enhance a variety of forms of group communication. These may include:

- different categories of conference membership corresponding to different participant roles, for example: observer (read only membership); participant (read and write membership); chairman (with powers to add and remove members, and to edit messages); and so on;
- the ability to delete or revise messages previously sent in to a conference, and to assign to others the right to do this for one's own messages;
- procedures for threading one's way through related messages in the same conference – via branching or message-linking options;
- structured message facilities, for example, for polling conference members on topics of interest, for voting, or for advertising;
- facilities for cooperative production of reports and documents, where individual users can edit and modify drafts submitted by others, in an iterative process;
- the ability to 'customise' commands and various other aspects of the system so as to produce a tailor-made version for specific purposes and groups.

There are a number of conferencing systems which are currently available commercially – the best known include PARTICIPATE, PortaCOM, eFORUM, CONFER, COSY, and NOTEPAD. Some were originally developed for government and military applications; others for business use; others for enhancing communication amongst communities of university researchers and scientists. The earliest and best-known system, and still in many ways the most flexible (as it is undergoing constant evolution as a computer conferencing test-bed and laboratory) is EIES (Electronic Information and Exchange System), developed by Murray Turoff at the New Jersey Institute of Technology. Current work on EIES includes a project to develop a version specifically for education and training purposes, and which will include sophisticated branching facilities, and the ability to handle graphic inputs and outputs.

Computer-mediated communication for distance education

Electronic mail and computer conferencing are examples of computer-mediated communication. As has been shown, such systems allow individuals and groups of people to carry on discussions and conversations over a computer network, regardless of time and place constraints. This technology is in many ways an ideal medium for students, tutors and course developers involved in distance and open education courses. Four features stand out as being practically tailor-made for such clients.

1 Once the equipment (microcomputers, modems, mainframe) and necessary software and network facilities are in place, *communication costs can be very low.* For example, the great majority of OU tutors and students should be able to access the University's own national computer network at local call rates (less than 50p per hour at evenings and weekends). Even in cases where communications have to pass through public packet-switched systems, the charges are far less than for long-distance voice telephone calls.
2 Communications (whilst being virtually instantaneous to the mainframe computer) are *asynchronous*, unlike face-to-face meetings or telephone calls and conferences. Messages can be entered and retrieved when convenient to users of the system, permitting time for reflection and for thoughtful composition.
3 All communications are *stored* until deliberately deleted, and can be filed in such a way as to be immediately accessible when required – a feature not found with face-to-face and telephone communication unless burdensome recording procedures are employed.
4 The processing power of the mainframe computer and its CMCS software is used to *organise and structure* inputs, outputs, and communication patterns in a variety of different ways. (In addition to the computer conferencing features listed above, tools can include private notepads for personal documents and notes; signalling of current on-line participants, with the possibility of synchronous communication; and a directory of members with users' names, addresses, interests, etc.).

As far as pedagogical issues are concerned, there would seem to be three main challenges in trying to use computer-mediated communication in the distance education situation.

1 *Scale*: most current applications of computer conferencing in the educational field have concerned small groups of students (in the tens, say), rather than the much larger student populations typical of many distance teaching projects.
2 *Integration*: this new technology must be integrated, not only with existing print and audio-visual media, but also into complex course development and presentation systems, involving central teams preparing materials to be tutored by intermediares. To make best use of these new technologies, it will undoubtedly be necessary to re-think many of the standard course development and presentation methods, and this will probably involve major enhancements of tutors' roles.
3 *Optimisation*: it makes little sense to use these technologies merely to replace existing procedures (e.g. electronic mail as a substitute for postal correspondence or phone calls, computer conferencing as a substitute for face-to-face tutorials). The unique characteristics of computer-mediated communication should be used where they can provide maximum benefit in terms of the quality of learning which they can promote.

The problem of *scale* can be tackled in several ways. A clear distinction should be made between one-way and interactive use of computer-mediated communication in the former case, one could envisage, for example, the use of a database under the control of a designated member of a course development team, to be used for stop-press and updating items (thus helping to alleviate the problems of inflexibility and 'fossilisation' of mass-produced course materials, referred to at the beginning of this chapter). Course developers and tutors might be invited to submit suggested items for inclusion to the database editor, and students would have read-only access. Such a facility would work equally well regardless of the total number of students on the course – in fact the cost advantage of computer-mediated communication over postal mailings increases with numbers in this case.

In the latter case – interactive use in the individual or group mode – the tutor group might be considered as the basic unit within which communication occurs. The OU norm of 25 students to one part-time tutor fits well with what is probably an optimal group size for computer conferencing applications such as on-line seminars and tutorials. It is also a size which easily permits the establishment of self-help groups, especially as the students would have had the opportunity to meet face-to-face and thus get to know each other personally.

However, this does not imply that communication should occur *only* within individual tutor groups. One could envisage, in addition, the setting up of a conference which could permit all tutors and course developers to share information. Such a facility could be used for briefing, comparing marking and tuition practices, obtaining specialist help, evaluation, and feedback. Finally, on relatively low population courses, it would not be out of the question to have a general course conference to which all students and tutors could contribute.

Integration of computer-mediated communications into an existing distance teaching system is a more problematic issue than that of scale. It is probably only through the experience of using the technology that the best ideas will appear for integrating the medium with core course materials. In this context, it might be useful to explore the potential of computer communication for course development. Experience of use of EIES by groups working on common projects demonstrate that computer conferencing can be a very effective medium for achieving consensus and for joint preparation of working group reports. Such a facility would certainly make it easier for dispersed members of development teams to contribute to discussions on course content and objectives. And out of such an experience, ideas for using computer conferencing in teaching may well develop.

Optimisation of computer-mediated communication technologies for distance education will flow from two key features – the potential for group communication, and the fact that all information can be stored, organised, and retrieved at will. Straight away, this provides an opportunity for learners in the system to contribute and share their own knowledge and experience, changing a course from an inert set of pre-packed materials in to something much more dynamic and learner-centred. Research is needed to investigate how computer-mediated communication can best be used to facilitate cooperative learning, discovery learning, and development of problem-solving and critical thinking skills. On the negative side, it will also be necessary to identify ways of helping users deal with the potential information overload which often occurs on systems using these technologies.

Conclusion

In general, computer-mediated communication has the potential for being more than just an electronic substitute for correspondence tuition and face-to-face meetings in the distance education context. This potential will be increasingly realised as the necessary equipment and software, coupled with access to low-cost communications networks, becomes more widely available. And, although this chapter has concentrated on applications in large-scale distance teaching institutions (because this reflects the author's current preoccupations) there is no doubt that many of the more flexible and smaller-scale open learning projects could also use these technologies to enhance the learning process. Initially, this would probably be in cases where frequent face-to-face group meetings are difficult, inconvenient, or expensive to organise, but as experience with using these technologies for educational purposes builds up, so new applications will develop – cooperative networking projects, skill exchanges, and peer teaching are some of the more exciting examples which come to mind.

Further reading

For a general presentation, discussion, and evaluation of computer-mediated communication, see:

E Kerr and S Hiltz, *Computer-Mediated Communication Systems. Status and Evaluation*, New York, Academic Press, 212 pp, 1982.

For information on computer conferencing systems and software, see:

The special issue of *BYTE Magazine*, December 1985 – this contains a number of articles, including an excellent overview of currently available computer conferencing systems.

IEEE Transactions on Professional Communication, March 1986, Vo. LPC-29, No 1: Special Issue on Computer Conferencing. (This contains eight papers on computer conferencing.)

For publications specifically on applications of computer conferencing to education, see:

L Davie and P Palmer, 'Computer Teleconferencing for Advanced Distance Education' in *Canadian Journal of University Continuing Education*, X VOL 2, 56–66, 1984.

J Harasim and M Johnson, *Research into the Educational Applications of Computer Networks for Teachers/Trainers in Ontario, The Impact of Technology on Education: The Impact of Computers on Teacher Training Staff*, Toronto, OISE/Ontario Ministry of Education, 1986.

University of Guelph, *Computer Conferencing and Electronic Messaging, Conference Proceedings, Jan 22–23, 1985* (contains 21 papers) 227 pp, 1985.

New Jersey Institute of Technology, *Telecommunications and Higher Education: Conference Briefs, April 1982*, Newark, NJ, 101 pp (contains 16 papers), 1982.

P Haile and A Richards, *Supporting the Distance Learner with Computer Teleconferencing*, Islip, New York Institute of Technology, Islip, Long Island, 29 pp, 1982.

PART IV EDUCATIONAL COUNSELLING

20 Educational counselling and open learning

David Grugeon

What is educational counselling in open learning?

Adults, studying full-time or part-time, need advice and encouragement on a broader basis than the content of the course that they are studying. Implicitly or explicitly, they ask themselves 'how am I getting on?', 'what are my skills and interests?', 'where might this lead?', 'what shall I study next?'. In conversation with friends, relatives and acquaintances, informal support is sought and given. Adult tutors, craft instructors and college lecturers are all drawn into providing advice, formally and informally, to the students that they are teaching and training.

With the development of specialised forms of teaching and learning, where a substantial part of the teaching comes from a distance, the provision of advice to the student in order to cope most capably with educational decisions, becomes a more complex, deliberate and organised activity. An efficient open or distance learning programme needs – both for the sake of the students and the management of the programme – to ascertain that the customers want this programme, both in content and teaching method, and that any crucial characteristics of individual learners have been taken into account (for example, physical disability). Jonathan Brown, in chapter 21, analyses the essential elements of advice and counselling at pre-enrolment stage for open learning.

The methods of provision of advice and counselling to open learners are diverse. Depending on the learner's location, advice can be accessible at local level, in person or by phone. Or it may be more distant, by personal correspondence or pre-designed, as in computer-based guidance. John Taylor, in chapter 22, surveys computer-based guidance in education and training and notes the developing ability of good programmes to help 'clients learn how to explore and clarify their learning needs'.

Perhaps the most interventionist approach has been adopted by the Open University (OU) in its open programme for adult students taking a first degree part-time where, as Judith Fage describes in chapter 23, the tutor–counsellor recognises 'a need for early contact, active participation, help with educational planning, guidance through administrative systems, and support in coping with the difficult combination of studentship and adult life'. There may be some advantage to open learners in receiving advice from adults who are not responsible for the total instructional programme: it may be easier for the adviser to consider how the learner is coping with instruction designed by others. Individual diagnosis and support becomes more central to the role. The counselling function assists the individual learner to recognise the nature of his or her learning difficulties and successes, and to become more articulate (and thus more deliberate) about what to do next.

Educators and trainers of adults can benefit from the wisdom of those already experienced in advising adults through open learning courses of study. One such is Sylvia Rhys,[1] one of the authors of the recent book on *Guidance and Counselling in Adult and Continuing Education*. I hope the flavour of the few following quotations will encourage you to go to the original source:

> A counsellor seeks to provide information in as unbiased a way as possible in order that a person in need may be better equipped to weigh up a situation and choose between alternative courses of action for him/herself.
>
> If a counsellor is to help another person, it is necessary to view life through the eyes of that other person, to enter into that individual's understanding of reality, and to be able to use his/her frame of reference. The counsellor can then stand back and use the knowledge so gained to help the person in need to find better ways of coping.
>
> Counsellors must therefore tolerate uncertainty about the appropriateness of the help which they are giving and the difficulties inherent in the process of relating to another human being. They also have to recognise that whatever help is offered may be rejected or interpreted in ways other than those intended.[1]

Roger Lewis, describing counselling in distance education,[2] sees the role as:

> . . . intermediate between the formal framework of the institution on the one hand and the very informal network of family/friends at the other. It is a role that has been most developed in the area of young adult support where it is variously called 'working coach', 'jobmate' or 'godfather'. A 'godfather', for example, is an ordinary worker who takes responsibility for one to two trainees, independent of the management structure, and who meets the trainee informally.[2]

He goes on to ask:

> What skills does such a person need when supporting learners in distance and open learning schemes? First, the skills of a befriender (if these are in fact 'skills') and, secondly, the ability to activate those parts of the learner's world which could themselves perform a support function – e.g. family and friends. We can add the ability to help the learner through the system, particularly as many distance learning systems are complex – though fortunately not all are quite as intricate as the OU! The supporter needs to know when to refer a learner and to whom. All these processes also have to be managed largely by distance means – support by telephone and letter.[2]

Educational counselling and the Open University

The Planning Committee of the Open University, reporting in January 1969,[3] recommended that adults coming in on open entry should receive counselling. They commented:

> Because of the range of choices inherent in the degree pattern, the 'open-ness' of the University, and the possibility that many students may wish to enrol who are not at a stage when they could profitably pursue degree studies, we consider the development of the counselling service to be of particular importance. It will, together with the preparatory courses which we hope to see developed, and the screening effect of the University's foundation courses, be the means by which the University can reduce to a minimum the number of students who embark upon courses only to find that they cannot continue with them.[3]

Robert Beevers, the first Director of Studies, Local Centres and Tutorial Services, described the OU Counsellor who was yet to be (April 1969[4]) as:

> rather akin to the academic supervisor in the traditional sense. He is an educator and he must have an understanding of the total educational process that the student is engaged in. Conceived of in this fashion, the counsellor is as much a part of the tutorial process as the tutor proper . . .[4]

The succeeding 18 years of theory and practice have seen many developments and a number of alternative interpretations of the core purposes of educational counselling in its application to the changing programmes of the OU. However, one point is clear: there has been no principle of separation of counselling from the tutorial process – if anything the reverse. It is not seen as an exceptional service to which students *in extremis* might refer themselves – or to which they might be referred. It is a standard element of the teaching package.

With over 2000 part-time counselling colleagues, and over 50 full-time senior counsellors based in the regions of the UK (as well as some specialists at the OU's central administrative base at Milton Keynes in services for disabled students and in vocational counselling), the OU has had a good opportunity to develop main-stream theory and practice in educational counselling. A review by Dr Michael Moore, in *Teaching at a Distance*, No 25[5], surveys 72 articles in that journal alone in its first 24 issues on the subject of counselling. An early analysis of the changed context within which educational counselling now takes place comes in a paper by John Davison[6] where he calls for a logical counterpart to a teaching technology system:

> ... a role that will give some corrective emphasis towards the social and interpersonal against the individualized and programmed system; towards concrete activity against abstraction; towards vocation (in its original sense of the application of insights and values to situations); towards the actual learning conditions themselves ... There is an immense power to reach out and to persuade that is present in educational technology; a tendency towards domination of those at the receiving end that is latent in the sheer effectiveness of such systems. If these opportunities are to be used to raise the standard of intellectual life there must be a countervailing force towards imaginative understanding and critical awareness. It is a predicament common to all counselling, whether its starting point is in the health services, social welfare or education, even though methods may differ widely from one field to the other.[6]

Davison defines the counselling function as an intelligent, critical faculty and refuses to limit it to a therapeutic or ameliorative role:

> The habit of conceptualizing the student primarily as a receiver tends to reinforce the tensions between the teaching and the learning components of the scene. Without a critical base, counselling loses contact with both, preoccupies itself with sustaining the system or helping the student to adapt to it, and performs an engineering rather than an educational function.[6]

How does it work?

Although the OU started by separating the functions of local counsellor from correspondence tutor (and class tutor) it quickly became apparent that it would be possible, and desirable, to combine these functions in the hybrid title of tutor–counsellor. He or she provides the full range of teaching and counselling services relating to each new undergraduate student's chosen foundation course, and continues as the student's local counsellor when the student proceeds to higher level courses with several different course tutors at varying distances. A recent review of the tutor–counsellor role has reinforced the emphasis on a combination of functions in the first year of a lengthy and demanding course of home study towards a degree; it has added a formal commitment to preparatory contact with newly registered students in the months prior to the start of the course itself; and has streamlined the formal demands on counselling after the first year to emphasise a growing independence on the part of the learner, with the counselling intervention becoming more selective and occasional. The combined role is seen to be much more powerful and effective than the original separation where counsellors were used less effectively, and cut off from direct involvement with the student's written work.

What is transferable?

Much of the OU experience and thinking about counselling has wider application for all who wish to consider the practical implications for adults embarking on demanding learning programmes. For example, Nigel Nicholson, Counsellor for the Social Science Foundation Course, writing in 1976[7] applied the terms of the Tavistock theorists, Hill and Torst, originally used to describe work relations, to the educational context of adult undergraduate students of the OU. The terms describe sequential stages in the development of relations between individual and institution. Three principal stages are identified: induction crisis, differential transit and settled connection. The earliest experiences of commitment to the OU are seen as fairly traumatic (induction crisis) for many students – coping with new material, new methods of study, the tutor–counsellor, other students, the first written work for assessment and practical work. This period requires sensitivity and delicacy to help the student survive the initial period successfully. There is still a difficult period of continuing adjustment for most students (differential transit) which some traverse more quickly than others, followed by a more stable relationship with the whole programme (settled connection).

I would want to add a further stage, mentioned in a talk by

Barbara Coltman, Counsellor at Deakin University, Victoria, Australia, in August 1985. She described a period of weariness that frequently overcomes part-time students during the long progress towards a first degree somewhere between half way and three-quarters of the way (in many systems, after three or more years). The adult has lost the initial enthusiasm and immediate rewards in the early stages of study, the family have come to regret the longterm withdrawal of sustained involvement in domestic activities, the study programme appears to be more a matter of grim determination and grind (possibly at the expense of others as well as one's own social life) and the possibility of drifting starts to lead to the likelihood of giving up. It is at this moment that Barbara Coltman advises a thorough review, initiated by the counsellor, of the considerable progress that has been made, leading usually to a renewed resolve to stick it through to the final phase.

When we move beyond an open first degree programme to a range of opportunities for continuing education, the case for an intermediary is just as strong, as Michael Moore argues:[8]

> ... the function of which is to help each individual to identify personal learning needs ... a system providing direct educator – client consultation about needs will be a source of new programme ideas which is likely to be more valid than those derived from secondary sources ... the very activity of needs identification, the process itself, is a major learning experience.[8]

He offers a challenge:

> ... too many adults enter learning programmes without personal needs assessment and as a consequence experience failure, dropout and poor motivation. Adults who work at their REAL needs are highly motivated, do not drop out, and rarely fail!.[8]

Dr Diane Bailey,[9] from a wide perspective in the provision of open learning in the UK, emphasises the shift of role that takes place when much of the teaching is pre-prepared:

> In those open learning models in which the main teaching artery is the package of linked texts, tapes, kits or programs, the tutor is displaced as main pedagogue or subject authority towards the guidance roles of counselling, encouragement, coaching in learning skills, advocacy or trouble shooting. A study of tutors in open learning has shown how wide is the interpretation of that title (Clarke, Costello and Wright, 1986). The Open University's title 'tutor–counsellor' reflects the integration of roles, as do titles of industrial counsellor, mentor and facilitator used in various Open Tech schemes. Significantly, in several Open Tech schemes learners can choose a tutored or an untutored study route.[9]

She reinforces Davison's 1974 analysis, 12 broader years of development of open learning later:

> ... tutors and counsellors are not simply mediators of curricula. They have their own meanings and agendas. As first-in-line helpers they also have responsibilities for helping learners to use the curriculum rather than be used by it, to question and appraise it within their own construct system.[9]

A common context

In much open learning for adults the basic context is common: Students:

- have negative or inadequate/unfulfilled previous educational experience;
- study part-time;
- are drawn from a wider age range than for conventional groups and have considerable family and/or work responsibilities;
- have work-related motives, in many cases, for completing courses;
- lack the regular support of timetable and institutional setting;
- lack confidence to handle institutions and teachers;
- lack the full range of conventional formal qualifications.

Such a context requires the provision of an educational counselling function; the method of provision will vary according to the programme.

References

1 S Murgatroyd, S Rhys and R Woolfe, *Guidance and Counselling in Adult and Continuing Education*, Milton Keynes, Open University Press, 1987.
2 R Lewis, *Counselling in Distance Education*, Milton Keynes, International Workshop Papers, D Sewart and A Tait (eds), Regional Academic Services, Open University, 1983.
3 *The Open University*, Report of the Planning Committee, HMSO, 1969.
4 R Beevers, memorandum to Planning Committee, 1969.
5 M Moore, *Teaching at a Distance*, No 25, Milton Keynes, The Open University, 1984.
6 J Davison, 'Educational Counselling in Academic Studies' in *Teaching at a Distance*, No 3, Milton Keynes, The Open University, 1975.
7 N Nicholson, 'Counselling the Adult Learner in the Open University' in *Teaching at a Distance*, No 8, Milton Keynes, The Open University, 1977.
8 M Moore, 'Continuing Education and the Assessment of Learner Needs' in *Teaching at a Distance*, No. 17, Milton Keynes, The Open University, 1980.
9 D Bailey, 'Open Learning and Guidance' in *British Journal of Guidance and Counselling*, 1987.

21 Pre-study counselling and advisory needs

Jonathan F Brown

Introduction

In one sense the needs of the student entering an open learning system are no different from the needs of all students. These needs involve finding answers to a range of questions about the process they are entering. Questions like:

– *What?*	e.g.	What is the subject? What is the level? What qualifications/knowledge are needed for entry? What qualifications are gained by taking this course? What does the qualification mean?
– *How much?*	e.g.	How much will it cost? How much time will it take?
– *Can I . . . ?*	e.g.	Can I really do it? (in terms of prior knowledge, ability, skills) Can I really do it? (in terms of who are the other students – are they people like me?)
– *Should I . . . ?*	e.g.	Should I do this course or another? Should I do a course at all? Should I prepare for the course?

Although the need for answers to these questions may be the same, for the distance students they are even more critical. For the conventional student when these questions are not clearly answered at a pre-course stage, answers can still emerge during the educational process itself, from tutors, fellow students and the operations of the 'college'. In short, the face-to-face mode often copes with the unanswered pre-study questions by its own dynamic. The non-operating or non-starting student is quickly identified by the simple test of attendance. The contrast with the open learning entrant is clear. Answers at the pre-study stage to a large extent determine whether the student actually engages in an educational process. Non-starting is difficult to identify in a distance system where as simple a test as attendance is not available. So for any open learning process a crucial issue is converting the intending student into an operational one.

The converse may well be true: if answers are received at the pre-study stage it is more likely that the students will start the course.

Although it is relatively easy to suggest the areas of need, providing adequate answers is subject to at least four difficulties.

1 The changing 'status' of the intending student.
2 An appropriate answer will need to cover the full range of guidance.
3 Not all students have the same needs even when following the same programme.
4 The student may not be able to articulate these questions.

Each of these difficulties will now be examined in turn.

1 *The changing 'status' of the intending student*

The changing status of students, from initial enquiry to the point of starting the course, puts the intending student into different levels of involvement in the process of becoming a student. The person making a tentative enquiry about a course has a different 'status' to that same person actually starting the course. Although systems will differ widely there is likely to be a time lag, an administrative process and probably a financial transaction. More important is the change in the level of commitment to becoming a student and in consequence the nature of the questions requiring an answer.

In the Open University (OU), for example, the potential student is seen as progressing through four different 'statuses':

- *enquirers*: those who ask for details of courses and who receive brochures and application forms;
- *applicants*: those who apply to join a course or programme;
- *offerees*: those who receive an offer of a place in response to an application;
- *initially registered students*: those who accept an offer of a place, sign an acceptance form and who pay a fee (or arrange for a third party to pay).

It is clear that there is an increasing level of commitment to becoming a student and, in the case of the undergraduate programme, the passage of a period of time. But it also involves declining numbers. The position for the OU's Undergraduate Programme in 1985 (for 1986 entry) was:

- enquirers 200 000;
- applicants 56 000;
- offerees 32 316;
- initially registered 19 788.

This rate of decrease may be atypical in that the OU is larger than most other institutions and has special features. For example, there is a strict ration of places on the undergraduate programme so that the number of initially registered students should be approximately the same as the quota (or ration). Not all open learning systems will have this sort of quota. Moreover the length of the 'gestation' period (formally a 10 months application period which is in practice much longer where applications are carried forward from the previous year) will usually be much shorter elsewhere. However, the OU example does show that pre-study guidance will need to cover the potential student at different levels of commitment to the courses. It is likely that most open learning systems will have to distinguish between at least two processes, as shown in Table 21.1.

Table 21.1

The changing status of intending students

Process	Open University Status
Publicity	Enquirer
Enrolment	Applicant Offeree Initial Registration

2 *An appropriate answer will need to cover the full range of guidance*

The question raised by the student may require an 'information' answer. *How much will it cost?* can usually be seen in this mode. In so far as the answer is '£x', information is an appropriate mode of response. However, it is unlikely that *Can I really do it?* can be answered in this way. It is likely to require a more personal answer which can only be approached after a considerable interchange of information between questioner and adviser and counsellor. Using the UDACE Report *The Challenge of Change* (1986)[1] helps to identify at least six overlapping activities involved in guidance:

- informing;
- advising;
- counselling
- assessing
- enabling
- advocating.

(The UDACE report also identifies a seventh activity, that of 'feeding back' which is also an important aspect of pre-study guidance. Any programme needs feedback on intending student response and their needs if it is to remain relevant and responsive, open learning programmes perhaps in particular. However, this seventh activity is not a direct service to the student.)

It is argued that to be effective the pre-study guidance system will need to be accessible in all these forms. In short the answers must be available in six modes. There should be *information* to answer the questions; the intending student will require *advice* to choose appropriate options; working with intending students to discover, clarify, assess and understand their learning needs will involve *counselling*; it may be wise to have some diagnostic facility by the use of formal or informal tests to enable intending students to *assess* their needs; intending students will need support to *enable* them to become actual students and negotiations on their behalf may, with *advocacy* of their particular needs, be desirable.

3 *Not all students have the same needs even where following the same programme*

It is argued above that answers should be available in all modes of guidance. However, the associated difficulty is that no two students have exactly the same needs. Some will have prior experience of distance learning and have no need to ask the questions, *What is the teaching method?* For others, whose only experience is of conventional courses, the need to ask will be absolute. Failure to comprehend how one is to learn within the system will probably inhibit a prompt start. The question voiced may be about the plausibility of distance learning.

4 *The student may not be able to articulate these questions*

This difficulty is closely connected with the prior issue (the need for answers in different modes). Intending students will articulate questions with varying facility. Some will quickly identify their needs and ask the relevant questions. Others will have great difficulty in knowing what their questions are. To some extent this depends upon opportunity to articulate and, of course, their prior learning experiences.

Answering the questions

So far we have identified the probable questions and the difficulties in providing answers. How in the light of this does the open learning system meet the pre-study guidance needs of intending students? Not, it is suggested, with a uniform response. Answers will need to be more available in a flexible fashion to acknowledge:

- the range of question;
- varying levels of need from intending students;
- the changing status of students.

Guidance should be available in all modes and develop methods of contact which are accessible and 'user friendly'. The system will also have to provoke questions (or assist their articulation). This probably means that the guidance needs will have to be reflected in all 'output' from the open learning system, reflected, that is in:

- written documents;
- telephone calls;
- media output;
- personal (face-to-face) contact.

One way of expressing this is by use of a checklist on pre-study guidance. Two checklists are given here in terms of the student status.

Publicity checklist

- *Informing*
  Is promotional literature clear and welcoming?
  Are the purposes of the programme introduced?
  Is course-specific information given?
  Is it clear who the courses are for?
  Are sources of further information about courses given?
  Are sources of further information about alternative courses given?
- *Advising*
  Is advice offered?
  Is requesting advice suggested?
  Are alternative methods of getting advice (telephone, written, personal) offered?
  Are 'outside' advisory networks suggested
- *Counselling*
  Is counselling offered at this stage?
  Is counselling by another organisation suggested?
  Is counselling active (open learning system intervenes) or reactive (potential student requests it)?
  Is counselling suggested by materials available e.g. (videos, work-books, checklists)?

- *Assessing*
  Is assessment offered at this stage to the student?
  Is assessment imposed?
- *Enabling*
  Are there 'pre-entry' programmes to assist the potential learner to join?
  Is someone available to assist with filling in form and/or obtaining sponsorship?
- *Advocating*
  Does the system itself act on the potential student's behalf?
  Is some other organisation able to act on behalf of the potential student?

Enrolment checklist

- *Informing*
  Are enrolment processes clear and encouraging?
  Is information on fees, payments, sponsorship, liabilities, time and place also clear and encouraging?
  Is preparatory material available?
  Are sources of further information indicated?
- *Advising*
  Is advice available at enrolment?
  How does the enrolling student obtain advice?
  By what media is advice available?
- *Counselling*
  Is counselling available at enrolment?
  Is counselling active or reactive?
  Is counselling aided by other materials?
- *Assessing*
  Is assessment available at enrolment? If so:
  Is the assessment by and for the student? (self-diagnosis) or
  Is assessment for the open learning system? (i.e. a condition of entry)
- *Enabling*
  How is enrolment assisted?
  What ways are used to encourage and assist joining?
- *Advocating*
  Who can act on behalf of the enrolling student?
  How far can the advocate go?

These two checklists owe much to the ideas developed by Diane Bailey in a NICEC occasional paper *The Nature of Guidance and the Open Tech Programme* (1985).[2] Dr Bailey uses a slightly different but not dissimilar tabulation of the guidance activities and her lists are not confined to the pre-entry phase.

It is argued in this paper that guidance at the pre-study stage for the intending open learning system student is more important than for students entering a conventional educational course. Although the difficulties in devising an appropriate pre-study guidance system are acknowledged, such guidance is essential, essential not just as a desirable 'extra', added on to the open learning system but as an integral part of the system itself. Not only will such guidance be necessary to meet the intending student's need for advice but the feedback from the guidance process should inform the development of the open learning system itself. It may also assist in making that system aware of, and its relationship with, other learning processes.

References

1 Unit for the Development of Adult Continuing Education, *The Challenge of Change: Developing Educational Guidance for Adults*, UDACE, 1986.
2 D Bailey, *The Nature of Guidance and the Open Tech Programme*, NICEC, 1985.

22 Computer-based guidance

John Taylor

Introduction

This chapter brings together computers and guidance – yet one is about machines, the other is about people. Some would question their compatibility; others might doubt whether machines can attain the level of understanding and knowledge that a real live guidance worker must have. But computer-based guidance is already here – as a support tool to professional guidance workers; as an alternative to, but not a replacement of, the convention guidance sources; and as a spur to thinking about how established guidance facilities can be developed.

While this chapter cannot cover all the present realities and future plans, it can point to some of them and show where more information can be found out. First, however, what is bundled together in the word – guidance – and the adjective – computer-based?

Guidance

Guidance can be regarded as having three main components or stages: information, advice, and counselling. Some would add a fourth – evaluation or feedback.

Information records the facts of what has been, is, and is expected to be. *Advice* begins to relate these facts to what the enquirers or recipients believe to be their circumstances, abilities and aspirations, so that some rational choices are clarified. *Counselling* goes further to ensure, as far as possible, that those seeking guidance are asking the right questions in the first place, and then fully understand the relevant information and consequent choices open to them. No small job!

The final stage of feedback links guidance staff to educational providers by informing the latter about some of the outcomes of guidance work. This gives education providers hard information from actually expressed needs and demands by potential or actual students, about, for example, how many enquirers cannot, or will not, physically attend a college – and thereby identifies the need for open learning.

This may suggest a sequence of distinct stages in guidance work. In practice that is rarely true. Stages blend into each other, but the search for, and the provision of, information is often the starting point.

Information technology

Information technology, as its name implies, can play an important part at the information stage. It can also help provide advice. At the counselling stage, however, it remains much more limited – at present. Feedback, on the other hand, can be greatly enhanced by the use of computers as information handlers. Guidance workers can store and analyse the outcomes of their work, and pass relevant information to the education providers.

Any computer equipment installed primarily for guidance purposes can equally be used, with appropriate software, for other related administrative purposes such as record keeping, statistical analysis, budgeting and book-keeping, wordprocessing and electronic mail.

Guidance for 'what' and 'how'

On the guidance side the fundamental questions are:

- *what* are people being guided about, into, through or towards?
- and *how* are they being guided?

The answers could be as big as a library full of education, training and careers reference books. In relation to open learning the answers might be:

- it is about what knowledge and skills can be learnt in what ways;
- what (if any) educational and professional qualifications can be gained, through attendance or otherwise at what institutions;
- in what study mode;
- over what period of time;
- with what (if any) entry pre-requirements;
- with what (if any) special provision or facilities for adult students;

- at what financial cost;
- with what (if any) student grants;
- and – more and more these days – with what job and career prospects.

A kaleidoscopic and encyclopaedic list like that suggests that computers may already be becoming a necessity, rather than an add-on, for effective guidance work. But that list still only answers the question about *what* guidance. The *how* question brings in the dimension of the enquirer's learning through the enquiry process, which can be harnessed to help with computer-based teaching of such obvious things as decision-making skills, personal assessments, and the preparation of *curriculum vitae* and job applications.

The three main areas where guidance is relevant – education, training and careers – are so closely related that many enquirers often do not, and sometimes cannot, tell them apart; and why should they? However, most of the present generation of computer-based guidance systems do make these distinctions, but that has as much to do with the separate development over time of the different guidance services, as with the current state of information technology.

Computer-based guidance systems about education and training already cover much of the information kaleidoscope shown above, and there is a parallel provision of careers information, advice and learning about relating abilities, attitudes, aspirations and qualifications to jobs. These two parallel streams may soon begin to converge.

Such developments underline the speed at which computer-based guidance facilities are nowadays being brought into use. Alongside that is the speed at which the capabilities of the smallest computers are being enhanced, while the time they take to do things is being dramatically reduced, and, even more important, their prices continue to fall. The present and future power and speed of the microcomputer, which can sit unobtrusively on the guidance worker's desk or in the enquirer's own living room, is one reason why computer-based guidance can no longer be dismissed as unworkable.

Computerised systems

This is not the place to look at what happens 'under the bonnet' of a computer. In any case, the important thing is not so much the 'engine' as the component parts of any computerised information system. These are fundamentally three. The first is the database, both the information itself and where it is electronically stored. The second is the data retrieval or processing system, whereby the data are accessed from the database for enquirers to see on the screen or printed-out on paper. The third, sitting between the database and data retrieval, is the communications link that joins them.

Databases can be stored on any computer from the largest mainframe to the smallest micro. In general, the larger the computer, the bigger the database that can be stored, although the latest laser storage and retrieval techniques are changing this equation.

Computer-based guidance needs to be technically sophisticated. Even at the basic information-giving level, guidance work can be quite complicated and is not easily reduced to mechanical transactions. Thus most of the successful developments so far have usually started on large (and thereby expensive) computer systems, the economics of which have generally dictated that the data held has to be applicable to, and accessible by, large numbers of enquirers. This means that national systems predominate.

The size and power of these mainframes and their databases are available to enquirers through telephone communication linking the enquirer's terminal directly with the mainframe. The very latest technology actually frees enquirers from the need for this telephone link. Laser techniques make it possible to store vast quantities of data on a compact disc (CD-ROM) which can be searched very quickly and simply by a special disc player attached to a personal computer. Thus a relatively cheap computer can now access enormous databases transferred from mainframe computers onto a single compact disc.

National services

The following descriptions of existing or planned computer-based guidance systems divide into three broad groups: those dealing with essentially educational data; those concentrating on information relevant to training; and those aimed at careers guidance. Most are either nationally available or nationally produced for local application. At the end of this descriptive listing there is reference to locally-grown systems.

The two main telecommunications systems in Britain which link mainframe-stored databases and searchers sitting in their offices or homes, are both the offspring of British Telecom: Telecom Gold is only a telecommunications network; Prestel is both a telecommunications network and a vast database with a third of a million screensfull of information from 'distance shopping' to railway timetables, weather forecasts and the latest cricket scores.

Almost any currently manufactured microcomputer (with a modem to transmit and receive telephone signals) can 'talk' to other computers through these systems at local telephone call rates, provided that the enquirer has paid the (relatively small) annual subscription to use the system.

Prestel has defined a part of its enormous database as 'Prestel Education' (Prestel Education, Telephone House, Temple Avenue, London, EC4Y OHL) so that any enquirer wanting educational data (which, among other things, covers courses and careers information) can home-in immediately on that part of the database.

The Educational Counselling and Credit Transfer Information Service (ECCTIS, PO Box 88, Walton Hall, Milton Keynes, MK7 6DB) offers a useful extension to the information already stored in Prestel. It simply uses Prestel as a communications channel which passes enquiries through a 'Gateway' to allow them to access directly the ECCTIS mainframe computer at Milton Keynes, while only paying the usual Prestel rate of a local telephone call charge wherever the enquirer is in Britain. This brings within easy and immediate reach the ECCTIS database of information about all further and higher education courses leading to qualifications throughout the UK. At the end of 1986 over 30 000 courses were covered. By the end of 1987 this courses database will be largely complete with over 70 000 course records and details of their standard entry requirements and their non-standard credit transfer entry opportunities.

This development has attracted the National Educational Resources Information Service (NERIS, Maryland College, Leighton Road, Woburn, MK17 9JD) to share the ECCTIS Gateway. Thus its database of teaching materials (resource packs, worksheets, computer programs, video films and other audio-visual and printed materials), with notes about their availability and case studies of their uses, is also publicly and cheaply accessible from anywhere in the UK.

Similar developments have occurred on the training front. The PICKUP Short Course Directory of over 6000 records about the availability of short work-related courses is now also searchable through the ECCTIS Gateway, and on a floppy disc for microcomputers. The PICKUP (Professional Industrial and Commercial Up-Dating) Directory is managed by Guildford Educational Services (GES Ltd, 164 High Street, Guildford, GU1 3HW).

Another training courses database sharing the same Gateway is the British Institute of Management's directory of management courses (BIM, Management House, Cottingham Road, Corby, NN17 1TT).

The Materials and Resources Information Service (MARIS, 1 St Mary's Street, Ely, CB7 4ER) has established, under Open Tech sponsorship, the MARIS-NET database covering the availability of open learning materials, training organisations and services, and resources and trainers. Direct telecommunications access to these databases is available to MARIS-NET subscribers and there is also a public search facility through a Prestel Gateway.

An example of a specialist subject computerised database is AVMINE (Audio-Visual Media Information for Nurse Education, 55 Broomgrove Road, Sheffield, S10 2NA), which invites enquirers to write or telephone for information to be printed-out from their computer, or to visit the computer office and conduct their own personal search of the database. These limitations on access must inevitably reduce usage, but they illustrate what can still be done without incurring the capital expense of telecommunications links. A similarly accessed database about training opportunitues for working in the travel and tourism industry has been created by the Local Government Training Board (LGTB, Arndale House, Arndale Centre, Luton, LU1 2TS).

This begins to illustrate the diversity of information available and the consequent difficulty of identifying what guidance is available where. Attempts have been made to produce directories of databases (in book form, of course!). On the education side the latest attempt is the *Databases for Education Directory* (Information Centre, School Curriculum Development Centre, Newcombe House, 45 Notting Hill Gate, London, W11 3JB). For training information a useful source is the Training Resources Information Providers network (TRIP, British Association for Commercial and Industrial Education, 16 Park Crescent, London, W1N 4AP).

By far the most ambitious attempt so far to pull together databases relevant to training, or vocational education, is the initiative of the Manpower Services Commission to create a nation-wide network of Training Access Points. The TAP scheme began experimentally in 1986, with a number of local networks in operation, to find out whether a coherent whole can be created out of the existing separate databases about education and training opportunities plus locally relevant and locally created databases. All these databases can then publicly be accessed through 'Training Access Point' computer terminals in such places as Jobcentres, public libraries and high-street shops, with a separate supporting network of advisory agents. More information about TAP, described in one MSC paper as 'electronic windows into the world of complex and fast-changing information on training opportunities' is available from the TAP Unit, MSC, St Mary's House, Moorfoot, Sheffield, S1 4PQ).

The emphasis in most of the computer-based guidance so far described has been on information retrieval and information processing. The other aspect – learning – is currently more evident in careers guidance work, where enquirers can be 'computer-assisted' to learn more about their own abilities and how to present them most effectively. These career learning systems, which first appeared in North America, have been developed separately in Britain. They are mostly still aimed at school-leavers, but some are now being adapted and extended to offer guidance to adults.

JIIG-CAL (Job Ideas and Information Generator/Computer aided Assisted Learning, 5 Buccleuch Place, Edinburgh, EH8 9LW) was originally designed as part of a careers education programme for school-leavers, but an 'adult version', already available as an 'interim programme', is to be introduced in 1988. This system helps enquirers to learn more about their own interests, to get ideas about suitable jobs, and information about what is involved in doing those jobs.

CASCAID (Careers Advisory Service Computer Aid, County Hall, Leicester, LE3 8RF) has similar aims and is developing a higher education version of its present school-based system. Both JIIG-CAL and CASCAID are moving from being only available through a mainframe system to becoming usable on a microcomputer.

An ambitious system also now under development is CACGS (Computer-Aided Career Guidance System, Scicon Ltd, Wavendon Tower, Milton Keynes, MK17 8LX). This is aimed initially at graduating students, but there are plans to extend into general adult guidance. It will provide learning in career planning and decision-making, self-assessment techniques, and preparing such things as job applications, in addition to other information about occupations, further study opportunities, employers and job vacancies.

DOORS (Data on Occupations Retrieval System, MSC, St Mary's House Moorfoot, Sheffield, S1 4PQ) is another computer-based system which is about to become available on discs for microcomputers and on-line through a Prestel Gateway, to give a wide range of information about hundreds of different occupations. Signposts (Careers and Occupations Information Centre, Moorfoot, Sheffield, S1 4PQ) is a similar easy-to-use system available on Prestel and as a microcomputer package.

There are a large number of software packages aimed at careers education and guidance teaching, mostly at school level. Over 50 of these packages are listed and assessed in a booklet, *Careers Software available on Micro-computer* (available from the Careers Service Office, Education Department, County Hall, Taunton, TA1 4DY at £2.50 post included). An interesting exception to the schools context is Careers Builder (Lifeskills Associates, Ashlings, Back Church Lane, Leeds, LS16 8DN) which is currently used in staff career development work within companies, but is likely to become publicly available.

Local services

Locally created computer-based guidance systems are still relatively rare, not least because of their high development costs. There must, however, be great scope for them in the future, if only because of the demand for locally relevant information. The difficulties of setting up local computerised services and the associated problems of a proliferation of non-standard and incompatible systems (which applies equally to national systems) are among the matters investigated in a recent report prepared by Linda Butler on *Information and Technology*[1] (published by the Unit for the Development of Adult Continuing Education, 19b De Montfort Street, Leicester, LE1 7GE, at £4.50 post included).

That report concluded, as this chapter has sought to show, that not only could computer-based guidance systems provide 'vast amounts of information in a form readily accessible to clients', but also that they could contribute to other aspects of guidance like 'advising, assessing, and even some aspects of counselling such as helping clients learn how to explore and clarify their learning needs'.[1]

References

1 L Butler, *Information and Technology in Educational Guidance*, Unit for the Development of Adult Continuing Education, 1986. A thorough investigation of general principles and practices, in relation to educational guidance for adults, with recommendations for the development of common standards nationally.

Further reading

D Bailey, *Technology – Assisted Guidance and Open Learning Systems*, National Institute for Careers Education and Counselling, 1986. The most comprehensive available consideration of the current state of the art, with a very useful reading list.

L Butler and J Allred, *Handbook of Managing, Collecting and Using Learning Opportunities Information*, Unit for the Development of Adult Continuing Education, 1987. A practical handbook for those planning to create a local computer-based guidance system.

D Hall, *Adult Learning by Choice*, Council for Educational Technology, 1986. Study based on the outcomes of a two-year practical project in developing computer-based guidance programs to encourage participation in non-formal learning opportunities.

E Gerver, *Computers and Adult Learning*, Milton Keynes, Open University Press, 1984. A knowledgeable survey of the strengths and weaknesses of the various aspects of computer-based learning, with some references to using computers for 'social information'.

23 Foundation Studies counselling and teaching – a case study illuminating the practice of integrated teaching and counselling for new learners

Judith Fage

Take four new Open University students

Pat is 28. She is divorced, with two young children and no paid job. She left school at 15, despite encouragement to stay and take 'O' levels, because she wanted to save up to get married. Her first child starts school next year and she hopes to prepare herself to return to work. She definitely does not intend to go back to her previous job as a shop assistant. She has always liked 'good' novels and has therefore chosen the Arts Foundation Course.

Granville is 45. He is Jamaican by birth, came to England as a young adult, and works as a laboratory technician in a north London hospital. He feels in a rut, bored with life; like Pat, he reads a lot, especially poetry. He is deeply involved with his church, and would like to enter the ministry. He has been told he needs an Arts and Social science degree for this.

Malcolm is a 37-year-old engineer, working for a large firm as a marketing manager. He has a Higher National Diploma, and has done well in his career. He has to travel abroad frequently. He is taking an OU arts-based degree because he feels his mental life is unbalanced: too much technology, not enough creativity.

Joy is 54, confined to a wheelchair since she contracted polio at the age of 12, which ended her schooling shortly after she started grammar school. Her right hand is also affected, so she finds writing difficult. She lives with her elderly parents, and sings in a good local choir.

These are not four typical OU students; after nine years as a tutor–counsellor, I realise there is no such person. But it is, of course, their differences – their varied experience and complex personal stituations – which make them typical adult open learners. I am going to consider the practicalities of teaching and counselling such students in relation to a group in north London taking the Open University Arts Foundation Course, and in particular Pat, Granville, Malcolm and Joy. There are 18 of them allocated to me in October, and my first job is to read through their application forms, and to make the kind of contact which will give them encouragement and the confidence to accept me as assessor and critic as well as tutor and counsellor.

It is tempting to think a friendly, open, enthusiastic letter or a warm and welcoming phone call will achieve that. However, for many students the tutor–counsellor is rather like the doctor: they are so afraid of being a nuisance that they let small, easily solved problems develop into large, serious ones. To overcome this requires not only the right initial contact, but persistence and development over the years, and students may have their own view of the desired relationship which is more distant. Letters and phone calls, the two mainstays of distance counselling, each have their own merits and drawbacks. Letters provide a record and do not force a response; but individual letters are time-consuming, and there is perhaps a hint of hypocrisy in a chatty, personal photocopied letter. Phone calls taken even longer, and can be an intrusion into the unseen and unknown; but they are a means of immediate personal interactive communication, and students without a phone are usually the most difficult to contact.

I decide on a photocopied handwritten letter with an individual comment at the end. One object of the letter is to invite people to the induction meeting at the local study centre in November. This meeting establishes, in addition to each individual student's contact with me, two more learning relationships: between peers in the form of the group, and between the group and the tutor-counsellor. Fourteen students are at the meeting, including Joy, whom I had telephoned, and met outside; two other students lift her wheelchair up the three steps and the group has begun to fuse.

Before my students' arrival I have dismantled the conventional 'classroom' seating arrangement of the room and rearranged the chairs in a circle, so that we start with an assumption that we are all going to be talking to each other, and not just me to them. I then begin by using the 'icebreaker' technique of asking students to introduce themselves to a partner and their partner to the group; this gets them talking and with luck laughing. Granville is very formal, but talkative. Joy is a lover of art and music with a gentle, middle-class voice. Pat is lively and cheerful. She has got her baby-sitting sorted out and seems very well organised. Malcolm is not there. Amongst the others are a teacher, a librarian, a policeman, a middle-aged mother of five children, and a young unemployed graduate. Gerald is retired and rather aggressive and scornful of what's going on. He wants to know my academic qualifications, and when we are going to do some work. The others are uncomfortably amused; then, as he ignores my reply, annoyed. I am afraid he will spoil the evening for everyone; I stop him, though not very gracefully. Karen has just moved down from the north, has a full-time job, two very young children, and is taking two foundation courses. My open expectations falter here. I feel certain that if she does not drop one course, she will drop out altogether.

After the 'ice-breaker', I talk about the course and try to convey my own thrill on first reading it, eight years ago. We discuss preparation, and we talk about the system. The sheer size of the Open University, which now has around 120 000 students studying about 350 courses and packs, with nearly 20 000 new undergraduate students in 1986, requires a host of rules, procedures and exemption arrangements regarding such matters as fees, registration for courses and summer school attendance. Interpreting and advising on these is an important aspect of the tutor–counsellor's role, and my students need to know this is a legitimate area in which to seek help and, if necessary, my active intervention on their behalf through my senior counsellor. At the end we join the two other arts groups at the study centre for coffee and to exchange addresses for shared transport and perhaps future self-help.

In the following weeks I contact those who did not come, or with problems to be followed up. Pat needs to talk about summer school: how does she feel about going? What are her fears? Can or should they be overcome? With young children she could be excused attendance, but would deprive herself of a valuable academic experience, as well as the social contacts she misses as a single parent. Granville needs help with essay writing: we discuss local courses and work he could do at home. My young unemployed student, John, is facing depression and a problem with fees. I cannot cure his depression, though I can try not to add to it. I can listen to him, and give him practical advice on financial help. I do listen – and listen – and as my projected 15-minute phone call extends to 45, I am conscious of my increasingly clamorous children needing supper. Winding-up phone calls graciously is a difficult counselling skill, but one which I need increasingly with John, who will be telephoning me almost weekly over the next few months. Being a tutor-counsellor is supposed to involve an average of 9.5 hours a week, and not more than 15 in any one week: not untypical later on when 14 assignments to mark may coincide with a number of student needs which must, if I am to help effectively, be met with an immediate response.

Malcolm is full of apologies: he is very busy at the moment, but things are likely to improve and he hopes to start preparations soon. I ring Karen to discuss her workload, and ask if she might consider taking only one foundation course. She refuses almost curtly, saying she is sure she can cope. I recognise the 'superwoman syndrome' and its defence mechanisms, but feel unable to press her further at this stage. I ring her tutor on the Social Science Foundation Course and we agree to keep in touch.

In this initial period I have seen my roles as tutor and counsellor as indistinguishable. New students themselves do not have a divided role – they see their entry into both course and University as the same activity; and while as a tutor I am introducing them to the course, as a counsellor I am preparing them to be University students.

In February we meet again for the start of the course. At our study centre we have three arts groups, and I and my two colleagues have met beforehand to plan our joint timetable. We work and teach together as much as we can: it keeps us fresher over several years of teaching the same course, allows us to share our specialisms, try out different styles and approaches, learn from each other, discuss problems, and be more flexible and rational in our use of the study centre sessions. We can also compensate for each other's weaknesses! It is more fun for us and helps achieve a relaxed, informal, shared-learning atmosphere.

The task ahead of our students at this stage is enormous. In nine months they must move from their current position, which at its extreme will be one of no experience whatever of academic work – a few will never have written an essay – to that of a full-time undergraduate with 'A' levels, after a few months at University. Realistically our students are likely to lack study skills and confidence, but do possess experience, which they need to harness towards academic ends. By the end of the first session I hope to have begun to move in this direction and to establish certain habits and expectations.

The Arts Foundation Course (A101, now, after a life of 9 years, superseded by A102) is in two parts: the first block introduces students to each of six arts disciplines in turn: history, literature, music, philosophy, art history and religion. The last block is an interdisciplinary study of the industrialisation period in Britain. In this first two-hour session I try to help them understand what is being asked in the first assignment, and to express their ideas. I use today, as I will frequently in early sessions, the student-centred structured group approach pioneered by Northedge and Gibbs (individual work, followed by discussion in pairs, then fours, then plenary). It means everyone, even the shyest students, must speak, and can practise their ideas in the less threatening one-to-one encounter first, giving them confidence to do so in a larger group. It helps reduce domination by any one individual, including the tutor! It involves students in relevant activity – in this case looking at an extract from the course reader, analysing it, discussing ideas, and organising them for presentation. It also helps students get to know each other, though the three working with Gerald are not sure they wish to. His need to dominate is curtailed, but not completely.

This part of the session takes just over an hour: 10 minutes for welcomes and explanation, 10 minutes individual reading and note-taking, 10 minutes work in pairs, 10 minutes in fours, and finally 25 minutes for presentation and discussion. After coffee we have a 20 minute 'worry' session: a list of statements to tick and talk about in groups, about time organisation, note-taking, essay writing, or not being clever enough. It is comforting to see that others share their worries, and helps me to plan sessions to deal with them in the next few weeks. At the very end, we meet the other group to extend the self-help list and discuss ways of using it.

It is a full session, attempting to set a pattern of expectation of future sessions and of the three relationships described earlier: between me and each individual student, me and the group, and between students. Within these relationships, I have tried to acknowledge the range of needs likely to be experienced by my diverse group, and to create a basis for them to seek help and to feel their needs will be met.

Subsequent sessions will allow for more student initiative than the first: for example, most students can provide their own historical sources in the form of letters, artefacts, books and magazines; or their own choices of poems, pictures and music. This is particularly helpful when teaching a course rooted mainly in the middle and upper class Western European cultural heritage to a socially and ethnically mixed group. Until our foundation courses at least bridge that gap, we need to try through our presentation of the course to give it relevance and to validate students' own experience.

As the year progresses, my students will also need to experience other teaching styles, such as presentation plus questions and discussion; illustrated lectures; debates; problem-solving sessions; and the use of broadcasts. Part of their progress towards becoming more independent learners will be to enlarge their repertoire of learning skills through this variety, as well as through their growing ability to use different kinds of print and broadcast media.

I have mentioned, too, the catch-all phrase 'study skills'. This is a complex area, providing a focus of anxieties about incompetence and failure, and carrying the burden of students' past educational experience. An overt problem with reading and making notes, for example, may conceal fears about being stupid and unable to understand the material. Both aspects have to be tackled.

Study skills problems are often first apparent in an obvious way in the first written assignment. This is a critical moment in a student's career. Nigel Nicholson (1977) writes:

> from the student's view point it is not a piece of work that is being evaluated but his whole self–

and this is the only individual teaching all students are sure to experience if they are active on the course. Combining the roles of both teacher and assessor is not necessarily contradictory, but it does highlight some of the paradoxes involved in marking the work of adults. We have an ideal image of the tutor-counsellor as a model of andragogy based on constructive criticism to an equal, but in reality it can be hard to avoid completely the teacher–child 'could do better' attitude. Encouragement can slide easily into patronage.

In her first assignment, Pat writes clearly. I can see why her school teachers wanted her to take 'O' levels. She's understood the questions, and her answers are carefully structured. What is lacking is originality and spark. Later I will try to encourage her to take a few risks; this time I will try to open up a few possibilities.

Granville has more problems. He skirts round the question, first paraphrasing the passage under discussion, and then bringing in his own ideas unsupported by evidence and unrelated to the question. I suggest ways he could focus on it. Should I change his dialect word endings to standard English? I do, as a separate point, giving examples, but I am still not sure of the best way to tackle this. Granville has already phoned me twice; he is worried about failing, saying he has never failed anything before. The arts are, however, a new venture. His whole status in the family seems to be at stake. His essay is, thankfully, a bare pass.

Joy's is a clear A grade, and a pleasure to read – a relief, since it is the fourteenth assignment I have marked in the space of three days. The assignment question is too limited for me to take her on much further, but at this stage I hope the course units will do that. She already has a small self-help group meeting at her house.

What about Malcolm? No assignment from him. We have a lengthy phone call. He has been away again, but has started his assignment. It is just that he keeps getting half-way through, and then feels it is all wrong, so he starts again. I try to encourage him to risk writing and sending it. I hope that if he does, I can give him enough encouragement to continue.

By March the initial hurdles are past. At this stage, new students have to decide whether or not to finally register as an OU student. They have had a short while to test the water; now they must decide whether to commit themselves to the rest of the course (and the rest of the fees). Some students do drop out. They may, rarely, not like the course. Often they realistically decide they do not want to give so much of their life to it. Sometimes, of course, it is just too difficult. I try to help them make a rational decision whether or not to continue, unrelated to feelings of success or failure. I wish, rather unrealistically, that they could see their step into higher education as a brave and adventurous one, from which they can develop, in or out of the Open University.

March is also the time to make summer school choices. Three of our four students are concerned about this. Joy needs a campus convenient for her wheelchair, and special requirements: for accommodation, a helper, and travel. We complete a form for this, but a more difficult problem is her elderly parents. She is trying to arrange for her aunt to stay with them. I need to make sure the system responds flexibly.

Pat is also worried. Her sister will have the children, but should she leave them for a week? The four-year-old still misses her father and is rather insecure. I cannot advise her on that decision. What I can do is allow her to voice her worries so that she can assess them more easily, advise her on the procedures, and help her keep her options open. I am conscious of complex educational implications too: summer school is academically desirable, but it would not help her studies if her child becomes unhappy.

Malcolm is afraid he will be sent abroad when he should be at summer school. We discuss this. He finally sent his assignment in; as I thought, it was a good pass, and I gave it all the praise I could muster; but he is already late with the second.

Granville is looking forward to summer school, but he is having real difficulties with his assignments. Answering the question is again his problem, and I am not succeeding in explaining to him why. I ask my senior counsellor to authorise a special session to go through his assignment with him and try to make more progress.

By May, 13 of my 18 students are still with the OU (two never materialised at all, three have dropped out – one is Karen, whose children were ill, and she had left no leeway in her life for any problems). Surprisingly to most of them, who are amazed at the flight of time, they need to start thinking about next year. The structure of the OU makes course choice extremely important. In our modular system this is the area in which students may experience most learner autonomy, and the greatest freedom of choice. Once the course begins, however, autonomy declines. The University therefore commits heavy resources to course choice in the form of counselling, meetings and literature, and leaves students a long period in which to make up their minds. The tutor–counsellor, who knows each student's abilities, is in a unique position to advise, though there are several other resources: tutors on post-foundation courses, staff tutors, senior counsellors, advisors for students with disabilities, fellow students, summer school, vocational guidance, and the course choice meetings at which course units and specialist advice are available.

I talk to each student individually about their plans and ideas. Joy, a lover of the arts above all, does not want to take her second foundation course yet. She is such a bright student I am confident she can tackle higher level courses without difficulty. But her mother is not well, and she is not sure how much time she will have. She chooses two second-level half-credit arts courses, with a view to dropping one if problems arise.

Pat thinks she will take the Social Science Foundation Course: she is not sure yet what disciplines she wants to pursue further. We discuss her ideas about becoming a teacher. I suggest she needs to think about this more carefully before deciding on her next course – what would qualify her best for a place on a postgraduate course, and ultimately a job? I arrange for her to consult one of our vocational guidance counsellors. She also begins to think about the possibility of transferring to a full-time degree course when she has four credits and both children at school.

Granville is not sure what to do next. I strongly advise him to take his second foundation course. He will need two years of support at this level before he is ready to move on.

Malcolm is slipping further and further behind. He is always late with his assignments and has missed one completely. I can sense he may drop out. I ask him if he might prefer to withdraw and perhaps wait a year – I feel that might take the pressure off. But he says no, he will carry on.

Towards July, we are all getting tired. The pressure of assignments has been fairly unrelenting and motivation is flagging. For some students, the progress has been remarkable, and brought out talents they only half suspected. For others, it is still quite a struggle. Accommodating their OU work to the rest of their lives has not been easy, either, especially for those who get well and truly bitten by the OU bug.

Once they come back from summer school, however, they have crossed the great divide. They have benefitted from their separation from us and the experience of other tutors, particularly those specialising in areas we do not; and from the excitement of concentrated academic activity over a week. Even Gerald seems to have improved, and learnt how to fit better into the group, though he is still full of prejudices. Their increase in confidence is very noticeable;

just as well, because they are embarking on the last sheer slope of the mountain: the difficult interdisciplinary block of the course, and the feared exams. It is also a more complicated part of the course to teach, and I am especially grateful for collaborative teaching; I really need my colleagues now. The assignments are more demanding and I am consciously more critical, more challenging in my marking.

Our last session is an exams seminar for all groups combined: wine, crisps, a quiz, and a revision guide with suggestions on the content and process of revision for the exam, which we have prepared and modified over the years. We answer questions, offer tips, try to encourage the expression of worries. Some students are so anxious that they need special exam counselling. Fears of failure, mollified by reasonable grades so far, re-emerge.

Granville has just scraped by on continuous assessment; his assignments are better structured, more to the point, but he still has language problems. Malcolm has given up; he missed summer school, and I shall have to wait till he returns from abroad to find out what is happening. Pat has just recovered from her euphoria about summer school. All was well at home, and she came back tremendously excited, and having talked to some teachers there she has clarified her ideas about teaching. She has also decided, after discussion with the summer school counsellor, to try the Technology Foundation Course next year. Joy enjoyed summer school, but found it very tiring. She will take her exam at home. Her mother's condition is worse and she needs a lot of care. I send a form in for the attention of the exams board; there is no doubt about her passing, but there is a real stress in addition to her severe disability.

Immediately after Christmas the course results arrive. Joy has a distinction; she is thrilled, and, of course, so am I. Pat has passed and, to my relief, so has Granville. Malcolm did not take the exam. I finally spoke to him in late October; he had felt he had let me down and had not rung me. I wonder whether, paradoxically, my involvement with students increases their feeling of failure if they drop out. Malcolm has decided that next year will be just as busy, so he will not continue; he is probably aware that his motivation was not strong enough to overcome his workload and fears of falling below what he judges to be an acceptable standard. He feels he has gained from it, though: he will be reading, listening to music and looking at art in a new way – it is not a wasted year. (Is he reassuring *me* now that *I* have not been a failure?)

But that is not the end of the story. Next year they will be moving on to other courses, and I hope they are now ready to experience different tutors and teaching approaches. A good tutor may, in the course of contact with students, take on some of the supporting role I have filled so far. But I shall still be contracted to be their local counsellor, and ideally will remain so throughout their OU careers.

All the while I have been working with them this year, I have been counselling past generations of my foundation course students about their study problems, course choice, or tangles with the system. Eventually I hope I will see them graduate.

There is a great deal missing, of course, in this account. I have not referred to the forms to be filled in, the records to be kept, the time spent reading about new and changing regulations and helping students to interpret them. I have not talked about my students' experience of the joy of intellectual discovery. And I suppose every tutor–counsellor has a history of special cases. There are, occasionally, mentally ill students who often need a phenomenal amount of support; prisoners and ex-prisoners; the most severely disabled students (not all as bright or as easy to care about as Joy); those who encounter dreadful crises during the course; those who are rude and disruptive; and those who neither want nor seem to need any help.

With all of them, though, the job is the same: to look at their individual needs as students, and work from there to support their progress. In doing so, I would not choose, in my students' first critical year, to untangle the mesh which binds together my roles of tutor and of counsellor; it allows me to consider and respond to their whole experience as students in the context of their lives. This does, of course, carry with it some dangers, in entrusting students to one person with the considerable power involved in marking assignments, intervening with the University system, and setting the context for a range of learning patterns and relationships; which is why we are thoroughly monitored by our staff tutors and senior counsellors. But the value of the tutor-counsellor model in providing a strong focus of support for students does, I believe, outweigh the risk. Indeed, it has been adopted, usually through an extension of the tutor's role, by many other open learning schemes, of different lengths and levels, whose students share with OU students a need for early contact, active participation, help with educational planning, guidance through administrative systems, and support in coping with the difficult combination of studentship and adult life.

PART V STUDENT ASSIGNMENTS

24 Student assignments

Mary Thorpe

Introduction

Since its inception, the Open University (OU) has handled around seven million student assignments across a whole variety of courses and levels of study. This reservoir of experience relates largely to the undergraduate programme and it provides the basis for all the chapters in this section. However, the OU has itself benefitted from being able to apply this experience to the design of assignments and other student activities in non-degree courses. And the analysis in all four chapters identifies issues which need to be considered in a very wide variety of open learning programmes. This chapter, for example, draws attention to both intrinsic and extrinsic factors affecting student assignments. Intrinsic factors are related to the design of an assignment and the kind of learning which is the outcome; extrinsic factors, on the other hand, are the pacing function of assignments, their influence on what students study, on motivation, and so on. These and other factors are elaborated in this chapter because they create issues which are likely to arise in open learning generally, though the forms they take and the responses people make to them will differ.

In the whole of this section issues of assessment and of learning are closely intertwined. However, the emphasis in the title has been given to assignments, for several reasons.

Firstly, the educational significance of assignments is wider than that of assessment, a term used here for work which students do themselves (with more or less guidance from the institution) and submit for comment, and *possibly* grading. An assignment is always intended to generate the student's own, independent response, but it is not necessarily formally assessed, or related to certification in any way. Assignments discussed here are always submitted for external comment and/or grading, but can be related to activities in texts which students do for themselves only. In-text questions and assignments both seek to generate independent work by students and in that sense they involve comparable problems of design and meaning.

Assignments are an occasion, therefore, for the students to clarify their own response to the course. In the OU context from which much of this chapter is drawn, assignments are intended to be a medium for student *learning* as much as for student *assessment* and this dual goal very much accounts for the major significance assignments have for students, tutors and the course team. This is not to deny that there is a tension in maintaining both these goals in some form of combination, for the course team, the student and for the tutor, and some of these tensions are brought out particularly in chapters 26 and 27, in this section.

A second reason for focussing on assignments rather than assessment is that open learning courses are not always assessed, though activities or projects may be suggested to students as part of their studies and as a way of providing self-assessment of progress. One third of the projects included within the Open Tech Programme by January 1986, for example, did not include assessment as part of the materials produced (Hilgendorf, 1986).[1] Many of the OU's packs in its non-degree programme are also not assessed, though there may be optional assignment packs for completion with computer feedback but no grading provided to students who submit them. Thus, the design of student assignments may still be a concern for open learning providers, where course work is not formally assessed.

A third major reason for not focussing on the narrower field of assessment is that the assignment has a wider institutional significance for open learning generally and certainly for the OU, where it is probably the single most important mechanism for prompting and for pacing the individual's study and offers the only vehicle available to *all* students for feedback and dialogue with a tutor about their individual progress. The regular submission of assignments to a local tutor is perhaps the dominant feature of OU studies for most students.

Assignments and assessment

Having pointed to the central and wide-ranging significance of student assignments in open learning, I want to focus on some areas in more detail, beginning with assessment. For although assignments are about *more* than assessment, the fact that for most OU students they count for half of the overall assessment score on their course, inevitably shapes their significance and the status they acquire within students' study experience.

Each of the assignments on a course is part of the assessment structure of the course as a whole; even where assignments are 'formative' (i.e. they do not count towards final course score even where a grade is given), feedback to the student is usually related to helping better preparation and performance on another assignment which *is* assessed.

The pattern now established (though it is not mandatory and can be varied if course teams justify their case) is that up to eight Tutor Marked Assignments (TMAs) and eight Computer Marked Assignments (CMAs) can be set for continuous assessment on a full credit course (estimated study time 400 hours including assessment) and up to four each on a half-credit course (estimated study time 200 hours including assessment). Course teams are likely to assume on average around 12–20 hours for the completion of an assignment, though of course individual students may take less or very much more time to complete each assignment.

About two-thirds of the courses in the undergraduate programme do not use CMAs at all; all courses use TMAs, and about one-fifth use a combination of TMAs and CMAs. The work for several TMAs may be combined in the form of a project and about one-fifth of undergraduate courses in 1986 used them.

Another mechanism introduced by the University and now an established element in its assessment procedures is the idea of substituting an average overall course score for one or more TMAs or CMAs where a student has either failed to submit the assignment or gained a score lower than the overall course score.

All these features, taken together, offer considerable flexibility to course teams to design assessment which encourages the kind of learning desired. For undoubtedly flexibility in assessment features, and a wide range of options, are necessary in an institution offering such a range of courses with very varied learning objectives. For example, although the continuous assessment component counts for 50% of the final course score on most courses, it can be varied if the course team wishes. Four course teams have given the examination 40% of the final course credit and a fourth-level course based entirely on a project designed by the student allocates only 20% of the course score to the examination. Course teams can also decide to differentiate TMAs and CMAs by weighting them differently. For example, four TMAs on a half-credit course can each be weighted equally at 12.5% or greater emphasis can be put on the last by assigning it 20% and the first three 10% each.

Table 24.1 provides an example of how one course team has combined a variety of elements to create an assessment strategy appropriate to the content and structure of their course. The Technology Foundation Course has also incorporated the idea of an end-of-course essay which students write towards the end of their studies (not under examination conditions therefore) but which is marked centrally by those who also mark the end-of-course examination.

Table 24.1

TECHNOLOGY FOUNDATION COURSE

ASSESSMENT STRUCTURE

February	CMA (formative)	
March	CMA	TMA
April	CMA	TMA
	CMA	
May	CMA (formative)	TMA
	CMA	
June	CMA	
July	CMA	TMA
		TMA
August	CMA	TMA
September	CMA (formative)	
	FINAL ESSAY	
October	Examination	

3 assessment components

1 TMAs (6)	27%	
2 CMAs (7)	18%	
3 Examination	55%	end-of-course essay 10% unseen examination 45%

Students must pass continuous assessment and achieve at least 40% in the exam component to pass the course.

Every course guide contains a clear description of how the course will be assessed, and course teams can influence how students study a course by the design of a distinctive assessment structure, using assignments as well as an examination. Course teams can contribute to effective study, for example, by setting an assignment on parts of the course where there are particularly difficult concepts. This gives students feedback on their understanding and helps prevent their carrying forward misunderstandings into the rest of their studies. Course teams can also be helpful by setting one or two formative assignments. These offer students the benefit of more teaching and feedback on their performance, without the anxiety of formal assessment. Even where the tutor does grade the work, this will not count towards the final course score. This is especially important in the case of project work, for example, where students need an opportunity to rehearse what they plan to do early enough to be able to revise their aims or methods if this is what their tutor advises.

Course teams can also use assignments to influence student decisions on which parts of the course to skim or miss out. This can be particularly important towards the end of the course when students are likely to be behind schedule, and important new teaching material occurs. The final unit(s) in a course, for example, may often be integrative in nature, or provide an overview of major issues which helps the student put earlier learning 'into place'. By weighting the last assignment more heavily, or by not allowing substitution on it, the course team can signal to students the undesirability of missing out the final parts of their course.

These examples illustrate how assignments can be used by course teams to influence students' study, but they also have potential as a mechanism for inviting the student to take more responsibility for their own learning. From the early 1970s, course teams were designing (more or less structured) projects which counted usually for a double TMA or more, and which gave students the opportunity to undertake an extended piece of work on their own, appropriate to the educational goals of the course but not guided throughout by course material.

Extensive research into this feature of student learning demonstrated that they were popular with students who had done them and that the unstructured projects in particular (projects leaving most room for decision-making by the student) were consistently more highly valued than those which left students with fewer choices and which made up a smaller part of the course work (Henry, 1978).[2] The students' response to project work is taken up in greater detail in chapter 25.

Assessed assignments, therefore, can be developed as a means of influencing both what students choose to study as well as how, and in the case of projects, they become the means whereby students create their own course, to a greater or lesser extent. Furthermore, the educational significance of the assessed assignment for open learning is that, in being submitted *during* course work and not under the peculiar pressure created by end-of-course examinations, it offers a test of ability and understanding arguably truer to the everyday conditions in which students operate and therefore a more appropriate measure of performance. It has also been argued that while examinations are stressful for candidates of all ages, they are particularly so for adults and, in putting a premium on speed, could be seen as putting older candidates at a disadvantage (Cross, 1981).[3]

Assignments and pacing

The practical significance of assignments for open learning has often been put in terms of a pacing function, whereby students, having lost the routine for study provided by regular class attendance, are 'helped' by being set a number of assignments at intervals throughout the course duration. The task of completing each assignment by the 'cut-off date' for submission to the tutor or computer for marking, helps structure what might be a lengthy period during which the student must rely on self-discipline and self-motivation in order to keep studying and finish the course. Assignments are not just a hurdle: they help to get learning started and provide targets which structure it as it continues.

The submission of assignments is related, therefore, to issues of student drop-out as well as of learning and assessment. The first assignment on a course focusses all these issues sharply. Most course teams favour an early date (in OU terms within the first four to six weeks) for the first assignment as a stimulus to 'getting started', as a means (probably) of establishing the tutor–student relationship, and as an indication for the student of what the course will require. These are also important issues for students, some of whom may decide to drop-out if their first assignment grade is not very good. Even later in the course, assignments can still be associated with drop-out, if, for instance, heavy demands are made at a time when the students cannot expand their own time for study.

The timing of assignments generally is an important issue for students and similar problems have recurred in student feedback across many courses in different faculties. Such problems include the 'bunching' of assignments, especially at difficult times like the summer holiday period, the location of assignments before students have had the chance to study the relevant course material, and the location of the last assignment – too late for students to receive feedback before sitting the examination.

Pacing is, of course, also related to feedback and the need for a rapid return of assignments is one of the 'cardinal rules' in distance education which may come to apply to open learning with equal force. There is currently an experimental study in the OU of one means of (potentially) speeding up the turnround time of assignments. Although the final results of this study will not be available until 1987, it has already provided qualitative evidence that the issue of rapid turnround needs to be interpreted within the wider context of students' study experience. If it is possible to cut only two or three days off turnround time, this may matter little to a student if the tutor's comments are few or illegible, or if extra expense is involved to achieve it.

On average OU students receive their TMAs within 17 days. They send their scripts direct to their tutor, who marks them, sends them to the University (often in two or three batches) which processes them and returns them to students. Factors which affect the turnround time are the speed with which the tutor finishes marking each script (a factor difficult for the OU to control directly), the TMA cut-off date, postal services and the way scripts are logged and monitored by the University. Students may be prepared to resign themselves to a few weeks' turnround time and the consequent fact that they will often not be able to use feedback in preparing the next TMA, but they *do* want to be able to read the tutor's comments when they arrive and to have the kind of constructive comments they can use in studying what remains of the course, and in revision (Field, 1983).[4] Assignments provide not only feedback but feedforward, by indicating adjustments in approach and understanding which may be needed if the student's future study is to be most effective.

Some of these points are made in the qualitative comments of students participating in the turnround experiment referred to above.

> I have been very lucky in having Dr O as a tutor and this has influenced the answers [to the questionnaire]. She *always* returns TMAs quickly even if they are submitted early. I must stress that she is NOT representative: and I draw on 5 years' (6 credits) experience. In short, it is the tutor and not the system which results in quick feedback. Those who are slow will continue to be so even if you change the system.

> It would be helpful to be able to read the tutor's comments – most of the time the writing is so appalling that this is impossible.

> I enclose a pre-paid postcard with TMAs so I can get the grade back fast in order to see if I need to pull my socks up for the next TMA. This is important for the likes of TMA 04/05 which took eight weeks to come back! I feel the final TMA return date is close to the exam and if the TMAs could be spread better this problem wouldn't arise. I am annoyed that 2 TMAs arrived after the exam.

Having elaborated on some general features of the relationship between assignments, assessment and the students' experience of study, I shall now turn to the more detailed considerations of assignment design, the feedback provided to students on their assignments, and the tutor/student relationship.

Assignment design

OU course teams have characteristically under-estimated the amount of time students will spend in studying their courses, including the time spent in completing assignments (Blacklock, 1976).[5] Data collected from students studying courses in years 1971 to 1975, revealed that about three-quarters of the full credit courses where feedback was analysed were 'overloaded', in their first year especially, in the sense that most students spent more than the recommended study time of 10/12 hours per unit. The average overload accumulated across the year was 42 hours and in some cases, particularly high unit (study) times were related to time spent on associated assignments (Blacklock, 1976).[5] Although the report notes that course teams have been able to reduce this overload in subsequent years, this certainly requires regular monitoring and a willingness to modify assignments and study guides especially during student use.

The survey of project work in the late 1970s showed that students usually spent longer completing their projects than course teams estimated – up to five times as long. This suggests that course teams tend to overestimate what can be achieved by many students in the study time allocated and need to review their goals. However, it also reflects the fact that students are keen to get high grades for any assignment which contributes ultimately to their passing the course, and may give more time to this aspect of their course work than the course team would find desirable.

It is not only the amount of time students spend completing assignments that is important, but its quality. This will often be characterised by uncertainty and anxiety, as well as a mixture of enjoyment, boredom or interest, depending on the student and the circumstances.

Interpreting assignments

Students for whom the majority of study hours are spent on a campus with other students, often involved in face-to-face learning, have many opportunities to ascertain what is expected of them in their written work and perhaps to read the work submitted by others. Such opportunities are often much less available, if at all, in open learning contexts. For most students, therefore, the first stage in answering an assignment is working out what it really means: what is being asked and what might count as a relevant answer. To refer to this as a 'stage' is misleading; sometimes students may never feel confident that they are clear about the meaning of an assignment, or uncertainty may recur at one or more points in the preparation of an answer. This uncertainty is especially difficult for new students to handle, inexperienced as many are in completing any form of written work for evaluation.

This is certainly a practical difficulty, and various strategies have been developed to meet it. Foundation courses particularly have integrated into the course texts themselves teaching about the skills and approaches needed in answering assignments. And the Arts Foundation Course now uses an audio cassette to talk students through the various stages in answering the assignment which has been set. At post-foundation level the strategy most often used is to add explanatory 'student notes' after the assignment question, and these can be helpful, as suggested by this student reaction:

> I usually have to try and put the question into my own words before I can see what they're on about, and if they've said it twice in different ways I find it a bit easier . . . it's a sort of double check that I'm on the right lines . . .
>
> (taken from Durbridge, 1981)[6]

However, student notes may or may not resolve the problem. Lack of clarity in the wording of an assignment can be compounded by notes which further confuse and add to the complexity rather than clarify it. Students often find it more helpful to discuss the assignment with their tutor before starting, and many tutors incorporate such discussion into tutorial sessions. But attendance at tutorials is voluntary; some students cannot attend and many are rather nervous about revealing their own inadequacies by phoning tutors directly. The University encourages such contact, and certainly the more confident and cue-seeking students use it regularly. Unfortunately those who perhaps need it most, often do not, without exceptional encouragement from their tutor.

This means that the wording of assignments and the contextual clues provided by student notes and other related course materials, is a crucial issue. Students have to interpret the task they have been set before doing it, and a badly worded assignment (whether ambiguous, misleading or both) creates a negative experience for students, tutors and the course team. For students it creates not an opportunity for them to explore and demonstrate understanding, but an occasion for confusion and disappointment; for tutors there is the dissatisfaction of finding that what should have promoted and consolidated learning has not done so – and has perhaps even led many students astray; and for the course team (or authors of the assignment) who share this disappointment, there is the added embarrassment of poor student performance overall.

In full-time conventional education, the effects of assignment design are unlikely to be an issue outside a particular group of students and a small number of staff. However, in distance learning, assignments are a much more public issue and if for no other reason, course teams always discuss their assessment strategy and the type of assignments to be set, during course production.

Indeed, once course materials are produced, unless these can be changed from year to year, assessment and the preparation of each year's assignments is one of the major tasks (often the most important) for those with academic or teaching responsibility for the course. In the OU context, assignments are the chief aspect of the course which can be changed from year to year and many course teams have collected tutor comments in the first year especially, on the design of each assignment throughout the course, in order to improve the way their course is taught (Ryan and Thorpe, 1983).[7] Tutors have been able to offer comments, like the following, which synthesise experience in marking assignments from a whole group of OU students, often backed by years of exposure to students studying full-time in a similar area.

> Section 1 of TMA01 was an interesting and useful exercise, but it was too hard. I see the merits, very much so, of asking students to write a short argument in which they must confront the problems of the definition of an abstract opinion. 'What do you understand the term "civilisation" to mean?' was invariably read as 'What do you think civilisation ought to be like?'. If the question had read 'What does the term "civilisation" mean?', I am sure the students would have been instantly pushed towards a more neutral approach. One might argue that it was one of the purposes of this essay to make clear to them the difference between 'is' and 'ought', but I do think that careful phrasing of a question will force them to think about this difference. Second, the term chosen was probably too hard. Of course, it ties in with unit 1. But an interesting opening TMA might anticipate the next unit. 'What is the difference between opinion and argument?' I would have loved to see my students writing on this problem, and it would have given me teaching opportunities not afforded by the 'civilisation' problem.
>
> (Tutor comment)
>
> From A101 Tutor Feedback, 1978, PT5 Report (OU mimeo)

This kind of feedback has been used by course teams on occasion to improve assignments, and even to develop a radically different assessment structure for the whole course.

Active learning

Thus far I have discussed the student's experience of an assignment at the stage of initial response to the task, when a dominant concern for the student is to decide what is required. Although the completion of assignments is an immensely varied experience (not just between students but also for the same student between assignments on the same course, as well as across courses) the assignment process generally seems to provide for many students the most intense experience of their studies.

It has a particular significance in the context of open learning, because the assignment requires that the student be active by working at least to some degree independently from the material provided by the course. This may be in a context in which other ways that students make an independent contribution to their own learning are limited or non-existent – such as contributions to seminars, deciding which books/papers to read or lectures to attend, forming discussion groups or joining subject societies of one form or another. Therefore, much more may be at stake in the completion and marking of assignments for the quality of learning provided by an open learning course.

It is perhaps for this reason that OU tutors display a taken-for-granted assumption that assignments which encourage 'regurgitation of course texts' are by definition badly designed and a missed opportunity. In a context where students have to be given a pack of specially prepared material rather than lectures and lengthy reading lists, students who are allowed to study passively and who are not encouraged to be critical, are in danger of achieving only trivial understanding.

However, an assignment which encourages critical, even imaginative use of course content, is not necessarily an assignment which gives students no guidance. In the following example, which is an edited version of the last assignment in a second level inter-faculty course (Third World Studies), students will need to draw on many areas of the course in working on an exercise which has in no way been 'done for them' in the course materials. Nonetheless there is extensive guidance on which parts of the course are relevant to their answer and on what kind of answer is required.

Assignment Example

The Question

You have been asked by a socialist party in India to visit China and report back any evidence of the early effects of changes introduced there since the death of Mao Zedong in the area of household production. You are to present a proposal to the party members outlining the data you intend to collect (qualitative and quantitative) and why. Comment briefly on how you will collect the data and on how reliable you judge your findings are likely to be. Your proposal should be between 1500 and 2000 words in length.

Student Notes

You might find it helpful to structure your essay by deciding on 4 or 5 major issues posed by the changes of policy, introducing each one with a succinct account of the possible effects. You should then explain the data you hope to collect which could indicate the nature and direction of any change since the early 1970s.

In Block 5, Part B, Section 9, you will find an analysis of the effects of collective production within the commune system during the 1960s/70s. You might also need to remind yourself of the effects on peasant production of the Green Revolution: these are outlined in sections 5.2–5.5 of Case Study 5, and their implications are discussed in Sections 6 and 7. Remember that your study will be undertaken in China, where land tenure and social and political organization differ radically from India. You might also find it useful therefore to read the more general analysis of peasants and agriculture change summarised in Section 5 of Block 3, Part A...

(extract from U204 Third World Studies: Block 5 Study Guide, 1984)

This is not to argue that *all* assignments in all courses must make the highest intellectual demands of the student, but that the goal of the assignment structure overall must be to contribute to a coherent and well-integrated understanding of the course area at the level at which it has been presented, rather than to reinforce rote learning or an uncritical concentration on course materials.

In the context of the OU, for example, it is often the case that assignments later in the course are more demanding (and may be marked with higher expectations on the part of tutors, a point referred to below) with less prescriptive guidance than those at the beginning. But, even in the context of a foundation course, 'easier' does not mean 'reproducing course units'; it may often mean that the nature of the task is very clearly specified and structured by the course team and closely related to direct teaching provided by the course.

In the case of those foundation courses which rely on the essay as the dominant form of assignment, early assignments may not require a full blown essay from students, but offer practice in the component arts of essay writing, such as selecting relevant points from course material, presenting arguments for and against a particular point, making notes of the evidence in support of a particular theory, and so on. This strategy is one based on the idea that it may be more effective (especially for students returning to study after a break) to focus initially on tightly defined and limited exercises in intellectual enquiry, building up to more complex exercises as the student develops understanding of the content of the course they are working with and has more practice in making a response in assignments.

This judgement is based on experience, not research, but some of the arguments used in support of it are that students characteristically need early proof that their decision to take an OU course is not going to be a disastrous failure. Many are also inexperienced in most, if not all, of the skills of studying and it is extremely difficult to tackle all at once and to make progress.

An easier approach to manage (for those designing the course and the assignments as well as for the student and the tutor who marks their work) – is to build up understanding and skills incrementally. It seems more likely that students will perceive that they are making progress and that they will not be overwhelmed by the enormity of a task making numerous demands of them all at once and at a time when they may also be struggling with many new ideas presented in course material.

Computer feedback to students

Much of the educational and practical significance of assignments in open learning is that the student receives feedback on their progress, and this has been mentioned earlier in relation to 'turnround' time and pacing. In the OU feedback takes the form of either computer or tutor feedback. Since 1984 it has been possible to provide students completing CMAs with much fuller feedback than previously, when little more than scores right and wrong were returned to students. In 1986, nine undergraduate and twelve non-degree courses provided feedback which was personalised in the form of a letter discussing the reasons why particular answers were right or wrong and some guidance on what the student might do about it. The following is an example from the Technology Foundation Course. (This particular CMA was formative.)

An Example of Feedback on a CMA

Dear Mr Brown
You've done very well on this assignment (CMA 45) and can go on to the numeracy in the rest of the course with confidence. What follows are comments on the questions you got wrong so you can see what is causing you problems.

Your choice of answer (A) to Q1 was the wrong one. The correct answer is G, i.e. B=9. You seem to have chosen the original value at which A was set, rather than work through the algorithm to the end of the program.

Before looking at the answer given at the end of this letter, try having another go at the problem after looking again at Block 2 COMPUTERS. In particular, have a look at the sections devoted to programs. Section 3 should help you understand the basic instructions which a computer can carry out and 3.5 deals specifically with the use of LOOPS.

Try to think your way around ONE loop, writing down each value of A and what you think will be printed each TIME you travel around the loop.

For Q12 your choice of answer (B) was the wrong one. The correct answer is A; that is 56.9mm^2. The answer you chose seems to suggest that although you got the ratio of the problem right, you forgot that cross sectional area is proportional to (diameter)^2. Have another go, remembering that area is proportional to (diameter)^2. If you are still stumped, the solution is included with this letter.

The answer you chose for Q21 (C) was not the correct one. The correct answer is B, i.e. 24:4. Work through the relevant passages of STRUCTURES AND MATERIALS again and try and satisfy yourself that stiffness is proportional to cross-sectional area. A solution is included.

Your answer (B) to Q31 was not correct. The correct answer is D, i.e. 1/4. It looks as though you took 1/3 of the useful work, that is 1/3 of 1/4, to arrive at your answer. In fact the friction loss is 1/3 of the total loss. Try again!

I hope that this assignment helped you put right some things that were going wrong and provided a useful summary of the numeracy to date. As a summary it might also be useful when you come to revise later in the year.

Yours sincerely
T101 Course Team

(taken from Byrne, 1983)[8]

All except two of the courses using this full form of CMA feedback used CMAs for formative purposes only. Their function was primarily that of contributing to effective learning and reinforcing student motivation by providing an opportunity for self-assessment which would not count towards final course score. For some non-degree courses, questions are provided to which there is no absolutely right or wrong answer and feedback takes the form of a reflection on what the students' answers indicate about their attitudes and response to the course at that point.

Although this kind of feedback can be provided for assessed CMAs, these create a much greater workload for course teams since new assignments are needed each year for at least the first three years, together with a new set of teaching comments each time. It may be for this reason that as yet only two courses have used this facility for assessed CMAs. The impression of both course teams concerned is that students like this form of assessment. Evidence from other sources also supports the view that students are not 'put off' generally by the idea of a computer marking their work, and in some cases prefer it, because the response is at least always quick, courteous and legible (Baath and Manson, 1977).[9]

Assignments and the tutor–student relationship

All Ou degree courses use TMAs and therefore all undergraduates have some, if not all, of their assignments marked by a tutor. Indeed, the assignment is the main, sometimes the only means of access to a tutor and therefore to teaching which is particular to each student's needs and intents. Where, as in the OU, the tutor is required to teach through commenting on scripts as well as grading, the relationship between tutor and student constitutes in effect an additional medium through which the student pushes forward his or her understanding of the course and of his or her response to it. The quality of this relationship depends directly on the attitudes to learning and on the practical commitment to the OU work of each person involved. Inevitably therefore, the relationship and the kind of learning it can support, vary enormously.

This factor is recognised in a number of ways by the OU. There is, for instance, an extensive monitoring system using both statistical analysis of grades awarded by tutors (Murrell, 1976)[10] and peer commenting on the quality of teaching comments on a sample of scripts from each tutor. Also one of the main components of briefing and staff development work between full-time and part-time tutorial staff, is assignment marking – what to aim for in general as well as for a particular course. An exploration of these issues and of what tutors and their students might aim for in the assignment exchange, is offered in chapters 26 and 27 below.

Both these chapters provide insights into what it is to be an OU tutor and I will conclude by emphasising two issues which must surely occur with similar force in other forms of open learning which involve tutors teaching through marking assignments, whether they themselves have set them or not.

The first issue is that of how the tutors use their power, for OU students do not participate directly in deciding the grade awarded their work, and tutors retain their traditional position of authority over students. What is under discussion is not the existence of this power but how it is used. In some courses, for example, it may be desirable for tutor and student to negotiate an interpretation of an assignment agreeable to both, before the student begins. Course teams sometimes promote such an interchange where the student is meant to apply their learning to an immediate context relevant to them, most often their own work situation. The unforeseeable range of differences in the context of students makes it impossible for the course team and tutor to specify what should count as 'the right answer', except in the most general way. In these circumstances tutors can be asked to recognise formally the need for flexibility, and to negotiate with individual students a version of the assignment which enables them to use their own experience and which also satisfies the course team's educational aims.

In general, however, we must surely accept that the kind of tasks we set for students (perhaps especially on academic and degree level courses) are open to more than one interpretation, even when clearly expressed. I would argue therefore, that those tutors who base their grading of students' work on a narrow, predetermined range of what constitutes an appropriate answer for a particular assignment, are not using their power very productively or very creatively. While this view also applies to the tutor–student relationship generally, the phenomenon of an unproductive, negative use of power by the tutor of adult students in open learning carries greater risks, and may even be more likely to occur, than in conventional full-time education. It may be more likely because the range of answers submitted by students often varies widely in open learning, partly because of the difficulty for students (discussed above) in deciding what an assignment means and what it requires. Such difficulties do not simply reflect intelligence; tutors will certainly experience high scoring students who on occasion offer what *to them* may be an 'eccentric' interpretation of what an assignment is about. The issue for the tutor is how to react not only to the complete misunderstanding of a question, but to assignments submitted by students who have interpreted their meaning very differently from the tutor, or from the assignment author. Open learning tutors may have to learn that responses which say merely that 'this is not what was required' are especially unproductive in the open learning context.

Such a negative closure of the assignment exchange certainly encourages instrumental use of learning opportunities, where 'cue seeking' students attend the first tutorial merely to discover 'the line' taken by their tutor for the course, in order to write the kind of answer he or she seems to require. In addition, where a student perceives that their work has in effect been rejected, it is likely to be very difficult for them to use the experience in order to learn why and to make use of a conscientious tutor's comments. This may be especially unfortunate because students who offer interpretations of an assignment outside the range found acceptable or 'right' by a particular tutor, may still have grasped some of the meaning of the course. For the open learning tutor the challenge is to try to understand what it is that the student *does* understand and to build on it. The tendency which the open learning tutor should be aware of and try to avoid, is to focus always on what is wrong with the student's understanding and with the way they express themselves.

This is not to argue that tutors must abdicate their power, must never correct students, make negative criticisms or refuse to communicate or interpret the authoritative view of the course team. But the basis from which they may do all of these things, at one time or another, is that of recognising and accepting on its own terms, what the student has submitted. A student is more likely to 'listen' to a tutor's critical comments if there are also comments which show that their work has been given a reading sufficiently careful and open-minded for the tutor to have grasped what the student *has* understood of the course, and *why* they answered their assignment as they did.

Open learning tutors need to maintain a critical self-awareness, a point explored in much greater detail in chapter 26 which also touches on my final point here, concerning the link between assignments and independent learning, the second issue.

The idea of independent learning is neither new nor peculiar to open learning. It is a term used by different authors to mean different things (see Morgan, 1985[11] for an outline of some of these uses). In the OU it has been associated with the idea of 'being able to study without the regular support of a tutor' as well as with self-awareness, intellectual maturity and a critical attitude towards the curriculum prepared by the course team. I am more concerned here with independence in the last two senses. In commenting on assignments, tutors in open learning have an opportunity to encourage and consolidate an independent attitude in students, especially since their comments are direct to each individual rather than part of the general discourse of the course materials. Indeed some tutors in open learning define their major goal as the growth of intellectual independence in students (self-awareness, intellectual maturity, a critical attitude towards the curriculum), and again chapters 26 and 27 in this section explore the idea further.

Conclusion

> Assignments structure, focus and filter learning, and like hanging tomorrow, concentrate the mind wonderfully.[4]

In conclusion, student assignments are a crucial part of open learning. They usually require a different kind of effort from students, from that needed in other areas of course work. Indeed they enable students to test how effectively they have been studying their course, as this student comment suggests: 'It was only when I started my TMA that I realised how little I understood the units' (Field, 1983).[4]

The assignments students submit for assessment represent their own response to course work and often require a period of intense, emotionally-charged activity. The process of being assessed and taking feedback on performance, focusses for many students all their anxieties about educational failure and the appropriateness for them of further study of the course in question, or of any kind. Such feelings are exacerbated where study at a distance from the institution means that anxieties cannot be shared with other students and informal guidance on what kind of assignment is required is not easily available, if at all.

For the educational institution, the course team and the author of assignments, this is an area of crucial decision-making, both during course production as well as course presentation when assignments are often the focus of monitoring, evaluation and course improvement. The assignment structure should provide appropriate opportunities for students to pursue the kind of learning which is the goal of the course. It should also contribute to students' effective study by pacing their progress and by not overloading them, especially towards the end of a course. The assignment may also be the chief mechanism through which students receive evidence about their own progress and how to improve it, whether via computer feedback or tutor feedback. The tutor marked assignment is distinctive because of the opportunity it offers students for dialogue with a teacher who knows their work and the quality of this interchange may very importantly add to or detract from the quality of learning possible for the student.

References

1 L Hilgendorf, *Progress of the Open Tech Programme: Second Survey Report, January 1986*, Tavistock Institute of Human Relations, 1986.

2 J Henry, *The Project Report Vol 1, Findings and Recommendations*, Milton Keynes, IET, Open University (mimeo), 1978.

3 K P Cross, 'Learning as a function of ageing: Physical changes' in *Adults as Learners Increasing Participation and Facilitating Learning*, San Francisco, Jossey-Bass, 1981.

4 J Field, 'Course Research Researched' in 'Feedback and Evaluation in Course Presentation and Development', *Teaching at a Distance*, Institutional Research No 2, Milton Keynes, The Open University, 1983.

5 S Blacklock, *Workload. A Summary of Student Workload on Courses for which Feedback was Collected by the Survey Research Department 1971–75*, Milton Keynes, IET, The Open University (mimeo), 1976.

6 N Durbridge, *Essay-Writing and Higher Level Students: A strategy for providing situational help*, Milton Keynes, IET, Open University (mimeo), 1981.

7 S Ryan and M Thorpe, 'Tutors and Tutor Feedback' in *Teaching at a Distance*, Institutional Research Review No 2, Milton Keynes, The Open University, 1983.

8 C Byrne, *Guide to the Computer Feedback and Assessment System for 1984*, Milton Keynes, The Open University, 1983.

9 J A Baath and N Mansson, *Cade – a System for Computer-Assisted Distance Education*, Hermods Skola, Malmo, Sweden, 1977.

10 J Murrell, 'KOSMAT without Tears' in *Teaching at a Distance*, No 5, Milton Keynes, The Open University, 1976.

11 A Morgan, 'What Shall We Do About Independent Learning' in *Teaching at a Distance*, No 26, Milton Keynes, The Open University, 1985.

25 Project work in open learning

Alistair Morgan

What is project-based learning?

Projects are an established feature of undergraduate courses at the Open University (OU) and probably the majority of courses in post-compulsory education include some activity described as a project (Adderley *et al.*).[1] Also an increasing number of activities in school curricula are called projects. The familiarity of project work makes it important to examine the range of activities it encompasses and the implicit assumptions about how students learn through doing projects. At the most general level, project-based learning can be defined as an activity in which students develop an understanding of a topic or issue through working on an actual (or simulated) real-life problem or issue *and* in which they have some degree of responsibility in designing the learning activities.

Projects themselves are very varied, from small-scale exercises to one or more year's work at degree level. A more detailed conceptualisation of project activities has been made using two dimensions (see Morgan, 1983).[2] These dimensions are the *project intention* – whether based on academic topics or 'real-life' issues, and *control*, whether teacher centred or student centred. Two examples will expand this conceptualisation.

Firstly, for example, a common approach to project work occurs in the physical sciences, where the aims of this project are that students should apply knowledge and techniques *already* acquired to an academic topic in a subject area *already* familiar to them. The student is working almost as a trainee researcher. Although students will probably have control over their learning through choice of project topic, the range of options will be derived from the teacher's areas of interest. The approach and methodology adopted will most likely stay within existing paradigms in the discipline area. This type of project activity is common in the final year of undergraduate programmes, (or third and fourth-level courses in the OU). In terms of the two dimensions referred to above, these projects are based around academic topics and the main control of the learning experiences is in the hands of the teacher.

In contrast, many projects (especially in arts, education and social science) have a more interdisciplinary nature and aim for the broader objectives of developing problem-solving abilities and the capacity for independent work. This type of project will not necessarily build directly upon knowledge and skills already acquired as in the previous example. The methodologies students adopt in their projects will tend not to be closely defined – the interdisciplinary nature of the project topics being problem or issue based and thus associated with a less strong tradition of research methodology. The topics that students tackle in these projects will often be related to contemporary 'real world' issues. Also, students are likely to have greater freedom in choosing their project topics and deciding how to carry them out. In terms of the two dimensions of project-based learning *project intention* and *control* – project topics will tend to be based around 'real world' issues, rather than be purely academic topics and students will be empowered with greater control over their learning.

Although this analysis of project work and these idealised examples or models have been derived from degree-level education, they can provide a basis for reflecting on projects in open learning. The educational rationale for project-based learning appears to be relevant to the design of open learning schemes.

The development of project work

One of the main difficulties in distance teaching and learning systems is how to encourage students to take an active approach to their studies. In the OU, the specially prepared correspondence text attempts to engage students through the so-called 'tutorial in print'. Rather than presenting students with uninterrupted prose, various devices, drawn from the principles of programmed learning, were incorporated into the majority of course units. However, the effects these approaches have are uncertain. The research is unclear about the benefits of these in-text devices and suggests that students are not as easily manipulated in their learning as course writers perhaps imagine, (Gibbs *et al.*, 1982).[3] However, to complete a project the student has to take an active approach to study. Perhaps the main advantage of project work is that new aims come into prominence. While a traditional didactic approach (embodied in many of the OU's correspondence texts) may be adequate for the transmission of an established body of knowledge, project work not only allows for the building up of subject-matter knowledge, but also for the exercise and development of enquiry and communication skills and some degree of independence and self-direction in learning. The processes of learning become important as well as the products. These aims seem to be important for many forms of education, particularly if education is seen as more than merely the transmission of information. Project work introduces an aspect to students' experiences that contrasts with an ideology that assumes education involves the accumulation of expert knowledge at the centre and its rational distribution to students.

Paulo Freire (1970)[4] describes this all too common ideology as the 'banking concept' of education – 'knowledge is a gift bestowed by those who consider themselves knowledgeable upon those whom they consider to know nothing – the scope of action allowed to students extends only as far as receiving and storing the deposits'.

More detailed criticisms of the 'explicit pedagogy' of the OU have been made by Harris and Holmes (1977).[5] They are critical of much of conventional educational technology and rational curriculum planning and the possibility of students constructing personal meanings. The following extract highlights this criticism.

> Our point is that many course team academics have resisted the more obvious devices employed by the rational curriculum planners, and have managed to include in their courses material and arguments which were not intended to be authoritarian didactic pieces of expert knowledge. Some academics do intend their students to seek personal meanings in the texts, to begin to apply the arguments to their own surroundings and so on. However, given the immovable nature of the one-way 'at a distance' teaching system, and the strong possibility of a 'hidden curriculum' fostered by the assessment system, such liberating intentions seem unlikely to be realised. The reality of the OU teaching system for students is one where large quantities of printed material arrive which express necessarily abstract and universalised arguments. No dialogue with the writers can be held concerning the personal relevance of these arguments. The only kind of communication with the central institution takes place via frequent assignments, which often call for a personal response while being graded according to impersonal 'objective' criteria.[5]

Designing project-based learning

The educational rationale for project work seems to be well established – so how can it be put into practice effectively? How do students cope with projects? A study of students' experiences of projects in 20 OU courses, besides collecting data for feedback to individual courses, attempted to develop guidelines for designing project work. These were not set out as a prescriptive framework, but rather identified a number of strategies likely to facilitate project-based learning (Henry and Morgan, 1978).[6] The guidelines can be regarded as a set of key questions to use when designing a project. Besides subject specific difficulties many students' problems are associated with the practical process of project work. Various stages seem to be common to projects across a wide range of contexts, namely: (1) deciding on a topic; (2) collecting information/data; (3) analysing/interpreting data; (4) writing the final report; the research report suggests that these stages might take approximately 10%, 50%, 20% and 20% of students' time respectively.

1 *Deciding on a topic and getting going*

For many students the early stage of deciding on a topic and getting going are the most difficult. Students are often anxious and unclear about what is really required – so clear explanation and project guides are valued by students. Also, for many students, it is the first time they have had the freedom and responsibility for decisions about what to study and how to go about it. Indeed, the OU foundation courses (and many post-foundation ones as well) foster considerable *dependence* on the course team or institution for student learning. Perhaps it is not surprising that students are often anxious.

In choosing topics many students are over-ambitious. For projects which are allocated, say, 40–50 hours study time (approximately 3 unit equivalents in OU study time), students' outline proposals are sometimes more appropriate to a post-graduate degree. Experience in the OU suggests that guidance on the scope of projects is essential, and that ensuring students are not hopelessly 'off course' with their project ideas, *before* they have invested much time in them, is a key issue.

2 *Collecting information and data*

Students require some indication of the type of data to collect or the journal or library sources most likely to be of value. In structuring projects in an open or distance learning course, it is essential to allow sufficient 'waiting' time to enable students to find out whether they can collect the data they need. This stage in projects can be frustrating when students discover that they cannot really achieve what they wanted because of difficulties in getting hold of the right kind of data.

3 and 4 *Analysing data and report writing*

These stages, which could be called 'ending-up', create particular difficulties for some students. With some project topics (a project on media monitoring, for example), students may have little difficulty collecting vast amounts of data, but will experience problems with selectivity, focussing down and relating data to theoretical frameworks. The provision of sample reports from previous years' students can provide a form of guidance more closely related to students' experiences of struggling to write up, than formal guidelines emphasising procedures and formats. Tuition plays an important part here in open and distance learning.

The role of tuition

What demands are made of the tutor engaged in project teaching? How do these demands compare with those made by more conventionally taught components in distance education?

Students need guidance at the various stages of doing their projects. However, for the tutor this no longer requires some degree of 'role innovation'. The tutor must be primarily a facilitator. The tutor's responsibility is to provide a framework for support and guidance. Also, as students will be working on their individual topics, taking to some extent idiosyncratic approaches, tutors will not be in the position of expert in the sense of having more information than the student.

In the OU, some of the most successful projects have involved considerable effort and resources into ensuring that there is the necessary dialogue between students and tutors to negotiate a 'contract' or specification of the project topic. Non-assessed TMA (Tutor Marked Assignments) as project proposals, face-to-face tuition specially geared to the project, resources for telephone tuition, time allocated at residential schools can all contribute to this framework – thus providing a safety net to prevent students getting irrevocably stuck in their project work.

How do tutors cope with these different demands? A study of project work in the OU (Henry, 1977),[7] suggested that although projects tended to take more of their time than conventional course components, tutors welcomed the enhanced role and greater responsibility.

The changed nature of the tutorial role, and particularly the value students place on individual face-to-face sessions show the importance of a diversity of teaching provision in any open or distance learning system. Organising project tuition may be difficult; project work may not have the same cost-effectiveness (or need a different priority on resources), it may be seen as a compromise or lack of confidence by the advocates of 'pure distance education' (if it actually exists); but on educational grounds and to enhance the quality of the learning outcomes this tuition seems essential.

Students' experiences of project work

How do students cope with the new demands and responsibilities of project-based learning? We have already seen how students require help and guidance at the various stages of doing a project.

Evaluation studies of projects in the OU show that students tend to spend far longer on them than planned by the course team (Chambers, 1984;[8] Henry, 1984).[9] Two factors contribute to this. First, many course teams grossly underestimate the time actually required to carry out a project, and second, as students are working on topics of personal choice and interest, time spent on them is less onerous than on other parts of the course. There is no doubt that many students are apprehensive about starting a piece of independent project work – however, many students find projects the most satisfying and rewarding aspects of their courses. A number of evaluation studies confirm the value that students place on projects.

For example, as students interviewed by Chambers (1984)[8] commented)

> the project was the highlight of the course for me ... I enjoyed many hours in libraries, galleries and museums. Although the project took up a major part of the course, it was for me the most enjoyable and rewarding part. The project was regarded as a very important aspect of the course, and one felt that at least one could understand and enjoy the individual research, so it behoved one to make the most of it.[8]

Students' experiences of project-based learning (when well-organised with support and guidance for students) certainly match the educational aims.

In terms of the quality of the learning outcomes, projects make a unique contribution to students' development as learners. The experience of doing a project may well be a key aspect of enduring significance after the detail of much of what was learnt for formal examinations has been forgotten, years after graduation. Project work makes an important contribution to what Powell (1985)[10] called the 'residues of learning' – namely, the enduring changes in the knowledge, skills, attitudes and values of students which take place as a consequence of their experience of higher education.

Conclusion

Project work has a vital place in open and distance learning. It makes a unique contribution to students' learning experiences and the quality of the learning outcomes. This is particularly important in view of the predominance of transmission modes of teaching in distance education.

Designing successful project work in open and distance learning needs more than a commitment to its educational aims. Putting it into practice requires thoughtful organisation and timetabling to provide a framework for *dialogue* between the student and the tutor to provide students with adequate guidance and support.

References

1 K Adderley, *et al.*, *Project Methods in Higher Education*, Guildford, Surrey, Society for Research in Higher Education, 1975.

2 A R Morgan, 'Theoretical Aspects of Project-Based Learning in Higher Education' in *British Journal of Educational Technology*, Vol 14, No 1, pp 66–78, 1983.

3 G Gibbs, F Lockwood, A Morgan and E Taylor, 'Student Learning and Course Design I: In-Text Teaching Devices in Open University Texts' in *Study Methods Group Report No. 12*, Milton Keynes, Institute of Educational Technology, Open University, 1982.

4 P Freire, *Pedagogy of the Oppressed*, Penguin, 1970.

5 D Harris, and J Holmes, 'Open-ness and Control in Higher Education: Towards a Critique of the Open University' in R Dale, G Esland and M MacDonald (eds), *Schooling and Capitalism*, London, Routledge Kegan Paul, 1976.

6 J Henry and A Morgan, 'Guidelines for Designing Project Work' in *Project Study Group Report No. 11*, Milton Keynes, Institute of Educational Technology, Open University, 1978.

7 J Henry, 'The Course Tutor and Project Work' in *Teaching at a Distance*, No 9, pp 1–12, 1977.

8 E Chambers, 'A Project Component in Architectural History' in E Henderson and M Nathenson (eds), *Independent Learning in Higher Education*, New Jersey, Educational Technology Publications, 1984.

9 J Henry, 'Project Exercises in a Research Methods Course' in E Henderson, and M Nathenson (eds), *Independent Learning in Higher Education*, New Jersey, Educational Technology Publication, 1984.

10 J P Powell, 'The Residues of Learning: Autobiographical Accounts by Graduates of the Impact of Higher Education' in *Higher Education*, No 14, pp 127–47, 1985.

26 Teaching by correspondence in mathematics

Joy Davis

Introduction

As you settle down to the task of marking a correspondence assignment for the first time, what differences will you find from conventional marking? Most of your marking to date has probably meant assigning grades to indicate the extent to which the student is coping with the task, with occasional comments in the margin, but knowing that you will be able to discuss solutions with students later. Now, with pen in hand, you are ready to begin responding to an assignment from a student with whom you have little, if any, face-to-face contact. You are aware of the need to make the most of this written contact. You want to make it clear, when necessary, *why* the approach to a question may have led to errors rather than simply to point out that errors have been made. You also want to use the student's work as an opportunity to assist them to develop effective learning strategies. How do you set about this task of helping students to *learn* mathematics and to *do* mathematics, through commenting on assignments? What do you need to bear in mind as you begin to write?

Reading definitions, results and worked examples in a text can be like entering a dense forest. Students who learn largely from texts without regular access to tutors and fellow students commonly remark that they are 'unable to see the wood for the trees'. Rarely are they able to listen to tutors speaking the mathematics they have been reading, and so they miss the subtle changes of emphasis and tone which direct attention to unexpected connections and signal to students what is significant and what is peripheral. As a correspondence tutor, part of your task is to help students focus attention appropriately, to find the 'wood'. Your correspondence with each student is unique to that student and should try to meet that student's needs.

Students choosing to study mathematics through distance or open learning methods are usually mature, and initially approach their studies with some purpose or intention. Purpose includes ideals, such as the desire to find out what mathematics is all about or to understand some of the concepts that once caused difficulty, as well as pragmatic goals such as to obtain a credit towards a degree. Under pressure of time, and driven by assessment, some students find their study strategy beginning to conflict with their ideals. They find they have to abandon the attempt to try to make sense of texts, and to focus attention more and more on assessment grades. Texts are not studied for themselves, but are scanned for examples and results pertaining to assignment problems. For students with strong ideals, such a shift can lead to disillusionment, even if the pragmatic goal of successful assessment is being achieved. For example, it is quite common for students who seem to be doing well to surprise their tutors by suddenly withdrawing. The conflict between their ideals, and the study behaviour which they find themselves adopting, becomes unbearable. Others choose to continue, but admit to disappointment and a feeling that they have in some way been let down.

In order to strike a balance between ideals, and the pragmatism that goes with keeping to a schedule, students need access to more sophisticated studying strategies than those they used at school. They also need support from their tutor in identifying and using these strategies. The comments you write on scripts will reflect your view of what is important in mathematics, and how best to go about studying it. If your attention is on the fact that answers are right or wrong, this is where students' attention will also be. By focussing on what is *mathematical* in what has been done and, in particular, in commending students for evidence of good mathematical behaviour (even when the answer may be wrong) you can help students to resist superficial study habits and instead, to develop their ability to think and behave mathematically.

For these reasons it is important that you seek to articulate for yourself a coherent account of what constitutes mathematical thinking and how students can learn mathematics effectively. When your comments are permeated by your mathematical point of view and make *explicit* references to the processes underlying mathematical thinking, the students can themselves become articulate about thinking mathematically and will be able to reflect upon their own learning.

Some useful frameworks

Writing comments requires a language in which to communicate clearly yet effectively about learning and doing mathematics. Traditional classroom language is about right and wrong answers rather than about making meaning. The advantage of a technical language about learning is similar to that of a technical language in mathematics itself but, as in mathematics, it takes time for the terms to acquire meaning and significance. One important role of the language, or vocabulary, is to draw attention to distinctions which may otherwise be overlooked. For example, when we first work with a new concept we struggle to get a sense of what the concept is about. 'Getting a sense of' is the first, pre-articulate stage in the learning process, culminating in the feeling that we can *see* what the concept is all about. We can confirm the *see*ing, and make it firmer by giving it expression, that is by *say*ing what it is we have seen. Finally we capture our understanding by *record*ing it. Written records have a stiff formality quite different from spoken versions.

In doing assignments students are supposed to be working at *recording* what they 'see', but often they are not ready for it. They may not yet be 'seeing' the concept, in which case you could suggest that they give more attention to a particular part of the text. Avoid inviting them to re-read long extracts since they certainly will not have time to do that. Instead refer them to selected paragraphs, supported by particular examples. Remember in choosing these excerpts and examples, that the intention is to help students to get a sense of a concept. Encourage students to say to themselves what they have understood, to put a definition, a statement of a theorem, or an account of a section into their own words and to speak it out loud if possible.

Students sometimes believe they have understood nothing at all because they have such difficulty in writing down the formal mathematics required of them. Yet questioning reveals that often they *can* 'see' what is required, but the problem lies in the *recording*, the capturing of the *seeing* in mathematical notation. Saying what has been *seen* helps to forge links between the *seeing* and the *recording*. Even so, as tutors we may tend to place too much emphasis too soon on precise and succinct solutions to questions. The students may not be ready for such elegant written expression. Praise it when it is achieved but remain sensitive to the struggle inexperienced students have in writing out an argument. It is better to encourage them to write out what they are *able* to *say*, in plain and simple English words, than to demand such precision of expression in formal notation that they become despondent and feel unable to progress. Elegance and precision come with time and experience.

An awareness of the distinctions between *seeing*, *saying* and *recording*, and of the role each plays in the development of understanding, will help you to diagnose students' difficulties and will guide your comments on their scripts. They are equally valuable when responding to students' telephone queries and in tutorials. In response to the frequently heard remark:

> I think I can see it, but I don't seem to be able to get started . . . I don't know what to write down.

you can invite the student to say what they can see, in as simple a form as possible, before then writing down what they say. It is a remarkably helpful gambit, since the student no longer feels a sense of failure and impotence.

Similarly, by appreciating that students need to progress through *saying* to *recording*, we are reminded to encourage students to speak out loud their current understanding of a concept, or statement of a theorem, in their own words, rather than do all the talking in a tutorial yourself. When studying from texts alone at home it is often helpful to talk out loud to oneself. Encourage them in this, by encouraging it on the telephone and in tutorials.

There is a very simple and effective way of helping students to deal with being stuck on a problem – encourage them to begin every question by writing down what they WANT and what they KNOW and to return to them whenever they are feeling lost or stuck. Solving a problem very often consists of building a bridge between the KNOW and WANT statements. For example,

> Find the equation of the straight line passing through the points (2,9) and (11,12)
>
> Solution
>
> I WANT the equation of a line.
> I KNOW the points (2,9) and (11,12) lie on it.
> I KNOW a line has equation $Ax + By + C = 0$, so I WANT A, B and C.
> I WANT to force the two points to lie on the line . . .
>
> substituting $x = 2$, $y = 9$ and $x = 11$, $y = 12$ begins to build a bridge from KNOW to WANT.

By writing down what they know and want, students can always get started on a problem. If technical terms are involved, then definitions can be written down. Relationships between terms can be expressed in simple language. For example,

> Find a primitive of x log(x).

Getting started is often the most difficult part, especially if a technical term like 'primitive' frightens the student into inaction.

Solution

I WANT a primitive of x log(x).
I KNOW that F is a primitive for f if $F' = f$.
Thus I WANT F such that $F'(x) = x \log(x)$.

It is amazing how such simple acts of transcription can release paralysed thinking.

Often it is clear from a script that the student has jumped into the question too impetuously and floundered in a maze of symbols without taking account of a critical piece of information contained in the question. If you can, when possible, frame your comments in the language 'you WANT...' 'you KNOW...'. This will help the student to acquire the habit of organising information effectively.

In being aware of the distinctions between *seeing*, *saying* and *recording* and of the value of KNOW and WANT, we can keep our own attention partly on the processes of learning mathematics rather then entirely on the *content* of mathematics, and encourage students to do the same. In this context another importat and useful distinction to have available is that between *specialising* and *generalising*.

When examples are used in the text to introduce a new concept, they are there to provide special cases from which the 'theory' can be generalised. Where examples and exercises follow a piece of theory, they are there to provide an opportunity for students to specialise from the generality of the theory. By drawing students' attention to the way the processes are being used in the text we can help them organise their reading and develop their own ability to specialise and generalise appropriately. The 'forest' begins to emerge as more than just a collection of 'trees', and some of the types of 'trees' begin to be identified.

Specialising and *generalising* are also key issues in assignments but students do not usually notice them even when questions are specifically designed to highlight the processes. A carefully structured set of questions in which students are expected to notice what has been going on in some particular cases, and then use the information in a general context, is likely to be dealt with piecemeal, without any noticing, unless we bring the processes to their attention explicitly through our comments. Good questions are those which stimulate students to *specialise* and *generalise*, for example:

Give an example of ...
What is common to the following examples ...?

Encourage student to use diagrams as an aid to their working – another form of *specialising*. Encourage them too, when working on questions couched in very general terms, to begin by *specialising* to particular cases in order to get a sense of what the question is about and to get some clues as to how the bridge between WANT and KNOW may be built.

See, say, record; KNOW and WANT; *specialising* and *generalising* are examples of frameworks which contribute to our understanding of mathematical thinking, and provide us with a vocabulary for communicating to students about strategies for learning and understanding mathematics. Using the framework words explicitly with students can help them learn to examine their own progress and diagnose their own difficulties. They might also begin to become articulate about thinking mathematically.

Tensions

As you begin to comment on scripts, you may experience a tension between wanting to write plenty of comments, yet not having enough time; and between writing something helpful, and yet not overloading the student with even more reading. There are a variety of tensions in any teaching/learning experience, and it can be tempting to try to resolve these tensions quickly so that they don't block the learning. For example, if a student is stuck on a problem, it is tempting to 'push them on' by telling them the answer, or by making some pointed suggestion. Such an intervention may or may not actually help the student, but it may ease the tutor's tension that 'we should get on'. However, learning cannot take place without tension. To resolve a tension by deciding upon some cut and dried solution may be to throw away the energy which it contains, reducing teaching to a mechanical routine. By contrast, noticing where tensions arise and working *with* them maintains a flow of energy and of interest and relieves us of the need to decide categorically between 'right' and 'wrong' ways of doing things.

According to the tensions operating, what we do in one situation may be different from our ideal, or what we would do in another. The 'time' tension, for example, may result in our sometimes taking short cuts, perhaps by copying solutions for students rather than posing questions and making comments which would help them to do the problems for themselves. By living with the inherent tensions, noticing, reflecting but not judging, we can avoid being seduced into always taking the short cut and then feeling guilty, which simply drains energy.

Student confidence

For virtually all students, completing a mathematics assignment and submitting it to a tutor is, initially at least, extremely threatening. It is not easy for us to appreciate just how vulnerable students feel in exposing their work to another adult for 'marking', so attention must be given not only to what comments to make but to the tone in which they are made. In writing remarks which represent an overview of the students' performance on an assignment, I recommend beginning with positive comments. There is, though, a tension present between being supportive and resorting to cliché's: 'You have made a good attempt at these questions, but...'. Look for opportunities to commend students for being mathematical, e.g. for the effective use of diagrams or for the explicit use of KNOW and WANT, of specialising and generalising. Try to remember to thank students for letting you know, through informal remarks, what they had in mind. In this way you can be more responsive to the very good students too, for merely writing 'Excellent Script' does not offer them adequate feedback.

In dealing with weak students care must be exercised in finding what deserves to be commented upon. Overwhelming them with red ink is not helpful. Again it is often the case that you can be positive about a mathematical *act*, while correcting a computation. It is probably better to select for comment those items which enable you to offer the most constructive advice and support, and keep remarks about other points very brief indeed.

Developing a working relationship through correspondence tuition

The first communications with students should create an atmosphere of trust and begin to establish a way of working. Your first comment will set the tone for everything that follows. Students have to learn what is meant by correspondence tuition. You should explain that you will be focussing attention not only on answers but on the evidence of how learning is progressing and that your comments can form an important component of their learning. Reassurance is needed that this may generate more than the usual amount of tutor comments on student work, but that extensive commenting does not mean errors, but rather the opportunity for improvement. The traditional red ink tends to carry with it a sense of 'wrong', so that you may find it better to use another colour.

Our aim is to engender a relationship with students in which the student is willing to expose uncertainty and confusion, knowing that this honesty will be respected, and that positively helpful suggestions will be offered. Encourage students to communicate with you informally within the script, indicating explicitly where their uncertainties lie.

e.g. $\int x\,dx = \frac{x^2}{2} + C$ (but I'm not sure if I need that C.)

You can deal more effectively with a solution that has gone astray if you know whether or not the student is convinced about what has been written. You will, of course, have to reassure students that their actual mark will be the same with or without the informal comment, but that you cannot assist when you are not aware that assistance is needed.

The nature of your relationship with students has its roots in your perception of mathematics. If you see mathematics as primarily about reproducing standard techniques on standard types of questions, then this attitude will be picked up by your students. They will be reinforced in the belief that getting correct answers is all that counts, but the tension between their performance and their own assessment of what they actually know will not go away, and may easily lead them to dropping out. If you see mathematics as an activity which involves conjecturing and modifying conjectures, with struggling to see and to express, then assignments encourage students to further their understanding, rather than hide their ignorance.

So, to address the question 'What do you bear in mind as you begin to write on a student's assignment?', you will be looking for opportunities:

- to use the script as a basis for teaching and developing students' learning by focussing their attention where it is needed;
- to notice and commend examples of good practice, and evidence of mathematical thinking;
- to point out what is missing or inadequate in a particular approach.

I suggest that to do this requires each of us to develop our own account of what constitutes mathematical thinking and how students can be employing the processes of mathematical thinking while working on texts and assignments. The language of KNOW and WANT, of *specialising* and *generalising*, of *seeing*, *saying* and *recording* is a useful place to begin.

Notes

For those who would like to take these ideas further, the following sources are suggested:

1 *Learning and Doing Mathematics*, Unit of the Open University Mathematics Foundation Course, available from the Centre for Mathematics Education, Maths Faculty, Walton Hall, Milton Keynes, 1984.

2 J Mason, L Burton and K Stacey, *Thinking Mathematically*, Addision-Wesley, 1982.

3 J Kilpatrick, *Reflection and Recursion: Proceedings of the Fifth International Congress on Mathematical Education*, M Carss (ed), Birkhauser, 1986.

27 Reflections on the role of correspondence teaching

Margaret Miers

Introduction

Over the past 14 years I have marked hundreds (perhaps thousands) of student assignments whilst working as a a part-time tutor for the Open University (OU). There are days when the post in the porch is unwelcome and the pile of essays a source of pressure, but correspondence teaching remains a task to enjoy and a process of exploration and development of my own abilities as well as those of my students. Far from becoming routine, it is a task that still prompts questions about what it is I am trying to do as a correspondence teacher and about how I might evaluate what I have achieved. Recent experience of the other side of the fence, both as an OU student, and now as a student nurse, have led to reflections about how teaching as well as learning might be assessed and developed.

Goals in correspondence teaching

Perhaps the most obvious goal in correspondence tuition is to assess the student's work. Indeed, the OU's monitoring system, whereby a sample of scripts marked by each tutor is reviewed by an academic member of the full-time staff, was orginally developed as a means of attempting to ensure consistency in grading. But the OU's strength as a distance teaching system has been its strength in developing *teaching* at a distance as well as assessment. The OU *Handbook for Part-Time Tutorial and Counselling Staff* (p 24) informs tutors that:

> the most important part of your work is to teach by correspondence. Students attach great importance to your written comments on their work. They work in isolation and rely on you to inform them of their progress and the ways in which they might improve and develop their studies. In addition to constructive criticism, students also require encouragement and recognition of their achievements.[1]

Thus we are alerted to the difficulties of distance learning and to the students' need for praise and encouragement as well as criticism and advice. Certainly I aim as a correspondence tutor to teach by explaining course content and offering advice about assignment skills, and I seek to praise and encourage by recognising and acknowledging students' strengths. My monitoring reports suggests that I satisfy the criteria the OU uses to judge tutors' performance.

Each faculty in the OU uses its own monitoring form to report on a tutor's correspondence work. These forms thus indicate the specific aspects of a tutor's work that monitors are observing when reviewing a marked assignment. Table 27.1 summarises these aspects. All faculties are concerned with the tutor's assessment (grading) and all except Education note the time the tutor takes to return the marked assignment. All faculties are also concerned that the tutor should correct factual errors, refer to course material in script comments, and explain the grade awarded. Thus the importance of a tutor's expertise in the subject, and of assessment skills, is clearly recognised. In addition there is emphasis on the importance of making clear comments, comments that are 'likely to help student improve', and on developing a relationship with the student through distance teaching. Comments should be 'helpful', attitude 'encouraging', and tone 'sympathetic'. Unlike the part-time staff *Handbook*, however, the monitoring forms offer little direct acknowledgement of students' need for recognition of their achievements. The teaching model suggested by the monitoring forms seems to be that of 'tutor as expert'. Tutors, through their correspondence work, are expected to offer clear, constructive advice about course content in an encouraging manner.

A 'tutor as expert' model, however, is not the only model used in distance teaching, nor is it necessarily the most appropriate for teachers in adult education. Much of my own sense of development as an OU tutor is based on the recognition that much of the joy I find in teaching adults (now that I feel grown up enough to do it) comes from the excitement of finding out about individual students and discovering that they can use me, and the course, as a means of opening up new knowledge about themselves, and about the world. The excitement does not rest in the continual redeployment of my own expert knowledge, but in observing and sharing, and, I hope,

Table 27.1

Monitoring forms

		Tech.	Maths	Science	Soc S.	Ed.	Arts
Grading	Assessed (for leniency, etc)			√	√	√	√
	Monitors' own grade recorded	√				√	
	Too much or too little for partially correct answer	√	√				
Overall appraisal							
Script	Qualitative judgement (on quality and/or quantity)				√	√	√
PT3[1]	Qualitative judgement (on quality and/or quantity)				√	√	√
	Using PT3 well: referring to script	√	√				
	Using PT3 well: overall appraisal, guidance for future TMAs	√					
Basic competence	Writes legibly	√	√	√			√
	Quick return	√	√	√	√		√
Specific points looked for	Corrects spelling			√			√
	Corrects factual errors	√	√	√	√	√	√
	Comments on poor presentation	√					
	Comments on obscure expression						√
	Notes excessive/insufficient length			√			√
	Notes lack of examples						√
	Refers to course material	√	√	√	√	√	√
	Notes and explains irrelevance			√		√	√
	Comments on faulty argument			√		√	√
	Showing why approach is wrong		√				
	Showing why line of thought is wrong	√		√			
	Using script as a basis for teaching	√	√	√			
	Using opportunities to teach	√	√				
	Making specific comments				√		√
	Comments likely to help student improve			√	√	√	√
	Explains grade	√		√	√	√	√
	Itemises marks to show where and why lost	√	√				
	Clear and helpful comments	√	√	√		√	√
	Sympathetic (helpful tone)	√	√	√		√	√
	Encouraging contact		√		√		√
	Demands realistic	√	√		√		√

encouraging, the students' learning. In order to satisfy students' need for recognition of their achievements, and to facilitate learning, it seems to me that tutors must first of all arrive at an understanding of the students' abilities and the students' goals. If I have developed as a tutor it is in my ability to demonstrate an understanding of an individual's progress in skills as well as knowledge, and to encourage a student to be aware of his or her own abilities, own goals, and own learning. My goals in correspondence teaching, therefore, are not just to assess reliably, and to teach by explanation and through remedial advice, but to promote learning through developing a mutual sense of positive regard, and offering each student an individual response.

Levels of tutoring: a flexible approach

In Table 27.2 I identify three aspects of a tutor's work which I regard as important. These involve (*a*) knowledge and understanding of course material; (*b*) knowledge and understanding of the skills involved in studying the course, and tackling the assignment; and (*c*) awareness of the assessment criteria used in the course and for the assignment. The first concern of any tutor would be to ensure that he or she has a firm grasp of the knowledge area, skills and assessment criteria (*a*, *b* and *c*), but I would see this as only the *first* stage of the teaching enterprise, and I would identify additional 'levels' of teaching, including levels 4, 5 and 6 in Table 2, for facilitative and reflective practice.

It is not enough for a tutor to demonstrate his or her own knowledge. Teaching involves identifying the student's understanding of (*a*) course content; (*b*) skills, and (*c*) assessment criteria (level 2), and explaining (*a*), (*b*) and (*c*) to individual students (level 3). Such explanatory or remedial work may be approached with more or less concern to develop the student's own awareness of his or her own knowledge and skills. Thus, in the table, I identify (tentatively) a fourth level, wherein a tutor shows how the course knowledge and skills link to the knowledge and skills the student already demonstrates. This stage I see as *en route* to level 5, where a tutor may be prompting a student to think about how much he or she knows about how much he or she knows. Levels 4 and 5 may be termed facilitative, whereas levels 1, 2 and 3 may be mainly explicative and remedial, based on a model of tutor as expert rather than facilitator. Finally I would identify a sixth level of correspondence teaching with adults wherein the tutor is able to reflect openly and critically on his or her own knowledge, teaching strategies and uncertainties, and join with the student in 'cultivating a garden', using Northedge's analogy (Northedge, 1976),[2] taking

Table 27.2

Correspondence teaching

	Knowledge (*a*)	*Skills* (*b*)	*Assessment* (*c*)
Level 1	1*a* Tutor's knowledge and understanding of course material	1*b* Tutor's awareness of academic, study and studentship skills	1*c* Tutor's awareness of assessment criteria
	KNOWLEDGE CENTRED, TUTOR AS EXPERT		
Level 2	2*a* Tutor's awareness of *student's* understanding of course material	2*b* Tutor's awareness of student's skills	2*c* Tutor's awareness of student's grasp of criteria
	REMEDIAL, TUTOR AS EXPERT		
Level 3	3*a* Tutor's teaching *re* course material (explicatory, remedial, etc.)	3*b* Teaching comments *re* skills	3*c* Ability to *explain* assessment criteria
	EXPLICATIVE, TUTOR AS EXPERT		
Level 4	4*a* Ability to *link* course knowledge to student's knowledge	4*b* Ability to link course skills to student's skills	4*c* Ability to link course's assessment criteria to student's own criteria
	FACILITATIVE MODEL OF TEACHING		
Level 5	5*a* Ability to further student's *own* understanding of course and own knowledge	5*b* Ability to further student's awareness of own skills	5*c* Ability to further student's self-assessment and awareness of own criteria, and that of the course
	FACILITATIVE MODEL OF TEACHING		
Level 6	6*a* Ability to acknowledge uncertainty about own knowledge and see uncertainties as a source of learning	6*b* Willingness to learn from and with student about methods of approach, study, etc. Able to acknowledge uncertainty	6*c* Willingness to *debate* with student relevance of assessment criteria
	REFLECTIVE PRACTICE		

Relationship – helpful, sympathetic, encouraging contact (Levels 1, 2 and 3)
– sense of individual concern (4, 5), unequal equals (Level 6)

Basics – clarity, legibility, quick return

seriously the view that knowledge is actively constructed by the learner and that it is not just the student who learns. This level of teaching can be termed 'reflective', following Schön in *The Reflective Practitioner* (1983).[3]

Correspondence teaching and open learning

But, as I have argued elsewhere (Miers, 1986),[4] we cannot review teaching without reviewing learning and my concern about what 'good' teaching practice is really like is related to concern about what our views of learning really are. I share Morgan's view that in a university:

> we are trying to foster 'quality' in learning ... We want students to go 'beyond the information' presented, to apply knowledge to new situations, actively to construct meaning, and to build on their existing understandings and experiences so as to relate ideas and information together. (Morgan, 1985, p39)[5]

We seek to encourage a deep rather than a surface approach to study (see Marton and Säljö, 1984)[6] in order to maintain quality in learning, and to do this we seek to understand our students as individuals. In my view tutoring at levels 4, 5 and 6 (Table 27.2) is about encouraging deep learning.

As I tutor I am not content with surface learning although I have my battery of techniques to ease the pathways through course material, assignments and exams. As a sociologist I am not content with surface learning although I can proffer checklists for comparing grand theorists. Surely no social scientist can see the memorising of theorists' ideas as sufficient, however important the ideas to the discipline? Students have a social world to look at too, and sociology is formed by, and reflects on the world in which we live. Deep learning takes time but for many students it is not something that can always wait for more knowledge, more skills. Thus it is respect for my discipline, my knowledge base, that provides the impetus towards independent, deep learning. It is the recognition that this involves identifying students' own knowledge, through which the discipline filters, that gives my interest in self-directed deep learning a fresh imperative, every course, every year, every student.

Teaching levels and the teaching relationship

A tutor's methods of teaching will reflect a tutor's view of his or her work. A distance teacher concerned with transmitting knowledge may concentrate on writing comments referring a student to course material that has been overlooked. Such a tutor may emphasise the cognitive aspects of learning. A tutor concerned with developing a student's *own* awareness of the skills necessary for a particular assignment in order to facilitate learning may ask direct questions about how the work was done and make suggestions about why problems arose, thus involving the student in trying to identify the source of difficulties. In doing this a tutor may be stressing the behavioural aspects of learning. But the learning process can be seen as having affective as well as cognitive and behavioural elements and awareness of students' need for encouragement and recognition reflects an awareness of ways in which affective elements facilitate learning. How students *feel* about the course and the tutor will be related to performance, and thus the tutor-student relationship is itself a factor to be reviewed.

Tutors and students principally concerned with developing knowledge of a subject, through remedial and explicative tuition, may work together in mutual sympathy, but in a relationship that is likely to be relatively formal and impersonal. However, a tutor interested in an individual's learning, and able to work as a facilitative and reflective practitioner would demonstrate, in addition, a strong sense of individual concern, writing to 'the person', not just to 'the student'. Thus tutors interested in teaching an *individual* rather than a subject will seek ways of making an individual response, but at the same time, a tutor's ability to do this will influence his or her ability to facilitate individual learning. Thus the teaching relationship both reflects and constrains the teaching approach. But it is individual tuition that can 'push' for independent, deep learning within a distance teaching system.

I do not underestimate the difficulties of this. There are no short cuts to individual tuition, and no blanket use of christian names, or routine 'best wishes', or 'contact me by letter or telephone', can substitute for the recognition of individual worth. I see a key characteristic of individual tuition as an ability to seek to recognise a student's starting point for an assignment and a willingness to accept a student's choices about how to tackle a piece of work as having some validity, even if the work itself cannot satisfy the requirements of the course. Such an ability seems particularly important for reflective practice which asks the tutor to reflect on his or her own choices and decisions, and thus asks for willingness to see students as equals. Students and tutors would aim to work together in a spirit of 'reflective reciprocity', sharing and debating their own perspectives on the course, teaching and learning.

Teaching with a sense of individual concern seems to me to demand personal qualities of empathy, warmth and genuineness, the qualities seen by Rogers as essential for a counsellor to possess. (Rogers, 1957).[7] This does not mean that all students require counselling help from their tutor, but an ability and willingness to see study material and difficulties from a student point of view (*empathy*), to criticise a student's work whilst still conveying a positive regard for that individual (*warmth*), and the ability to be open (which does not mean all thoughts and feelings must be expressed) in a tutor-student exchange of views (*genuineness*) seems to me an effective way of working with adults in teaching or in any other relationship. In the example below I attempt to use knowledge that I have gained about an individual to help identify and resolve difficulties with assignment skills. Knowing that the student wrote poetry, and that she had already put her thoughts about the course into verse, I tried to prompt reflection about the demands of poetry and prose.

> I have come to see reading your essays as something of an adventure. These adventures have become more enjoyable as I become more used to your style. But they are adventures because I am never sure where you are going next and nor am I clear which route you've taken in order to get there. With this essay I find the route fairly easy to follow . . . But someone unfamiliar with the ideas would find the essay hard going. You don't make the links between points clear; (the links are in your head but not on paper!) You write in a disjointed style, in short, sharp paragraphs which often seem to be quite separate from each other in terms of content. Try to see your argument developing in bigger chunks, with clear links between each chunk! (This is difficult to explain!) Whereas poetry can afford to be cryptic, indeed may be part of the pleasure, assignments have to be clear to any passing reader. (?)

I like to think that my interest in that particular student led to a quest for a different and individual teaching strategy, which helped foster a constructive tutor–student relationship.

An additional counselling quality or strategy important in teaching may be what Carkhuff has identified as 'concreteness' (Carkhuff, 1969),[8] which, in the teaching context, I see as the ability to reformulate vague and imprecise thoughts and feelings into more specific statements. Tutors can help students express themselves more precisely by attempting to reformulate vague ideas. This may also involve empathy and imagination. In the example below I attempt to encourage a student to pinpoint reasons why she'd failed to produce an assignment she was happy with. The student's letter accompanying the assignment stated:

> since I spoke to you everything seems to have gone wrong, not least that I developed a total block on the question and very nearly gave up on it. I have the feeling that it's all rather vague and

that I ought to have re written it in a punchy way with plenty of references, but of course I haven't any more time.

I think you'll realise that I'm not really happy about the assignment, not because I don't understand the course material but because some of the question, or rather the way of answering it has eluded me.

My comments:

You are quite right. You could have written this differently, 'in a punchy way, with plenty of references', and it would have gained higher marks. You know it's rambling, and that this is a fault, and that you could have rectified this with more time (which was lacking!) I am puzzled by *why* the appropriate approach eluded you since you seem to be interested in the issues raised and you have clearly read and understood the course material. Maybe the mental block and nearly giving up was a reflection of other pressures, or maybe you were genuinely uncertain about whether to approach the topic from your own standpoint as a patient/member of society, or from the standpoint of a *Health and Disease* student. I confess I'd like to think it's both (student/person being inseparable) but it is safer (as I think you know) to start from the standpoint of student whenever in doubt. Show off your knowledge of the *course*.

OU tutors themselves recognise a wide range of qualities necessary for good correspondence teaching. In a survey of OU part-time staff employed in 1976 and 1986, the results of which are currently being analysed, many tutors, when asked what they think makes a good OU tutor, identify attributes that attest to the importance of warmth, empathy and openness. Some tutors do retain a 'tutor as expert' model and refer only to the importance of knowledge of the subject, but many tutors comment on the importance of the tutor's approach to the student, seeing necessary qualities as, for example:

being able to empathise with the student. One must be reliable and discreet.

knowledge of the subject(s) and willingness to confess ignorance. Enthusiasm and friendliness. Availability. Ability to draw out students.

empathy and patience, (wish I had more!)

sense of humour, flexibility, imagination and intelligence. Alertness to students' vulnerability and sensitivity.

Thus I offer this account of correspondence tuition as an individual view of what I think I, and many colleagues, attempt in our correspondence work, and as a means of opening up debate about teaching through assignments. It may be that the teaching 'levels' are indistinguishable but I contend, however, that good tutors are aware that they seek to offer a range of tutoring styles, a range of relationships, giving them flexibility in responding to different student needs. Teaching with a sense of individual concern involves learning about an individual student, and acknowledging one's own individuality as a tutor.

Evaluating tutoring

But a further concern as a tutor is how can I evaluate my own work? How do I know the quest for individual tuition is worthwhile? One problem in evaluating tuition is that the model of teaching we adopt determines the criteria we use for evaluation. My model of teaching (and of learning), sees students as equal, rational and responsible, and since my aim is to facilitate their own independent learning, then it must be the students themselves who are arbiters of my abilities as a correspondence tutor.

A student perspective

A major influnce on my views about correspondence teaching was my experience as an OU student, studying *Popular Culture* (Miers, 1984).[9] I learnt much about correspondence teaching and learning through submitting essays for assessment. Writing the first essay was a revelation. My first shock was that my expectations about the amount of time required to produce a good essay were quite unrealistic. My second shock was that broad, interesting essay topics are well-nigh impossible to answer within usual word limits, except at a (to me) frustratingly simplistic level. My third shock was that I resented the time it took to produce a legible version for my tutor. Even though I recognised that this resentment marred my performance – in a more patient frame of mind I might have reworked and rewritten more successfully – I failed to quell it. Nor did I resolve my time difficulties, although they ceased to be such a shock.

Coping with the frustrations of writing essays under the constraints of lack of time and lack of knowledge opened my eyes to the effort and energy part-time mature students must put into their work. In my tutoring, my empathy with students over essay writing led to more discussion of feelings and methods concerning essay preparation and I became more alert to the different skills necessary for tackling different forms of assessment. Both essay writing and examinations require analytical skills and an understanding of course material, but whereas a student demonstrating knowledge and clear thinking should do well in an exam, high assignment grades require, in addition, time, patience, and a zest for evidence and illustration which encourages the necessary sifting and shifting of course material. I began to think more seriously about my students' discrepant abilities in relation to examination and assignment performance, and encouraged them to recognise the importance of time in essay preparation, and of rapid thinking and clear argument in an exam.

I learned, too, about correspondence teaching, through my reactions to being marked and assessed. My tutor successfully conveyed and fostered what I saw as mutual respect in his marking, and I thus welcomed his advice. The simple technique of rendering suggestions into questions (develop by example?) conveyed a clear impression that we were both working together. Only once did I wince. The comment, 'obviously – aim to keep this up!', after an A grade, smacked of paternalism. Surprised at my own reaction I began to find it difficult to find the right words of praise for my students, fearful of sounding patronising. Viewing marked assignments from a student standpoint did alert me to the difficulties of writing comments that will be received with eager attention. I have a sneaking sympathy for students' exasperation and apprehension when faced with thorough and copious advice. To be read, the comments should relate to the students' concerns and not to the academic quibbles of the tutor, and must hold and sustain their interest. During my student year I developed a student perspective on reviewing teaching which, once found, is hard to lose.

But it is a perspective which needs reinforcing by talking to *students* about how correspondence tuition is received. It was (and is) as an active student that I learnt the importance of mutual respect in tutor–student relationships, the extent to which mature students deserve that respect, and the subtle ways in which it can be undermined. I learn from tutors who win my confidence, tutors who show empathy, tutors who are open, tutors who listen. Perhaps the most obvious way that student confidence and tutor–student respect can be undermined is through a tutor's over-emphasis on criticising a student's work in what can appear to be a negative way. Despite the OU official encouragement of a positive approach and recognising students' achievements, in practice, correspondence comments can still discourage and depress by the tutor's concern to provide thorough, critical tuition. One OU student in her fourth year has commented, after reviewing a selection of tutors' summary sheets attached to assignments,

> In quite a few cases the tutors neglect the relationship building aspect of their role in favour of critical comment and advice. There are many reasons which might account for this but if a generalisation is allowed then I would say it is because being critical, etc. is the easier part of the job.

Being critical may indeed seem the easier part of the job, perhaps because criticism is one of the skills highly developed and prized within the academic community. 'Preference for judging ideas rather than generating them' has been identified by Adams as an 'emotional block' which can interfere with the freedom with which humans receive, explore and manipulate ideas. (Adams, 1974, pp 53–8).[10] Academic tutors do, of course, seek to develop their students' critical abilities, but correspondence teaching should surely avoid temptations to use marking as a cheap way to demonstrate mental superiority, a danger Adams identifies.

From my limited experience of being a student, and from asking for students' views, I would suggest that students themselves are aware that they learn more readily from tutors who are able to offer encouragement as well as criticism. Students are also alert to the importance of the teaching relationship, and are interested in their own learning, as well as their grades, as the comments below suggest.

> I'm not sure if the student would be able to follow the comments let alone put the advice to good use . . . There does not seem to be any encouragement given or any hints as to what was right about the assignment, just emphasis on what was wrong.

> Some mention of personal pleasure at reading or seeing a particular point made would, of course, be on a personal level, and make the most bitter of critical pills a lot easier to swallow.

Developing tutor-student dialogue

OU students have no formal role in monitoring OU tutors but individual tutors can and do develop their own ways of noting student feedback as a means of evaluating their own work. Any thoughtful tutor will reflect on his own performance as a variable that may influence students' ability and willingness to keep up with course requirements. Noting attendance at face-to-face meetings, noting the telephone calls in relation to meetings and assignments marked can give us clues as to what we are doing right, if not what we are doing wrong. I suspect I judge my success by the extent to which a dialogue develops between tutor and student, and to that end, over the past year, I have sought ways to encourage students to respond critically and positively to the course material, assignments, my assessments, and teaching. One such method has been that of asking students to add notes with their assignments, telling me how well they think they've performed, what difficulties they've had and why. I saw the purpose of this as to encourage students to become aware of their own learning, and to improve their ability to assess their own performance. But I also saw it as a means of opening up opportunities for an exchange of views between tutor and student, about the course itself, and about teaching and learning.

Perhaps the main effect of encouraging tutor–student dialogue is that it enables a tutor to make an individual response. Knowing more about a student can alert a tutor to individual difficulties and provide the challenge of seeking individual solutions. But in addressing comments to a student who has opened up his or her own uncertainties, understanding and difficulties, a tutor must respond in kind, by making assessment criteria explicit, and explaining reaction. Such open teaching can afford to be bold if the dialogue is established and the tutor knows the student will respond if the teaching advice is misplaced. Consider, for example, a colleague's forthright probing in writing to a student she clearly knows well.

> This was, incontrovertibly, a clear and sound exposition, leading to basically acceptable conclusions. But I would so much like to see you develop ideas more extensively, more critically, and more aggressively. Only then will you be doing yourself justice ... I wonder whether it's your role as a teacher which has led you to develop the virtues of order, clarity and reinforcement without allowing, or provoking, you to raise issues which are problematic ... In the context of the OU you're playing it too safe. Don't limit yourself to those questions which give rise to easy or organised answers. Ask yourself whether you really believe what you write ... It's going to be courage of this kind that will shift your work from the good to the excellent. It's only because of the frustration I feel at seeing you rather stuck (and you yourself did ask me how you could progress), that I've allowed myself to sound so critical. You will find some more appreciative comments on my sheet. Come back to me how you will.

Consider, too, the extracts from a student letter, sent to me with an assignment, and the effects of the letter on my own comments on the marked work.
Student's letter:

> I am enjoying the work; some bits more than others and find it difficult not to use my own knowledge at times, but to stick to the text.
>
> I'm not so keen on the numerical bits. I seem to move into a 'blank minded' phase at the mention of statistics, although I felt that the book was very lucid. I don't feel that I have done all that well with this TMA. I thoroughly enjoyed the reading but find it hard to be precise in my answers. Perhaps I am too much of a rambler.

> Time was also a problem this section as we've had a very hectic time buying a house ... I hope to have a run of uninterrupted work for a while now.

My comments:

> You certainly don't seem to have answered Q.2. in a 'blank minded' way. Your answer to 2e) is very good – clear, precise and concise, and your other answers are on the right lines but don't go far enough ... or miss important points ... Answering data analysis questions, knowing how much to include, etc. is largely a matter of getting used to how to do it. My comments are meant to show you what you need to do to gain high marks ... (Is fear of statistics an old fear? Time to banish it!) You have controlled your own knowledge and any tendency to ramble well here. You *could* have made more use of course material with Q.1 e.g. ... I think sticking to the precise question is difficult with Q.1 ... Yes, selecting points for short answers *is* difficult, but I see progress in keeping to the point here. Do you?'

But developing tutor–student dialogue about students' learning doesn't necessarily develop dialogue about tutors' teaching, although I suspect the latter is unlikely without the former. Although I attempt to encourage this, in practice it is rarely broached directly, and I infer my success by students' progress in assignments, and their views about what they've learnt. But one OU course, due to start in 1988, *Professional Judgement*, will ask for students' views about tutors' teaching, as part of course requirements, and tutors and students will aim to work together in a spirit of 'reflective reciprocity'. Such an approach may bring tutors and students the necessary basic confidence in the teaching relationship which enables each side both to acknowledge it as a relationship, and to express what they see as going on.

Perhaps, therefore, encouraging a spirit of reflective reciprocity is now my main aim as a correspondence teacher. It is an aim only likely to be achieved if tutors bring to their work openness, empathy, and a sense of individual concern, as well as a sound grasp of the course's knowledge, skills and assessment criteria. It is tutors who are prepared to reflect and to learn who are likely to provide the positive and challenging tuition which pushes for independent learning at a distance. But reflection, like learning, and teaching, is its own reward.

Acknowledgements

I would like to thank Kathy Collier, Jack Dowie, Sarah Fisher, Tracy Richardson and Sylvia Rhys for their help in the preparation of this chapter, and for giving me free rein with their own comments and ideas.

Suggestions for further reading

The Journal *Teaching at a Distance*, and its successor, *Open Learning* discuss teaching models and assumptions quite extensively. A discussion referring to facilitative practice can be followed in articles concerning what actually happens in tutorials in *Teaching at a Distance*Nos 18, 20, 21 and 23.

Readers interested in teaching and counselling would find R Woolfe, S Murgatroyd and S Rhys *Guidance and Counselling in Adult and Continuing Education*, Open University Press, 1987, particularly chapter 4, helpful.

The implications of reflective practice for professionals are discussed extensively by Donald Schön in *The Reflective Practitioner: How Professionals Think in Action*, Temple Smith, 1983.

References

1 Open University, *Handbook for Part-Time Tutorial and Counselling Staff 1985/86*, 1985.

2 A Northedge, 'Examining Our Implicit Analogies for Learning Processes' in *Programmed Learning and Educational Technology*, Vol 13, No 4, pp 67–8, 1976.

3 D Schön, *The Reflective Practitioner: How Professionals Think in Action*, Temple Smith, 1983.

4 M Miers, 'What Do Tutors Learn from Monitoring?' in *Open Learning*, Vol 1, No 3, 1986.

5 A Morgan, 'What Shall We Do About Independent Learning?' in *Teaching at a Distance*, No 26, p 39, 1985.

6 F Marton and R Säljö, 'Approaches to Learning' in F Marton, D Hounsell and N Entwistle (eds), *The Experience of Learning*, Scottish Academic Press, 1984.

7 C Rogers, 'The Necessary and Sufficient Conditions of Therapeutic Personality Change' in *Journal of Consulting Psychology*, Vol 21, pp 95–104, 1957.

8 R R Carkhuff, *Helping and Human Relations: Volume 1: Selection and Training*, 2nd edition, Holt, Rinehart & Winston, New York, 1969.

9 M Miers, 'How it feels to be a student' in *Teaching at a Distance*, No 25, pp 101–105, 1984.

10 J Adams, *Conceptual Block-Busting*, Norton, 1974.

PART VI LEARNING IN GROUPS

28 Tutorial groups in open learning

Patrick Kelly

Introduction

Tutorial contact can have a major role to play in open learning programmes. The Open University (OU) experience shows that there is strong student demand for opportunities to discuss course issues with a tutor and fellow students; and it is clear that students view tutorial contact as an important and valuable component of the OU teaching system.

One of the characteristics of many open learning systems is the use of a wide range of teaching and learning techniques. In many instances the traditional pattern of full-time class-based study has undergone radical development and students in open learning schemes may be studying part-time, working with a variety of teaching media including printed texts, television and computer assisted learning and may, for much of their time, be engaged in independent study.

The selection and integration of teaching media and strategies is of major concern in the design of open learning programmes. One issue of interest across many systems is the role of the group tutorial and the balance between class tuition and independent study built around distance teaching materials, library or other learning resources.

The origin of the Open University as the University of the Air and the high visibility of the correspondence materials and the link with the BBC have tended to overshadow the contribution made by face-to-face tuition. It might be more appropriate to regard the OU as a multi-media teaching institution rather than as a pure distance teaching institution.

The OU does have a highly developed distance teaching system which includes correspondence texts, television, video, radio, audio-cassettes, computer assisted learning and home experiment kits. Although the teaching system has been designed to be accessible to the home-based student and there is no obligation to attend tutorials, the University is also aware of the value of opportunities for contact and discussion. A majority of the population live in or within reach of the large urban areas where most institutes of further and higher education are located. Very few OU students would be able to attend classes on a full-time basis but many are able to go to occasional evening or weekend classes scheduled at times convenient for them.

From the beginning there has been an extensive framework of locally-based tuition and counselling provision. Over 5000 part-time staff are employed by the OU and they are supported by 200 full-time academic staff in 13 regional centres. On the five foundation courses, 40 hours are allocated for tutorial and counselling support and approximately 15 hours tutorial time is available on full credit post-foundation level courses. In addition, each foundation course and a third of all post-foundation level courses have a one-week residential summer school as an integral part of the course.

Although attendance at tutorials is voluntary this does not mean that tutorials are a marginal activity. Considerable efforts are made to encourage attendance. On foundation courses tutorials are held weekly or fortnightly in parallel with the main themes introduced in the course units. There are far fewer tutorials on post-foundation level courses but the tutorial programme is usually geared to key concepts or particularly difficult aspects of a course. Some courses also use tutorials for group work or practical activities which cannot be carried out easily by distance teaching methods.

Tutorials are closely linked not only to course content but also to assessment. Tutors and students use tutorials to discuss assignments and exam revision and tutorials are often scheduled to coincide with assignment submission dates. Students are very conscious that the tutor–counsellor or tutor who organises their tutorials also marks their assignments which account for approximately half of the final grade awarded for a course. Thus the tutorial provision is a significant element of the OU's teaching system and many studies have confirmed the need, demand and value of tutorial contact for students.

The need for tutorial groups

The benefits of open learning are well known but the difficulties which learners may face should not be minimised. Students welcome the increased access to education offered by open learning but they may lack confidence and study skills if they have not studied for many years or have little formal educational background.[1] Many adults will be unfamiliar with modern teaching techniques and the range of teaching media used in open learning. Students may welcome the chance to learn at a time, place, and pace convenient to them but miss the interaction with other students and with a tutor which is provided by a conventional course. The danger is that the independent learner could so easily become the isolated learner.

The success of the OU follows in large part from a determination that the open door should not become a revolving one which dumps students back where they started, labelled as failures. It is generally accepted that new students need encouragement and personal support as they come to terms with the academic demands of undergraduate level study and the distinctive OU system.[2] Regular tutorial meetings on the foundation courses are seen as helping to ease students back into academic study and reduce drop-out. Does the need for tutorial contact wither away after the first year as students become self-sufficient learners requiring only the course units and audio-visual materials together with correspondence tuition? The available evidence suggests otherwise.

After taking one or two foundation courses students usually go on to courses at second level and may then proceed to third (honours degree) level courses. Studies of tutorial use indicate that at post-foundation level attendance is generally higher on the more demanding third level courses, and on those individual courses students consider most difficult, (Kelly, 1981).[3] The first national survey to examine tuition at post-foundation level revealed the key role of the tutor and tutorial contact for most students. Student responses to a number of attitude statements are particularly striking (Kelly and Swift, 1983*a*)[4]:

58% agreed that 'some aspects of most courses can only be taught effectively on a face-to-face basis' (17% disagreed);

67% agreed that 'a good tutor can make a course; a poor tutor can spoil one' (14% disagreed);

68% agreed that 'without a course tutor there would be no-one in the OU system to whom I could turn for help with study problems' (17% disagreed);

68% agreed that 'if there were no provision for contact with a course tutor, the OU would lack credibility as an academic institution' (14% disagreed);

8% agreed that Apart from having my TMAs (assignments) graded and commented on I don't want or need any other contact with a tutor' (77% disagreed).

In addition to the general attitude statements students were also asked about the help they had needed from their tutor over and above the grading of assignments on the last course they had taken. Less than a quarter reported that they had needed no help at all, whilst more than three-quarters needed some or a great deal of help. Between 30 to 40% felt that their tutor's help had been essential for sorting out a sticking point in their studies, a problem with assignments or for getting to grips with a major course topic.

In view of the emphasis on distance teaching media accompanying the recent announcement of the Open College, it is interesting to note that the majority of OU students believe that some aspects of most courses can only be taught effectively face-to-face and that they link the academic credibility of the University with opportunities for tutor contact.

The variety of needs for tutorial groups

The needs and objectives of tutorial groups are likely to vary in open learning study programmes according to the character, duration and level of courses and the interests, background and requirements of students. This diversity is also evident in different OU programmes. The group tutorial is an important component of the undergraduate teaching system but has a more limited role on some continuing education courses, and many short continuing education courses and study packs have been designed specifically for individual study.

Even within the Undergraduate Programme there are a range of attitudes towards tutorials and the role of the tutor. Three broad student orientations are discernible though there is considerable overlap between the second and third.[5]

1 *The student at a distance*

The OU route is attractive because it offers a home-based alternative to those who are unable or unwilling to study at a conventional university. Those who prefer to work on their own or have learned to become self-sufficient because they cannot go to tutorials may see no need for contact at all:

> I have no desire for any contact other than correspondence. I am taking an OU degree although I have been offered day-release at work. I prefer correspondence tuition.

2 *The student needing back-up*

Most students lead busy lives and have limited time available for study. They accept that they will usually work alone but want occasional contact. This becomes particularly important if a serious study problem occurs. However well designed, course materials are not truly interactive and cannot be interrogated:

> I try to go along to the first tutorial to see what the tutor and other students are like and I may go if there is a tutorial linked to a difficult unit. I usually go to any revision sessions. You need to have someone you can talk to when you're stuck and can go no further.

3 *The student needing contact*

For some students the existence of a tutor and personal interaction with tutors and students makes the OU a 'real' university. Some students would not study with the OU if they really were at a distance:

> Without support and encouragement from tutors and fellow students I might not have completed my degree course. I do not like studying alone, without being able to discuss problems or ideas with others. The Open University course should be more than just a correspondence course; these are already provided by other bodies.

The importance of the human dimension in study has been examined more fully in a study carried out last year, (Thorpe, *et al.*, 1985).[6] Some may see student demands for tutorials as evidence of a lingering and unhealthy dependence on the tutor, or, view the satisfaction which most tutors and students gain from tutorial interaction as incidental to the main educational function.

However, research findings lend support to those theories of education which emphasize the close relationship between cognitive and affective aspects in the learning process. The demand for contact arises in part from a (predictable) desire for help in mastering the course content and the assessment requirements. But the majority of students also find it important to be members of a live academic community and able to share ideas with others, and this is greatly valued by the many OU students who are seeking quality in the learning experience.

The human dimension is conveyed in many ways and is strongly identified with the group tutorial even though some tutorial experiences are better than others. The tutorial programme gives students access to their tutor and others taking the course, and enables them to compare progress, share experiences, problems and ideas and to discuss matters of group and individual interest.

The relationships established at tutorials help to promote other forms of contact. Student self-help or study groups are a valuable source of mutual support and almost all are set up at the early tutorials. If there were no tutorial provision it is likely thta there would be fewer study groups. Similarly, once students have met their tutor most find it easier to get in touch later on by letter or telephone if they have study problems or want advice. Few students seem willing to initiate contact with someone who is just a name on a list. There is also an important feed through to correspondence tuition. Tutors can draw on their knowledge of students gained in tutorials to address their teaching comments to a known individual rather than to an unknown 'student' and are better able to present their comments in the most effective manner for the individual concerned.[7]

Possibly the best case for including a tutor in distance teaching/ open learning programmes was made some years ago by Hilary Perraton:[8]

> The thing which a live tutor can do, which we can't mechanise and we can't mass-produce, is to enter into a dialogue with his students.

A more detailed picture of the student's need for dialogue is provided by survey and interview findings. To summarise:

Subject expertise

There is demand for access to an expert who can give an authoritative explanation of course concepts, provide feedback on progress and can pass on the academic skills of a discipline.

Help with study difficulties

It is essential to be able to get help to deal with study problems. Tutorials and other forms of contact can be used to clarify ambiguities in the course material and assignments, to overcome learning blocks, and to develop study and essay writing skills.

Maintaining motivation

Tutorials offer a partial solution to some of the drawbacks associated with the learning environment of the student at a distance. It is easy to lose heart and get depressed studying alone for the period of time needed to obtain a degree. Face-to-face meetings with a tutor and other students can sustain motivation and inject fresh enthusiasm for study. Dialogue breaks down the dry impersonal effect of the printed material.

Guidance through the course

Tutorials aid the integration of the different elements of the course package and relate individual topics to the principal course themes. Many students find the volume of printed material intimidating and value assistance to 'sort the wood from the trees'.

Broadening horizons

Tutorials allow a more extensive discussion of issues of interest to students than that offered by the course units. Tutors may also add to a course by contributing their own specialist expertise and by relating course themes to current events. It is also likely that tutors will be more in touch with the latest research and other developments than texts possibly printed some years ago.

In other words, through their correspondence tuition and tutorial work tutors occupy a key position as the intermediary between the student studying alone and the remote course materials.

Tutorial planning

Visitors who come to the OU to discuss the role of tuition ask eminently sensible questions about tutorial planning and organisation but rarely receive simple answers. How much tutorial support do students need? What are the merits of different tuition methods? Is it better to have regular contact throughout the year or a small number of intensive periods of tuition? Are evening sessions preferable to day schools? Is there an ideal length for tutorials? How far are students willing to travel? How many students attend tutorials?

The answers to many of these questions are bound up with the particular history, structure and financing of the OU and the tutorial planning issues which confront a national university relying primarily on distance teaching media will be very different from those faced by a college or university developing open learning programmes within the local community. Nevertheless there may be a few general lessons to be derived from the OU experience.

If the tutorial programme is optional it must be learner centred. If we look at a two-hour evening tutorial from a student's perspective, it is perhaps a commitment of three or four hours, allowing for travel. Then there is the financial cost of travel, sorting out arrangements at home, and other competing demands on time. The two-hour tutorial has to be worth the effort involved in getting there and offer more than an evening spent in private study. When post-foundation students were asked to indicate all their reasons for attending tutorials, eight aspects were mentioned by between 40 to 60% of those responding (Swift and Kelly, 1983*b*).[9]

Students' reasons for attending tutorials (in rank order)

1 To meet my tutor and discuss course/study matters.
2 To get help with difficult aspects of the course.
3 To meet other students and discuss course/study related problems with them.
4 To extend my understanding of the subject beyond the units/scope of the units.
5 For discussion and help with tutor marked assignments.
6 To sustain my interest and motivation.
7 For revision and preparation for exams.
8 For general support for studies.

A quarter of the students gave 'to meet my tutor and discuss course/study matters', as their *most important* reason for going to tutorials. This was followed by 'help with difficult aspects of the course' (given as the main reason by 15%) and 'to extend my understanding of the subject beyond the units/scope of the units' (mentioned by 12%).

These findings suggest that students look to tutorials to satisfy a wide range of needs. At foundation level the amount of tutorial provision is fairly generous. Although there is some variation a new student might expect to be offered weekly evening tutorials at one of 250 study centres from February until Easter, then a mix of weekly/fortnightly tutorials until the end of June, a break in July and August during which the student attends summer school, and tutorials most weeks from September until the examinations in mid October.

In contrast, after foundation level, the student may be offered between four and eight tutorials and these will be held in only a few study centres in the larger cities in each region. There is less tutorial time (approximately 15 hours on a full-credit course and 7 or 8 on a half credit) and many students have to travel further to attend.

The challenge at post-foundation level is to design a tutorial programme which is academically coherent and accessible to the greatest number. The University wisely decided against a model of centrally planned tutorial provision and instead devolved responsibility to the faculty staff tutors in the regions. In deciding the number of tutors and planning a tutorial programme the staff tutor takes account of the number of hours allocated for a course, the nature of the course and any particular requirements (e.g. for practical work or visits), the number and geographical distribution of students and significant local factors including the availability of public transport and the nature of the road network.[10]

It is difficult to answer questions about the distance students are prepared to travel because 30 miles is a short hop on a motorway but a long haul on country roads, and five miles across a city can be a very long journey by public transport.[11] In practice a choice is usually made between evening or Saturday morning tutorials and Saturday

day schools. A programme of evening/Saturday morning tutorials at regular intervals throughout the year provides continuity and reasonable coverage of course content. The main drawback is that if tutorials are held in just one or two locations in a region, many students will not be able to attend, or will consider the effort and cost involved disproportionate for a two-hour tutorial.

The advantage of the Saturday day school is that students receive several hours of intensive tuition. A number of tutorial groups may be brought together and by pooling resources tutors can offer a number of options. In addition, it may be possible to invite course team members or outside speakers to give a guest lecture. The day school gives 'good value' but has two drawbacks: fewer tutorials can be provided and this weakens continuity, and no matter how attractive the day's programme is there will be students who wish to attend but cannot because of the distance, time or the cost of travel.

The main alternative to face-to-face tuition is the group telephone tutorial but this has not fulfilled its promise as a tutorial method. The technology to link a tutor and several remote students together is cheap, and simple to use.[12] In Scotland, for example, where about a third of the students would need an overnight stop to get to a study centre, group telephone tutorials have been running effectively for many years. However, tutors and students generally seem to consider telephone tutorials as 'second best' to face-to-face contact and appear reluctant to put much effort into acquiring the skills of teaching and learning by telephone as long as face-to-face tuition is a viable option.[13]

The OU has sought to develop many tuition methods and in the future will make greater use of computer tutorials. These other methods will complement but are unlikely to replace the class tutorial.

Tutorial attendance and value

Tutorial attendance is regarded by many as the acid test of the level of demand and value of tutorials. Many regional and national studies have examined attendance but there are serious problems associated with attempts to use attendance rates to measure the effectiveness of the tutorial provision.[14]

It is difficult to talk about tuition in terms of national provision. On post-foundation courses the multiplicity of factors which determine the tutorial programme can produce a situation in which one student is offered sixteen hours tuition organised as eight two-hour tutorials and another student on the same course in a different part of the country is offered ten hours tuition organised as two day schools.

It is straightforward to measure how many students turn up to a tutorial but more difficult to assess the baseline to which this figure should be related. Once students register for a course there is no incentive to formally withdraw and some of the 'live' students who do not attend have in fact given up. Regardless of the care given to tutorial planning, it is inevitable that there will always be a proportion of students who cannot attend because of personal or work commitments.

There is a relationship between the amount of tuition offered and student take-up. Where regular tutorial contact is available locally attendance is higher than where students have to go far (in distance/time) for infrequent tutorials. Moreover, value cannot be equated simply with the number of tutorials attended since some students find it valuable to attend all tutorials but others find it just as valuable to attend selectively in response to interests and needs. Within these limitations it is possible to give a general indication of tutorial attendance rates.

The national survey of audio-visual and other media was carried out annually for many years. In 1979, 16 000 students studying 91 courses were sampled and the findings revealed that 75% of foundation students made use of face-to-face tutorials and 42% claimed to use tutorials extensively. At post-foundation level the figures were 59% and 29% respectively (Grundin, 1980).[15]

The 1983 national survey of post-foundation tuition examined attendance in relation to the type of tuition which students were offered. Seventy-five per cent of those for whom evening/Saturday tutorials were available said they used them as did 62% of those offered day schools. The most frequently mentioned reasons for *not* going to tutorials were personal, family and work commitments. This was followed by the distance/time spent getting to tutorials which was cited as a deterrent by nearly a third.[16]

The most recent survey, in 1985, was sent to a random sample of students who had gained two or more course credits. The responses, from over 2000 students, revealed that 76% had attended at least one tutorial (the rate was 80% amongst those who had passed their courses). Less than one in ten had studied alone without going to tutorials or having any other contact with their tutor, counsellor or other students through study groups (Thorpe *et al.*, 1986).[17]

Putting all the findings together it appears that between about two-thirds and three-quarters of the student population attend at least one tutorial and that perhaps a third or more attend some or most tutorials. Whether this is proof of worth is a matter of interpretation. What is not disputed is that the main cause of dissatisfaction with face-to-face tuition at post-foundation level, by a very considerable margin, is the lack of sufficient tutorials to give adequate coverage of courses.

What is the value of tutorial contact relative to other elements of the OU teaching system? As might be expected, the compulsory core of correspondence materials and assignments is considered most crucial to students' success, followed, on those courses which have them, by summer schools.[18] Tutorials are regarded as being more helpful than television or radio and despite the public attention which broadcasting attracts as a teaching medium, there is significant student demand for more face-to-face tuition at the expense of broadcasting.

Another way of approaching the question of value is to try to assess the consequences of removing tutorial support completley so that the only contact was through assignments posted to a correspondence tutor. It is apparent that although there is some dissatisfaction with individual tutors, the amount and accessibility of tutorials and the content of some sessions, most students attach a high value to tuition. The majority of students believe that face-to-face tuition is the most effective means of teaching at least some parts of most courses and feel that their ability to study would be impaired if the amount of tutorial support was reduced. Most students say they get a lot from face-to-face interaction with tutors and other students and a quarter of post-foundation students claim that without the help of a tutor they would probably have dropped out of at least one course. And, if students are to be believed, some would not wish to study with a correspondence university.

In the OU the primary teaching responsibility is carried by the correspondence texts. The central function of the tutor is to provide correspondence tuition and it is only through the marking and commenting on assignments that tutors are in contact with all of their students throughout a course. The role of tutorials is to support and complement the course teaching materials. Remedial help is one aspect of this role but it does not define it.

It is clear that at undergraduate level the overwhelming majority of students have needs for dialogue throughout their study career. Meeting in a group with a tutor helps students to understand course themes and to resolve study difficulties. Equally important, students like dialogue and feel that it fulfils a role which cannot be performed by course materials. Personal contact makes the learning process more effective for the individual and more enjoyable.

Enthusiasm for open learning and innovative teaching techniques has to be tempered by an awareness that few students turn to open learning because of interest in or commitment to novel teaching methods. For the great majority open learning is the only or the most convenient mode of study available to them. If the door is to be genuinely open the design of extended study programmes must address the full range of learning needs of adults studying mainly on their own over a number of years. OU students are drawn from a broad cross section of the community and it is likely that their perception of the role of tutorial groups and the value of dialogue will be shared by many adults attracted to open learning modes of study.

Notes and references

1 In 1984 36% of undergraduate students possessed less than the two 'A' levels normally required for university entry and 65% had completed their full-time education at the age of 18 or under. Source: Institute of Educational Technology, The Open University.

2 See for example (a) R Beevers, 'The Function of the Part-time Academic Staff in the Open University Teaching System' in *Teaching at a Distance*, No 3, Milton Keynes, Open University, 1975; (b) J Field, 'Tutor–Counsellor Evaluation: a preliminary note' in *Teaching at a Distance*, No 12, 1978; (c) P Henderson, 'The Tutor-Counsellor Role: a Case Study' in *Teaching at a Distance*, No 14, 1979.

3 P Kelly, *An Overview of Student Use and Appreciation of Tuition, Regional Tutorial Services Research Group*, Open University internal paper, 1981.

4 P Kelly and B Swift, 'Post Foundation Tuition: Student Perspectives' in *Teaching at a Distance*, No 24, 1983*a*. A postal survey to examine student perceptions of the role and value of tuition at post-foundation level was sent to a sample of 5763 students from 24 post-foundation courses (four from each faculty) with a representative mix of half and full credit courses at second and third level. 3411 usable questionnaires were returned, a response rate of 59%.

5 The quotations used are from students' open-ended written comments in the Survey of Post-foundation Tuition (Kelly and Swift above). The general orientations are confirmed by other studies e.g. S Clennell *et al.*, *Older Students in the Open University*, 1984.

6 M Thorpe *et al.*, 'The Human Dimension in Open University Study' in *Open Learning*, Vol 1, No 2, Longmans, 1986.

7 For discussion of the importance of writing to 'the person' not just 'the student' see e.g. M Miers, 'What do Tutors Learn from Monitoring?' in *Open Learning*, Vol 1, No 3, Longmans, 1986.

8 H Perraton, from a conference address in 1973 quoted in *Teaching for the Open University*, Milton Keynes, The Open University, 1982.

9 B Swift and P Kelly, *Tuition at Post-foundation Level in the Open University: a Preliminary Report on a Survey of Students*, Open University internal research paper, 1983*b*.

10 For a vivid analysis of the problems of tutorial planning in a region where a relatively small number of students are distributed over a large geographical area see H Richards, 'Teaching Distance Learners in Wales' in *Open Learning*, Vol 1, No 3, Longmans, 1986.

11 The factors affecting tutorial attendance rates have been examined in many Regional studies, see e.g. (a) T Phythian and M Clements, 'Post- foundation Tutorial Planning' in *Teaching at a Distance*, No 18, 1980. (b) P Kelly and J Millard, *The Low Population Problem*, Open University internal research paper, 1982.

12 See e.g. (a) J George, 'Tutorials at Home: a Growing Trend' in *Teaching at a Distance*, No 14, 1979. (b) B Robinson, 'Telephone Tutoring in the Open University: a Review' in *Teaching at a Distance*, No 20, 1981.

13 For a national account of use and attitudes towards Telephone Tutorials see P Kelly, 'Regional Use of Telephone Tuition', Regional Tutorial Services, Open University Internal Research Paper, 1981.

14 For the approach taken in one Region see papers by:
(a) S Baker, *Tutorial Attendance of Post-foundation Technology Students in the East Midlands Region during 1980, 1981, and 1982*, Regional Research and Development Paper No 9. Regional Academic Services, Milton Keynes, The Open University, 1983.
(b) J Millard and R Sinclair, *Preliminary Results from a Survey of Post-foundation Tutorial Provision for Social Science and Educational Studies Courses*, Open University internal paper, 1982.
(c) J Ekins, R Baylis and T Lister, *Analysis of Maths Tutorials in the East Midlands Region*, Open University internal paper, 1981.
For a more general discussion of issues associated with measuring attendance see M Thorpe, *Post-foundation Tuition: Measures of Student Usage and Tutorial Attendance*, Regional Research and Development Paper No 10, 1983.

15 H Grundin, *Audio-Visual and Other Media in 91 University Courses: Results of the 1979 Undergraduate Survey*, Institute of Educational Technology Papers on Broadcasting No 149, The Open University, 1980.

16 B Swift and P Kelly, *op cit.*, 1983*b*.

17 Student Opinion Survey (1985) Institute of Educational Technology. Findings reported in Thorpe *et al.*, *The Human Dimension in Open University Study op cit.*, 1986.

18 These rankings have remained broadly constant for years. The results of the 1979 audio-visual survey are in line with earlier surveys carried out in 1974 and 1977. See T Bates, *Student Use of Open University Broadcasting*, IET Papers on Broadcasting No 44, Open University internal research paper, 1975, and H Grundin, *Broadcasting and the Open University Student*, Open University internal research paper, 1978.

Suggestions for further reading

Issues relating to tutorial groups are discussed in many papers in the journal *Teaching at a Distance*, including:

A Northedge, 'Learning Through Group Discussion in the Open University', No 2, 1975.

R Lewis, 'The Place of Face-to-Face Tuition in the Open University System', No 3, 1975.

G Gibbs and N Durbridge, 'Characteristics of Open University Tutors, Part 1', No 6 and Part 2 in No 7, 1976.

M Thorpe, 'Evaluating Tutorial Attendance', No 10, 1977.

J S Daniel, 'Interaction and Independence: Getting the Mixture Right', No 14, 1979.

S Murgatroyd, 'What Actually Happens in Tutorials', No 18, 1980.
D Sewart, 'Distance Teaching: a Contradiction in Terms', No 19, 1981.
O L'Henry Evans, 'The Anatomy of a Tutorial (or When is a Tutorial not a Tutorial', No 21, 1982.
S Brookfield, 'Independent Learners and Correspondence Students', No 22, 1982.
S M Rhys and C Lambert, 'Tutorial Systems and Tutor Assumptions', No 23, 1983.
R Winders, The Plymouth Audio Conferencing Network, No 25, 1984.

For practical guidance on tuition and student support services in open learning see the papers and guides produced by Roger Lewis for the Council for Educational Technology, especially:
R Lewis, *How to Tutor in an Open Learning Scheme: Self Study Version*, CET, 1981.
R Lewis, *How to Tutor in an Open Learning Scheme: Group Study Version*, CET, 1981.
R Lewis, *How to Tutor and Support Learners*, Open Learning Guide No 3, CET, 1984.

For broader discussion and an international perspective see e.g.
S Brookfield, *Adult Learners, Adult Education and the Community*, Milton Keynes, Open University Press, 1983.
M Tight (ed), *Education for Adults Vol. 1: Adult Learning and Education*, Croon Helm, 1983.
A R Kaye and G Rumble (eds), *Distance Teaching for Higher and Adult Education*, Croon Helm, 1980.
T N Kahl, and A J Cropley, 'Face-to-face versus distance learning: psychological consequences and practical considerations' in *Distance Education*, Vol 7, No 1, 1986.
ACACE, *Distance Learning and Adult Students*, Advisory Council for Adult and Continuing Education, 1983.
J S Daniel, M A Stroud and J R Thompson, *Learning at a Distance, A World Perspective*, Council for Correspondence Education, 1982. See papers in the section on Student Support and Regional Services.

29 Designing group work for professional updating

Janet Grant

Although the ratio of individual study to group work might vary considerably, depending upon a variety of factors, distance learning usually involves some group work, even if the group is assembled by telephone conferencing, and open learning programmes often combine group work and individual study in some form. In this chapter, three courses which have a high proportion of face-to-face group work will be used to illustrate the design of group work for distance and open learning for professional updating.

The courses I shall discuss in this chapter are: P550 *Topics in Drug Therapy*,[1] P553 *Systematic Approach to Nursing Care: An Introduction*[2] and *The 1983 Mental Health Act in Practice*.[3] (All three courses are described in more detail in the References.) These materials were designed for the continuing education of practising health professionals and were produced with the intention of being self-contained and requiring no further input from the Open University (OU) or its staff once sold to the user. Accordingly, unlike undergraduate courses, the University does not award any certificate or grade to students who have studied the materials and no formal assessment is included within the package, although bodies other than the OU have chosen to give formal recognition of achievement to those professionals under their aegis who have studied the material with a locally recognised tutor. Tutors or course organisers for these materials are not OU employees, neither are they selected by the University. They are self-selected or selected by their own professional organisation and elect to buy and use the materials for their own purposes, often to fit in with some wider local plan of study. These factors make group work particularly salient and also provide special problems for the OU course designers who themselves are working at a distince from their intended audiences of students and tutors.

The first two of the three courses listed above are to be found within the OU's Continuing Education programme in Health and Social Welfare. The third was produced by the MSD Foundation in collaboration with the OU. In the following discussion of group learning at a distance, these three courses will provide examples of the principles and problems that arise. To do this, it will be helpful to consider the general purposes and characteristics of group work in the context of the continuing education of practising health professionals, as well as the role and preparation of the group leader, methods of pack production used to ensure that the group work components achieve their aims, and the integration of group work with individual study.

Group work for continuing education

The group work components of our exemplary courses have a variety of shared purposes:

- to increase the relevance of the course for professional practice by providing opportunities for discussion of personal circumstances in relation to course content;
- to facilitate a practical problem-solving and planning component in the course of study which is open to the comment and advice of other professionals and the tutor;
- to provide the opportunity for a change of learning method which includes immediate learning from peers;
- to identify and sort out planning or practice problems which students might encounter in relation to the course materials and their intention to facilitate change or development in their professional practice;
- to broaden and deepen the learning experience by providing different perspectives, either through group activities, audio-visual trigger material or guided discussion with peers;
- to provide the opportunity for students to discuss learning difficulties they might be experiencing.

The group work components of our exemplary courses also have a number of shared characteristics:

- group meetings are designed to occur at about fortnightly intervals during the course and serve to give it a temporal structure as well as providing some momentum. Between group meetings (with the exception of *The 1983 Mental Health Act in Practice*) students study a workbook individually at home;

- group meetings are relatively short, for pragmatic as well as pedagogical reasons given the professional audiences, and are designed to take 1–1½ hours only;
- each group meeting comprises a series of short exercises or activities designed to focus on and illuminate one or two central issues;
- some of the group meetings will contain short sequences of trigger material on video with associated discussion points. On average, each meeting would have no more than 10 to 15 minutes of video material spread across one or two exercises;
- each group meeting is integrated with the textual components of the course and builds on what the student has already studied as well as providing a link forward to the next part of the course.

The role and preparation of the group leader

The role and preparation of the group leader, who is also likely to be the course organiser, is of critical importance in the continuing education courses for health professionals described here. The role of the tutor would usually involve:

- acquiring the course materials;
- gathering and/or organising the group students;
- planning the timetable;
- booking teaching rooms and facilities for the group meetings;
- distributing the materials to the students and ensuring that they can keep up with timetable;
- introducing the course to the students and dealing with unforeseen problems;
- encouraging students and informally monitoring their progress;
- running the group meetings and taking care that both the content of the discussion and the interactions between group members are constructive and aimed at achieving the aims of the course and the students who are studying it.

The tutor's role, then, is one of pedagogue, administrator and educational manager, content expert and group leader. However, since local tutors are locally selected, the team producing the material's pack cannot readily make accurate predictions either about the degree of skill in group facilitation that any one person will already have or, as it has sometimes transpired, how much that person will already know about the subject or the course itself. It is therefore necessary to provide material designed specifically for the tutors, to inform them about the structure and content of the course and to help them run the group meetings successfully both from the point of view of content and the group process which will occur. The tutor's notes invariably recognise these problems. For example, the Group Leader's Notes for *P553 A Systematic Approach to Nursing Care: An Introduction* recognise the heterogeneity of tutors' skills:

> Some group leaders may already be very experienced in group work, while others may be relatively new to this style of teaching and learning; very few will have had any experience of running distance learning courses like this one.

The 1983 Mental Health Act in Practice Course Leader's Book addresses the problem likely to be experienced by tutors who are unfamiliar with the content of the course (as everyone will be to some extent, since even if they know the Act in question, they will not know the course which presents it):

> Since these learning materials are new to you, you will need to look through them in some detail before the first group meeting. Do this for a number of reasons:
> (a) There might be ideas which are unfamiliar to you now but will be needed at your fingertips during group meetings.
> (b) Points arise unpredictably in group discussions. You will need to decide ... which are built in later in the course and can be deferred.
> (c) The discussion points provided for you ... will cover most of the issues likely to arise ... so you will not be unprepared.
> (d) Further background information might be required of you and this is provided in ... this book. You will need to be more informed than your Course Members.
> (e) You will need to have the course content and exercises at your command so that your attention is free to deal with the way your group is interacting as much as to what they are contributing to the discussion.

Group leaders' notes tend to contain slightly different points, depending upon the assumptions that can be made about the people who will act as tutors and the characteristics of their students. However, in general the notes would cover information and guidance about the content and structure of the course itself, its aims and the materials, the intended pattern of study, what to expect of group members and the skills which the group leader should try to acquire, the tasks of the group leader in setting up and facilitating the course, helping students to learn, and conducting group meetings. The intended content of each group meeting is described in detail including the questions which should be put to group members, possible discussion points that might arise and suggested timings for each separate exercise within any one meeting. In addition, special background information can be provided for the tutor, as it is in *The*

1983 Mental Health Act in Practice where it would be unreasonable to expect that all tutors will be experts on this particular piece of legislation. This course also provides a transcript of the video for quick reference during the group meeting discussion, obviating the need for a preliminary search through the video itself.

Tutor notes attempt to support as well as guide, and involve the course team in identifying the minimum level of information and guidance that will enable all tutors, however inexperienced, to help all students benefit appropriately from the course. This can only be fully achieved by a process of drafting the materials and testing them out in practice so that a final version can be made which is based on practical experience.

Course production methods for group work

Regardless of the purpose or proportion of group work within any one course, the methods of course production used to achieve effective materials are substantially the same. The three exemplary courses described here underwent the same processes of development, each finally tailored to the course in question but each comprising the same components as follows:

1 *Needs analysis*

A sample survey of representatives of the course's target audiences is undertaken, using questionnaires, interviews and reference to published and unpublished documents to test out the idea and general outline and approach of the course. On the basis of the findings, the course is finally planned.

2 *First draft*

The course team prepares the first draft of the materials, including plans for learning activities or short exercises to be included in the individual study text, case material for illustration and study, audio-cassette exercises, if required, and ideas for the group work exercises and video trigger material, usually associated with the individual study text. This should all occur at the first stage of drafting to ensure that the course is an integrated whole rather than having unconnected and uncoordinated material in the textual and group elements. The degree of integration of group work is likely to be determined by actions taken at this stage.

The guide to authors of *P553 A Systematic Approach to Nursing Care: An Introduction* illustrates this point:

The importance of an integrated course has obvious implications for the way in which we plan, develop and write the course materials. It means that no part of the course can be planned and produced in isolation from other parts of the course. Authors need always to think about how the text will relate to the group sessions, the case studies, and all other elements. So, when drafting the text, part of the author's task is to make suggestions about related case study material, exercises and discussion points for the group meetings, things that the video should provide and so on. As you are preparing your draft, include notes on the following:

How does the text relate to the group session?
What points should be taken up in the group session?
What should the video show?
What exercises might the group session include?
Is there a place for audiocassette material?
Can the case study or audiocassette material be followed up in the group session?

The first draft of the course is criticised and commented on by members of the course team and recommendations for a revised draft are made.

3 *Second draft*

The second draft of the materials is then prepared. At the same time audio-visual components will also be made and for the three courses concerned here, this involved both video and audio-cassette production. The second draft is developmentally tested in two ways. Firstly, the text alone, possibly with a description of the group work, is sent to a group of people representative of the target audiences of the course, who work through it and report detailed comments and criticism to the course team. Secondly, the group meetings themselves are tried out and their evaluation used in preparing the final draft of the course. This process is described for *P550 Topics in Drug Therapy* in Gale (1983):[4]

> The modules were tested with an established, informal continuing education peer group of general practitioners and a vocational training group. Each module requires two group meetings. The tutor in each case was given a set of workbooks, a videocassette and the draft tutor's notes. As it would be in practice, each tutor planned and used the module and ran the group meetings according to their own needs and those of the group. The group meetings were observed by evaluators and notes taken. A series of specific questions and issues were raised with each tutor concerning the adequacy of the tutor's notes in preparing him for

each session, his feelings about running the module and the sessions, special difficulties, the need for further guidance, advice and information about either the process or content of the meetings.

Group try-out does not always involve observation and interviewing by evaluators. For *The 1983 Mental Health Act in Practice* the whole process, from recruitment of test groups to collection of feedback, was done by post and telephone, using questionnaires to both tutors and group members who also copiously annotated their course notes and course leader's book before returning them to the course team.

Integration of group work and individual study

Although group work might sometimes be designed as an optional element of the course (indeed, students of *P553 A Systematic Approach to Nursing Care: An Introduction* are advised that it is possible to study the course without attending group meetings), it is usually designed as an integrated part of it, closely related to every other element and learning experience which the course presents. Such integration can achieve a depth and breadth of understanding as well as a personal relevance which parallel streams of individual and group work could not attain.

Integration of group work and individual study can be achieved in a number of ways.

1 Group work can follow the line of argument or information presented in the text for individual study and take that further by introducing new argument and information.
2 A new perspective can be put on the work that students have already completed. For example, by presenting the same situation or circumstance of a case study from another person's or agency's viewpoint. In this way, the student's learning can be broadened.
3 Illustrations can be provided of circumstances, situations or phenomena studied in the text by means of video, role-play or other teaching methods and media which are suited to group work. In this way, the student's learning can be deepened.
4 Students can be asked to bring to the group meeting examples from their own professional practice which are relevant to the material they have been studying individually. They can then analyse or reinterpret their practice from the new perspective of the course and in the light of other students' experiences and professional practice. Group work is thus a powerful force for making individual study take on a personal relevance. For example, in *P550 Topics in Drug Therapy*, group members were asked to prepare for one group

meeting by completing a Psychotropic Drugs Score Grid for at least three surgeries prior to that meeting so that the discussion of prescribing habits at that meeting would have data that were personally derived and practically relevant.

5 The group environment can be used to advantage to help students to realise the practical possibilities for change in their own professional practice by planning the introduction of changes and developments, discussing these with peers in the group to ascertain their views of feasibility and making a commitment to the implementation of change that is supported by the group. For example, the final exercise of the final meeting of *The 1983 Mental Health Act in Practice* is described in the guidance to the course leader as follows:

> Introduce the exercise by explaining to course members that to end the course they will look at themselves again in relation to their work with other professions. They can do this in three stages:
> *Firstly,* what specialist support does each member feel that he/she could offer towards building good team working with other health professionals to implement the 1983 Mental Health Act effectively?
> *Secondly,* what support/contribution towards team working could each course member hope for from other professionals?
> *Finally,* ask course members to state some improvement that they intend to make in their own professional practice, i.e. to commit themselves to action to improve their team working. Each course member might like to write a 'commitment statement' or plan of action on page 34 of their Course Notes.

This exercise is accompanied by group discussion at each stage, and the whole exercise is designed to take 30 minutes.

An excerpt from a planning document for *P553 A Systematic Approach to Nursing Care: An Introduction* illustrates that the options for group work listed here are not mutually exclusive and that group work can be used simultaneously for a number of purposes:

> Group sessions provide the main opportunity for the students to use their new learning to analyse clinical situations to be portrayed on video and to consider their own experience. The sessions will also provide the opportunity for students to undertake exercises that will cause them to use the steps of the nursing process. Group sessions will also be a forum for discussion, so that learning problems and difficulties can be sorted out. Some exercises during group sessions could also be based on students' own clinical practice. For example, they could be asked to bring along a patient's history or assessment taken during the previous week and work with that during the session.

Evaluation of group work at a distance

After so much planning, design and production effort, to what extent do the course teams achieve their aim of producing distance learning materials which include a viable, effective group work component? This question can only be answered by field trials or specific evaluation of the courses in use. Data are available for two of four exemplary courses, so far.

P550 Topics in Drug Therapy was evaluated in use by means of observation, interview and questionnaire (Gale, 1984).[5] Group leaders' opinions were generally very favourable about the group work component. Seventy-five per cent of leaders in the study reported that group members, who were practising or trainee general practitioners, attended meetings regularly and the general feeling was that setting the group meetings within a wider programme of planned and integrated study was of positive benefit in keeping attendance rates high in comparison with other courses. The course team had predicted that not all group members would be able to attend all meetings, and had designed the course in a modular way to take this eventuality into account. So those who missed some group meetings, or even some of the individual study, found that not all was lost. Some groups so appreciated the group format that they decided to continue meeting after *P550 Topics in Drug Therapy* had finished for them.

The course, with its modular structure, had also been designed to be flexible in use. Some modules and some group meetings were presented as optional. It transpired that this format was used creatively by group leaders who did make selective decisions about which group meetings to hold. It was popular to conduct the first group meeting by post, since it was largely organisational. Some leaders also took the opportunity of adding original group sessions of their own if the need and interest was there.

Group leaders found that the discussion which followed on from the video trigger material generally kept close to the given questions, but where it did range more widely, it did so in a controllable and relevant manner.

Some problems were experienced by leaders. Working out when meetings should occur in relation to the text, and which meetings were truly optional and which not, did cause some difficulties. There is probably a case for simplifying the distance learning format for group work to one meeting following each period of individual study. Occasionally, a leader reported a lack in factual knowledge to deal with some issues that arose unexpectedly during the group sessions. This lesson was learned so that the later course, *The 1983 Mental Health Act in Practice*, includes substantial background information for both group leader and students.

Group members' opinions were also elicited and generally they reported that the group meetings had reduced individual isolation, enabled reconsideration of habits and actions, widened horizons, facilitated comparison with colleagues and consolidated study of the workbook.

P550 A Systematic Approach to Nursing Care: An Introduction also underwent an investigation of its use (Gott, 1985)[6] which concentrated on the views of the course leaders rather than the students. The more straightforward linking of one group meeting to each period of individual study with no optional sessions made course organisation and management 'generally easy'. Group meetings were generally organised during work time, and students had usually completed the requisite individual study beforehand. Distance learning materials of this type were seen to overcome the problems of time, finance and distance which beset more traditional courses.

Group leaders also reported using the materials flexibly and each element was reported as being used in some way not planned by the course team. This will be the case inevitably even if the course team suggests that it would be inadvisable to use certain elements of an integrated course independently. The key to success is therefore to produce materials which not only can, but also should be used flexibly to suit local and individual needs and conditions.

Summary

Group learning methods for the continuing education of professional audiences have a special role in facilitating practice relevance, shared experience and depth of personal understanding. Such achievements can only be ensured, however, by close analysis of the needs, circumstances and characteristics of the target audience, provision for the adequate preparation of the local group leader, full integration of individual and group work, testing the materials in draft form and evaluating them in practice.

References

1 *P550 Topics in Drug Therapy*, Milton Keynes, Open University, 1987.

This course was made for practising or trainee general medical practitioners. The course materials consist of:

* *An Individual Study Pack* made up of
- a distance learning workbook in three chapters, complete with distance learning pedagogical stylistic features such as frequent learning activities to engage the student in active learning and to draw out the personal practice relevance of the material being

presented, graphics, a personal style of writing, engaging layout and short, approachable sections;
- a supplementary booklet of factual information about drugs;
- and an audio cassette for individual study.

*_A Group Work Pack_ made up of
- an individual study pack for the tutor's personal reference;
- Notes for the Guidance of Tutors;
- a video cassette for use as trigger material during the group meetings

Each period of individual study was designed to take about four hours. Six group meetings were offered. These were to be an introductory meeting, two meetings associated with each of the first and second chapters of individual study, and one with the third chapter. In addition, a seventh optional meeting was suggested based on one side of the audio cassette. Group meetings were designed to last for 1½ hours.

2 *P553 A Systematic Approach to Nursing Care: An Introduction*, Milton Keynes, Open University, 1984.

This course was made for post-basic, i.e. practising nurses in any field. It consists of:

*_An Individual Study Pack_ made up of
- a distance learning workbook in seven chapters;
- a supplementary booklet of Case Files containing case notes and nursing documentation with associated learning activities;
- audio notes for use with the audio cassette which is also provided for individual study.

*_A Group Work Pack_ made up of
- an individual study pack for the tutor's personal reference;
- some Group Leader's Notes;
- a video cassette for use as trigger material during the group meetings.

Each period of individual study was designed to take about four hours. In addition to an introductory group meeting, one meeting was planned to follow on each period of individual study. Group meetings were designed to take 1½ hours.

3 *The 1983 Mental Health Act in Practice*, MSD Foundation in collaboration with the NHS Training Authority and the Open University, MSD Foundation, London, 1986.

This course was made for multiprofessional or uniprofessional groups of general medical practitioners, psychiatric nurses, psychiatrists and social workers. The course consists of:

*_A Course Leader's Book_ providing detailed guidance about setting up and running the course as well as background information about the Act, its history and related practical and professional issues.

*_A video cassette_ of trigger material to be used during group meetings.

*_Course Members' Notes_ providing a summary of the course, background information and various charts and notes to be filled in as part of the planned sequence of group exercises.

This course has no workbook or audio cassette and no individual study other than a small amount of preparation between group meetings. It entirely consists of three 1½ hour meetings each of which comprises a series of specially developed exercises, some using brief sequences of own experiences, opinions and attitudes, and aims to plan some changes in their practice.

4 J Gale, 'Topics in Drug Therapy: An Open University Pilot Course for Doctors' in *Medical Teacher*, Vol 5, No 1, pp 18–24, 1983.

5 J Gale, Field Study Report: *P550 Topics in Drug Therapy*, Unpublished report, Department of Health and Social Welfare, Open University, 1984.

6 M Gott, 'An Investigation of Nurse Educationalists' Use of the Learning Resource' in *A Systematic Approach to Nursing Care: An Introduction*, Unpublished report, Department of Health and Social Welfare, Open University, 1985.

30 The tutor's role in group learning

Andy Northedge

Face-to-face teaching within an open learning system tends to take on certain distinctive characteristics relating to the heterogeneity of the student population, to the many external pressures on their studies and to their uncommon enthusiasm for participation in discussion. The variations in students' age, experience, education, ability and motivation require a broad-based approach. The inevitable irregularities in attendance, in timekeeping and in preparation for classes demand a flexible method, while the breadth of experience and an adult commitment to a 'point of view' call for the opportunity to speak out. In this chapter I shall be considering discussion as a means of teaching in open learning systems and I shall focus on one particular strategy which is widely used in the Open University (OU) owing to its simplicity, flexibility and robustness.

Group discussion promotes a kind of learning that the processes of reading and listening do not readily produce – an engagement with underlying meanings and an active exploring of implications. While reading and listening to lectures may offer students a fairly fleeting and superficial contact with the ideas embedded in the subject matter, active discussion can bring them into direct involvement with fundamental issues, principles and structures. Collectively the group can construct meanings of a breadth and sophistication that individual members of the group could not achieve in isolation. Discussion can therefore develop concepts and sort out misapprehensions. The students also gain insight into how meanings within the academic subject are created as an active dynamic process. They see first hand how the ideas and language work. And crucially they learn to 'speak' the academic language, learning how to use its concepts, structures and logic.

Apart from *intellectual* gains many students value even more the *social* support of group work in much the same way as members of Alcoholics Anonymous or Weight Watchers. The group discussion lessens the sense of isolated struggle with studying. It allows a sharing of 'survival' tips and fosters a commitment to group goals.

As compared with the lecture, teaching through the medium of group discussion can be an uneasy business. Without that comforting sense of an ordered progress through a well established body of academic material, unwelcome questions loom up as to what exactly one is attempting and what, if anything, is achieved. Although one can set against such doubts the strong 'gut feeling' of intellectual stimulation, enthusiasm and general *bonhomie* which may follow a particularly successful discussion class, there are surely also those occasions when the issues fail to ignite, when some egotistical boor persistently stifles promising developments to press on down unproductive and distracting pathways, when the session sputters to an inconclusive end and even the keen students look relieved to depart. Why then take such risks? Why expose oneself to the sense of inadequacy that such failures can produce?

Why indeed! Some teachers manifestly avoid any such risks, even in small group settings, by recreating the lecture in a modified form. Though physical proximity may create an appearance of accessibility the social structure of classroom proceedings can create felt distances as great as in any lecture theatre. A teacher can fend off the dangers of open discussion by putting on an impressive solo performance, which gives the appearance of 'delivering the goods', while distracting students from the 'theft' of their opportunity to learn to speak for themselves. What I am concerned with in this chapter is how teachers can defend against the pressures to take on the mantle of the all-knowing fount of wisdom, by setting up group discussions which consistently produce results.

There have been interesting and sophisticated studies of the processes at work within group discussions! However, translating these findings into practical guidelines for teachers is no easy matter. It is one thing to be able to *identify* such processes as questioning, criticising, re-focussing, gate-keeping, time-keeping, observing, self-reflecting, etc. – quite another to be able to '*manage*' the processes and '*produce*' them as required. Given the overriding interest of both teacher and students in the *subject matter* of the discussion, rather than the *process*, and given also the power and pace of developments in group processes once set in motion, it is asking a great deal to expect the participants in a discussion to apply the insights of group process research directly, within the full flood of debate. Even well trained and highly skilled group participants would be severely taxed. In the absence of training and skills, what we know of group discussion processes needs to be applied at the stage of advance planning of sessions rather than wheeled out on the spot.

There are many ways of pre-planning a group learning session, some of them directly linked to the subject matter under study (e.g. focussing upon a rock specimen, a maths problem or a poem). However, I want to outline one particular device which has gained wide currency in OU tutorials, at summer schools and even in our own staff meetings.[1] It is a device so simple in concept that its power and its breadth of useful application are easy to overlook. The central principle involved is the sub-division of the learning group into small independent sub-groups for part of the session.

The basic sub-grouping method

In practice teaching sessions organised according to the sub-grouping approach can take a variety of forms. However, I will give an illustrative example. After a brief introduction the tutor asks each student to work on her or his own for five minutes on a set task. The student then joins a group of two or three others to compare notes and attempt to produce a common response to the task (which may be different for each group). After 15 minutes a member of each group writes a few notes or headings on the blackboard. The whole class then listens to a brief report from one sub-group and discusses the conclusions they have drawn. There follow reports from each sub-group with accompanying discussions. Finally the tutor spends 15 minutes leading a discussion which aims to pick out various key points from the preceeding discussions, drawing out their relevance within the broader context of the course.

How the process works

I shall come later to various ways in which this basic sub-grouping structure can be varied to achieve different end, but first I want to consider what is achieved by this deceptively simple device. I shall take each stage separately.

Individual work

Although this short initial stage can be left out, particularly in a well established group, it has much to contribute. By giving students a few minutes to engage with the task on an individual basis each becomes more committed to the subsequent discussion. Many students are inclined to approach the rather awe inspiring setting of an academic discussion with an expectation of keeping a low profile, staying out of the main action for fear of exposure and embarrassment. They are only too ready to believe they have nothing worthwhile to contribute, and they habitually confirm their belief by contributing nothing. The act of writing down notes immediately dispels this myth, providing concrete evidence to the contrary. It also gives the student a preliminary commitment to a point of view. For reticent or inexperienced students this stage can be crucial.

Work in small groups

The most immediately obvious characteristic of a class working in sub-groups (particularly when all have been 'primed' by a period of individual work) is a healthy 'buzz' of noise. This might seem a trivial observation. However, the atmosphere of active engagement in purposeful discussion makes a sharp contrast with the subdued, formal tones of many group discussions. Students who habitually remain mute in the larger group can bring another side of themselves into the classroom, revealing their interests and abilities. They can also practise at speaking the language and ideas of the discipline in a less threatening context. These processes are important both in the development of particular students and in the development of the group, since students begin to discover how much more other students have to offer than is generally apparent. Indeed, in the first meetings of a group, and particularly when the students are new to studying, it may be useful to restrict the group size to two, immediately after the individual work. One can then insert an extra stage where the pairs of students re-group as fours. Some very shy students will adopt a passive, subordinate role even in a group of three, whereas in a pair it is virtually impossible to avoid contributing. This opens up the possibility that the other student will see merit in what the shy student says and eventually promote the ideas at the level of the group as a whole. In this way all students come to have a chance to have their ideas incorporated into the discussion of the whole class. This develops confidence as well as enriching the discussions by bringing a much wider range of experience and ideas into play.

It is important to emphasise the contrast here with the way groups of people normally carry on discussions. Typically one or two people take up a leading role as spokespersons, promoting certain ideas and positions. The group then functions on something like a model of representative democracy, where for most of the time, most of the people 'participate' by proxy, listening and putting their support behind certain propositions sketched out by the spokespeople. This kind of 'silent participation' can be quite active and engaging for all its appearance of passivity, and it is hard to see an alternative to such processes in large-scale public discussions. In the classroom, however, active 'silent participation' easily breaks down.

Because of the context of academic striving, student

'spokespersons' tend to pitch classroom debates at too high a level. It may be that such students are more able than most, or alternatively that they are unconsciously attempting to boost their images and to conceal their doubts and deficiencies. In either case tutors, given their own familiarity with the subject matter, are easily misled as to the appopriate level of discussion. When this happens a pattern may quickly become established for subsequent classes, such that the majority of students never even contemplate breaking out of a condition of mute incomprehension, while the self-chosen few repeatedly raise unsuitably broad questions or alternatively tug the discussion towards very particular ground on which they happen to feel comfortable. Since the students not contributing cannot follow the moves made in the discussion, because the material is difficult, unfamiliar or idiosyncratic, they cease even that 'silent participation' whereby they listen and align themselves with positions being presented. Consequently they learn very little. By contrast, very small groups of students working on a fairly tight specified task *have* to find a level at which they can engage usefully with the subject matter. Since the work of the small groups provides the basis for the discussions of the larger group, there is a much great likelihood that those later discussions will begin at a level at which students can follow them.

Apart from the effect of small group work in engaging the students with the subject it also serves an extremely valuable function for tutors. It releases them from the strain of being the perpetual source and pivot of all developments within the class. In a general discussion it is easy to become trapped within those descending spirals in which one puts a question, an inadequate response comes forth, one steps into the confusion or the silence to answer the question oneself and then reaches hurriedly for another question, which again draws little response and so on – until, under the constant pressure of finding new questions as well as answering them, one gradually loses track of the central issues. With the sub-grouping method the tutor hands the students much of the responsibility for producing substance for the discussion. Moreover, while the sub-groups are at work the tutor can quickly pick up a sense of the level at which they are dealing with the issues and the points they are struggling over. There is also time here to plan strategies for later on, to deal with difficulties and clarify points in the course texts.

Preparing a 'sub-group' response

The sub-groups are reminded of the need for a group response to the task a few minutes before their work together ends. (For example, by giving each group a piece of chalk for writing up their notes.) This process of producing a joint response requires a sharpening of debate and, whether the students are conscious of it or not, they become involved in negotiation over the meaning of terms, exploring the compatibility of different approaches and other very useful intellectual processes. They also gain practice (very useful for essay writing and exams) in finding ways of encapsulating broad issues and ideas in a few brief notes which other people will be able to understand. The final step of putting the notes on the blackboard has the incidental effect of requiring students to enter the 'territory' by the blackboard which is normally occupied by the tutor. As students take over the tutor's space and write on the 'official' blackboard, they break the pattern of passive deference to the tutor. This can have a very useful effect in loosening up the structure of roles within the group. The tutor is also freed at this stage to take up any position within the room and may very legitimately choose a seat at the opposite side from the blackboard, to get a good view and incidentally to alter the pattern of social dynamics within the room.

The report-back stage

The details of procedure at this stage can be quite varied. Since a lot of the more penetrating analysis and vigorous interaction will have gone on in the sub-groups, the reporting back stage might deliberately be kept very brief. It cannot, however, be dispensed with since at minimum it provides a target towards which the earlier work is directed. However, it can also serve other useful functions. Students' horizons become broadened beyond the limits of their own discussion, their ideas are put into play at the level of the larger group and any misunderstandings or problems can be discussed. More importantly the tutor gets a chance to enter the process (bringing a more advanced knowledge of the subject matter to bear on the ideas of the students). Thus, as the larger group is re-created and its dialogue reconstructed, the tutor's more sophisticated grasp of the ideas and language can be brought into play alongside the ideas produced by the students. This allows a very fruitful interplay between the abstracted level of academic theory and ideas at the level students can produce and use them. To achieve this, it may be helpful for the whole class to discuss each sub-group's report as it is produced. The public display of notes on the blackboard helps focus the minds of speakers and listeners during the debate and assists comparison of the findings of different sub-groups. Furthermore, the notes stand as a symbol of the work of each sub-group, undercutting again the myth that only a few students are capable of producing useful ideas and demonstrating the common commitment to the work of the group.

Drawing conclusions

Since a key characteristic of the sub-grouping process is to produce a wide range of involvement and of thinking, one problem which may arise is a sense of incoherence and incompleteness at the end of the sub-group report-back. Here the tutor can very usefully undertake the responsibility of drawing threads together. Some students lack confidence in their own thoughts on academic issues and want to hear the tutor talking in the 'official' language of the discipline, showing how the ideas produced in the sub-groups can be extended and used as part of a more general debate. If the tutor finishes with a 15 minute overview of the broad issues using the notes produced by the student groups as a springboard for each major point, the students are able to make a lot of sense of the subject matter very quickly.

Variations on the theme

The basic parameters of the sub-grouping method – timing, tasks, group sizes and style of report-back – can be shifted around to create very different kinds of sessions. With regard to timing for example, the bulk of the time available might be spent in small group work with only a short report-back session at the end. Alternatively, the sub-grouping exercise might simply be a warming-up device at the start of a session, providing raw material for an extended general discussion. As far as tasks are concerned they need to be clearly specified (preferably with a fairly concrete element) to enable the students to engage quickly in spite of the absence of supervision. On the other hand a wide range of material can be used. For example, a question can be posed which is designed to raise fundamental issues from the set reading. Often a past assignment question will serve this purpose. Or the students can be given a poem or a newspaper article or a sample essay to work on. They can be set a decision to make, or a problem to solve. They can be asked to recall personal experience to provide material for discussion. They can be invited to bring along an essay of their own or some notes on a text to share experiences of studying. They can even be asked simply to find out about each other as part of an 'introduction' exercise at a first meeting. One of the most popular and most straightforward uses is at revision time where individuals and then sub-groups can work on old exam questions, providing outline answers. This is a remarkably quick and effective way of raking up ideas from months back and pressing them back into active service. In this last case, as with many other kinds of task, it is an advantage to give each sub-group a different task to work on, so that at the report-back stage the group does not keep covering the same ground.

With many possible variations of timing, task and so on, this is far from a routine or repetitive method of structuring groups. On the contrary it offers a great many possibilities. The skills it requires of the tutor are the imagination and the knowledge of the subject to devise tasks which immediately engage the students. It requires the ability to handle the reporting-back so that the whole group is engaged all the time and not just the sub-group reporting at the time (this involves interrupting at times to ask for comments from other sub-groups, or inviting links to be made to earlier points or to the course texts). Finally it requires skill in drawing threads together and showing the relevance of the sub-group discussions to the debates and issues in the course as a whole. While this may sound quite a lot to ask, none of these skills is quite so sophisticated as the skill of digging an 'open' group discussion out of a slough of despond or of coping with the unfettered influence of a voluble scatterbrain. These last are skills some of us spend whole careers failing to master.

Caveats

Having pointed to what the sub-grouping method has to offer, it is also important to note some factors which can inhibit its use. Perhaps the most immediate is a certain sense of 'manipulating' the students, in that one cuts across their expectations and across prevailing group norms in requiring them to undertake a task and then be shunted around between individual work, sub-group work and reporting-back. It is easy to seem a bit 'school-teacherly' if one strikes the wrong note in introducing the technique. This may make some students reluctant to cooperate. Accordingly it is important to enter into the process with commitment and confidence. Indeed it is unhelpful to discuss the procedure at any length beforehand and certainly unwise to offer it as an *option*. Students will almost always opt to stay in the larger group format they already know, rather than move into any other social arrangement. Conversely, once the sub-group work has begun it is a perfectly comfortable structure. The problem only arises at that moment of switching from the 'traditional' format to a more artificial one.

A mundane technical inhibition can also arise in connection with seating. It is important that sub-groups gather round into a proper working arrangement. If, say, they try to remain sitting in a line down one side of a table, the work of the sub-groups is greatly inhibited. Again, it seems a bit school-teacherly to ask adults to move their chairs. But there is no point in being half-hearted over this. If you have taken the plunge into a sub-group format, people have to move or be moved into their groups. It requires a moment of decisiveness to establish what is necessary. After that there is usually little difficulty in setting up the groups.

Another inhibiting factor is the fairly long period when the tutor is out of the main action. It scarcely seems legitimate to retire from one's role as the fount of all wisdom and the controlling influence in all debate. Is one earning an honest living if one sets the students to teach themselves for lengthy spells? What if they are getting it all wrong? What if one left the classroom for ten minutes? In fact, there are useful things the tutor can be doing during this period, such as listening to what the students are talking about and 'gearing up' for the later discussions. As to any doubts over legitimacy, it is only necessary to 'eavesdrop' on one or two groups to recognise that a period of release from directly supervised discussion is a tremendous opportunity for students to try out ideas they would not dream of launching in the normal class discussions.

A final inhibiting factor is the difficulty of producing a tight sense of coherence in the final discussion, as well as the lack of time to undertake a really sustained analysis of any specific issue with the group as a whole. Indeed, if the method is used too frequently it does become rather mechanical, and the inevitably fragmented nature of a discussion divided up into several stages will be unsatisfactory. There is a danger, then, in overusing the technique and in allowing it to substitute for more 'natural' processes of communication and teaching within the group. If used sparingly and with imagination it enables a group to achieve a high level of participation, cohesion and confident engagement with the ideas of the course. But it should not become a hackneyed routine or a permanent substitute for more sustained tutor-led debates. If it does, dissatisfaction and resistance will set in.

Beyond the sub-grouping method

The sub-grouping technique is a very valuable way of tackling a number of common problems, particularly when either the students or the tutor are inexperienced, or when a new learning group is becoming established as a functioning collectivity. Insofar as group teaching is seen as a way of helping students achieve 'personal growth' as speakers, as group participants and as engagers with intellectual issues, the sub-grouping method is very helpful in creating space for those things to happen. On the other hand, insofar as group teaching is intended as an opportunity for students to be initiated into the modes of academic discourse within the discipline, the method has severe limitations. The exclusion of the tutor for long spells does indeed deprive the discussion of an important resource. The tutor can hold key theoretical positions in play and can press home challenges to everyday assumptions in a way students tend to find difficult. Students are often unable to develop and sustain a satisfactory version of the academic discourse without the participation of the tutor and so their analysis of the tasks set tends to have a rather rudimentary and makeshift character. This is fine so long as active student participation is the primary aim. But as satisfactory levels of participation are achieved the more pressing goal becomes that of providing experience of sustained involvement in a more rigorous level of debate; in that level of debate, indeed, which is to be found in the course texts and is required by the assessment process.

Nor should we ignore the tutor's own need to be involved in such discussions. To be permanently fixed in a role as facilitator to a sub-grouping process is potentially very frustrating. For their own intellectual health tutors need at least some chance to be at the centre of the action, demonstrating to themselves and to their students their capacity to use the language and ideas of the discipline. What fun is there in being a teacher if you never get to teach?

However, a tutor-led discussion *involving the whole class* calls for more subtle and sophisticated skills than does the sub-grouping method and these tend to take longer to acquire. I shall not attempt to examine those skills in detail here, but perhaps the most obvious and most widely useful is the posing of a sequence of provocative questions: questions sufficiently contained and yet challenging to allow discussion to move between the world of the familiar and the concrete on the one hand and that of theory on the other. Here is an extract from a recording of a tutorial.

> 'in what ways was Gladstone a *liberal*?'
> (suggestions are made, discussion of them)
> 'Who was the leading liberal around WWI?'
> 'Lloyd George.'
> 'What policies was he associated with?'
> (suggestions)
> 'In what ways were those *liberal*?'
> (discussion – leading to recognition of a very different liberalism)
> 'Is Mrs Thatcher a classical *liberal*?'
> (discussion – concluding that in some ways she is, in some ways not)
> 'Does *liberalism* then have any consistent elements?'
> (discussion)
> 'How does this tie in with X's ideas?'
> (discussion) etc. . . .

The use of a sequence of clear, simple questions, each followed by a generous pause to allow students to think and respond means that although the tutor is very forcefully setting the agenda, the students are actively engaged in thinking through some difficult issues. Successful tutors seem to develop a facility in formulating these questions on the spur of the moment, shaping the discussion as it develops and guiding it towards the major issues in the course.

One other technique particularly worthy of mention is the practice of turning questions and replies back towards the group, asking 'Do you all agree with that? What about others of you in the group?' This encourages students to interrogate each others' contributions and not simply to wait to see whether the tutor says it is the 'right' answer. It also creates valuable thinking time for the tutor to work out the next move. A combination of strategic provocative questions and tactics for spreading the discussion out among group members creates the possibility of having a discussion which both follows its own course through whatever issues arise and at the same time confronts and utilises the big ideas within the discipline. This is perhaps the most stimulating educational experience the student and tutor can hope for and the most compelling reason for having learning groups at all.

Conclusion

The procedure of sub-dividing groups allows a tutor to explore various ways of framing the group's *social* and *intellectual* processes to encourage the development of norms of active engagement in discussion. The group as a whole develops routines of work and does not form the habit of functioning simply as a passive audience for the tutor's central performance. This is especially useful for students new to study, or new to each other. On the other hand the 'technical' nature of this solution is its ultimate limit, in that it eventually gets in the way. It is like the scaffolding which is invaluable while building work is in progress but which eventually has to be cleared away so that the building can be seen. In the end it is the tutor's depth of understanding of the subject, imagination in framing questions and insight into group processes as they unfold, which produce the most powerful and memorable group discussions.

References

1 R A Northedge, 'Learning Through Discussion in the Open University' in *Teaching at a Distance*, No 2, 1974.

Index